ANTHROPOLOGICAL PAPERS OF
THE UNIVERSITY OF ARIZONA
NUMBER 33

INDIAN ASSIMILATION IN THE FRANCISCAN AREA OF NUEVA VIZCAYA

WILLIAM B. GRIFFEN

THE UNIVERSITY OF ARIZONA PRESS
TUCSON, ARIZONA
1979

About the Author...

WILLIAM B. GRIFFEN has done ethnohistorical work in northern Mexico with a basic focus on the culture change of native groups as they were influenced or dominated by the Spanish colonial system. In the late 1970s, he worked specifically on Chiricahua Apache contact under the late eighteenth-century Spanish presidio system at Janos, Chihuahua. He received his Ph.D. in anthropology from the University of Arizona and became chairman of the anthropology department at Northern Arizona University in 1965. After three years as associate professor at St. Louis University, he returned in 1971 to Northern Arizona University as professor and chairman of the anthropology department.

THE UNIVERSITY OF ARIZONA PRESS

Copyright © 1979
The Arizona Board of Regents
All Rights Reserved
Manufactured in the U.S.A.

Library of Congress Cataloging in Publication Data

Griffen, William B
     Indian assimilation in the Franciscan area of Nueva
Vizcaya.
     (Anthropological papers of the University of
Arizona)
     Bibliography: p.
     1. Indians of Mexico — Chihuahua, Mexico (State) —
History. 2. Indians of Mexico — Missions. 3. Francis-
cans — Mexico — Chihuahua (State). 4. Franciscans —
Missions. 5. Indians, Treatment of — Mexico —
Chihuahua (State). 6. Chihuahua, Mexico (State) —
History. I. Title. II. Series: Arizona. University.
Anthropological papers.
F1219.1.C46G74   972'.1   78-14546
ISBN 0-8165-0584-5

CONTENTS

MAPS

PHOTOGRAPHS

TABLES

PREFACE

This paper is a preliminary account, much of it in the manner of a technical report of basic data, of a few of the processes of disappearance – leading to either assimilation or extermination – of the native Indian population that was first encountered by the Spaniards at the time they occupied and settled the central river valleys of the present-day state of Chihuahua, Mexico. In the late 16th and 17th centuries much of this area, which was within the political province of Nueva Vizcaya, was called the Conchería, after the principal Indian group, the Conchos, who inhabited it at the time of the entrance of the Europeans. As the colonial period wore on, however, many non-Conchos were included in this Indian province – Jumano-speakers and a few others – before it became functionally defunct owing to the depletion of the native population and the general change in the Indian situation in this frontier region. The primary concentration here is upon the area of these "original" peoples and the Franciscan missions that ministered to them.

The overall aim in this study has been to illuminate some of the results, and to outline a few of the processes leading to these results, of the contact between cultures in this region. It must be emphasized that the present work is essentially descriptive and preliminary, and deals only with a narrow aspect of the implantation of the Spanish way of life and the effects of this implantation upon the native population. This is partly because of the restricted nature of the data that I have been able to turn up. Some of the results are discussed in a very general and conservative way at the end of the paper, but much more work needs to be done before any but tentative conclusions can be drawn on many of the facets of Spanish-Indian contact in this region.

Probably the main contributions of this study lie in the new historical data on the natives and the events that affected them, in the data on the population of the region, and in the summary histories of the Franciscan missions. It is hoped that in some measure this paper may serve scholars who carry out research into this quite exciting field.

The material presented on Spanish-Indian contact is quite uneven. It originally appeared that it would be possible to put together a culture history of the Concho Indians. However, because of the kinds of data that began to show up (and because of the lack of cultural information), it rapidly became clear that this would have to be changed to a history of the various peoples who lived within the general area of the Conchería, as the Spaniards thought of it. Because only the Spaniards – and only a few of them – were literate, information regarding Indians was recorded only in those situations where the natives had some particular kind of importance for the Europeans. The most obvious social units in which this was true were the missions, although in haciendas, mines, and a few other contexts such as war, Indians were involved enough so that they got put into the Spanish records in some fashion. However, because of the availability of some parish records, as well as other documents that contain references to the missions, and because limitations of time made it impossible to delve very far into other aspects of the contact situation, this paper focuses mainly on material concerning the mission establishments, and much of this is of a demographic nature.

Even the extant material on the Franciscan missions is quite haphazard. Nevertheless, all pertinent information that has been discovered on the location, number of settlements, and population of these religious establishments, as well as of a few other places, has been included. Information on the other social contexts of culture contact, such as mines, haciendas, and the military, has also been put into this report in order to provide some balance to the presentation, but these topics have not been the central concern here. The Introduction (Chapter 1) is an effort to give some chronological context for the other data.

I have attempted to pull together as much census and other types of countable data as possible. However, there has not been sufficient information of this kind to derive a very coherent demographic picture of Indian assimilation in this area of Nueva Vizcaya. While some quantitative data have been discovered for some sites for some periods, the best that can be offered for the time being is merely to coordinate them by setting them down in a list in order to gain a larger picture. This has been done in the various tables; more refined analyses, if they ever become possible, will have to wait until more and better information turns up.

This paper is not directed to any problem other than establishing the context and the trajectory of the assimilation or extinction of the native population of one restricted region of northern Mexico. Discussion of such things as the early explorations (their routes, who the people actually visited were, and the like), and of the weighty ethnographic complexities that have plagued workers for a number of years, such as the "Jumano problem," has been purposely and studiously avoided. Since this paper has been written mainly from unpublished primary historical sources, what data on language, group (band, settlement, etc.) names, and general ethnography have been found in these sources have been included here to assist in information retrieval for future researchers. I am aware, as are all those who have worked in this particular historical field, that there remain many unused or only partially used documentary sources; until these are more thoroughly investigated it seems futile to speculate on the location of this or that tribal group, or whether some group of people were really Athapaskan rather than Uto-Aztecan.

Thus I have also avoided getting into the history of the Apaches in the area in the 18th century; in my opinion (given all of the inadequacies noted above) there were few or no Athapaskan speakers in the geographical area under discussion here until about this time. For the present paper, it is sufficient to be aware that some outside warring bands of people entered the area in the 1700s; knowing their tribal name or names, their greater ethnic connections, or their specific history would not change the overall picture of assimilation and extinction as presented here.

Work that still needs to be done in this area might be mentioned here. It would seem that future research could profitably be directed toward: (1) a thorough analysis of the demographic makeup and history of the entire colonial population; (2) an intensive investigation of the nature of Spanish contact and social units (missions, mines, ranches, and so on), including analyses of specific locations, not just general statements (only a small amount of work has been done in this area, the most notable by West [1949] on the Parral mining district); (3) research on the climate and physical environment and their changes during this period; and (4) an analysis of the ecological changes that were brought about by the introduction of Spanish society and culture into the region and by the interaction between Spaniards and Indians. Not only historical, but also archaeological and geographical investigations will be necessary to contribute to this end. Indeed, each of the sites mentioned in the text (as well as many others) must be investigated by the techniques of these and other disciplines, as Dr. Charles C. DiPeso and the Amerind Foundation are doing for the area of Casas Grandes.

Probably the principal source of information for this study has been the archives of the city of Parral, the ancient administrative center of the province of Nueva Vizcaya during the colonial period. The major portion of these documents are on microfilm in the library of the University of Arizona, where I utilized them. The other principal archival collections that have been consulted are those of: the Archivo General de la Nación, Mexico City; the Centro de Documentación, Instituto Nacional de Historia, Castillo de Chapultepec, Mexico City; the Bancroft Library, Berkeley, California; the Colección del Padre Pablo Pastells at the library of Saint Louis University, Saint Louis, Missouri; and documents found at the University of Texas in the Latin

American Collection and in the Documents Division, Austin, Texas. (For comments on the relative value of the various sources employed, see Griffen 1969.)

On questions of population and ethnic identification and assimilation, major documentary adjuncts to the above collections were found in local archives, mostly at churches and former missions. The records of many of these places are quite incomplete, as well as in poor condition, and most do not go back before the 18th century. Nevertheless, I collected some data from the following locations: the municipal archives of the towns of Janos and San Francisco de Conchos, and the parish archives of Aldama, Aquiles Serdán, Bachíniva, Buenaventura, Camargo, Casas Grandes Viejo, Chihuahua City, General Trías, Julimes, Namiquipa, Ojinaga, Parral, Rosales, and Valle de Allende, all in the state of Chihuahua. Sr. José María Cano of Namiquipa also kindly lent me a document from his personal collection.

I visited a number of other places and spoke with many persons, mostly priests and local government officials, concerning local records. Almost invariably the municipal government archives contain little or nothing dating before the 1911 Revolution. I could locate no colonial records at the following churches that I visited: Nuevo Casas Grandes, Coyame, Galeana, Jiménez, Nombre de Dios, San Francisco de Conchos, San Pablo Meoqui, San Pedro de Conchos, or Santa Bárbara. Possibly further searching in the future will turn up documentary sources at these and other places.

The attempt has been made to exhaust these sources for descriptive material relating to the Franciscan missions, population data on the places cited in the text, tribal and group names, and ethnographic or cultural information on the native groups. For the most part the data dealing with historical events have only been summarized, to support the material on changing population and missions. The translations from Spanish are my own.

There are, as already partially noted, many factual gaps in the data regarding the culture history of the Conchería. One that deserves special note is the dearth of information on the first 60 years or so of Spanish settlement in the Santa Bárbara–Parral district. Particularly with regard to the historical ethnography of north Mexico, this period will have to be much more thoroughly researched. To date, the material contained in the Parral archives has been singularly disappointing in this respect, although understandably so, since by the time Parral was founded in 1631, the initial blow of conquest was ending and the Spanish system was quite well entrenched. Archival resources at Durango and other places that I did not have time to investigate may hold much valuable material for the solution of this problem.

For some areas, especially that of La Junta, which was properly part of the Conchería and the Franciscan mission system, practically no new information has turned up; consequently, published works on the region, mainly the excellent analyses of J. C. Kelley (1952a; 1952b; 1953; 1955), have been relied upon, especially in the realm of interpretation. I agree wholeheartedly with Kelley's ecologically oriented interpretation of depopulation of La Junta, and would only add that the Spanish empire should also be included as one of the changing environmental factors.

I would like to express my most heartfelt thanks to all of the people and institutions who assisted me during the course of this study. Expressions of indebtedness go first to the National Science Foundation, which supported the major portion of the research under grant GS-5. Also, thanks go to the National Endowment for the Humanities, under whose grant No. H-68-I-177 I collected a small but crucial part of the material included here on the Janos-Casas Grandes district. Appreciation is extended especially to the people at the various libraries and documentary collections consulted, and to a number of parish priests in the state of Chihuahua who permitted me to examine their extant parish records for the 17th and 18th centuries.

Dr. Charles C. DiPeso, of the Amerind Foundation, Dragoon, Arizona, deserves my most sincere gratitude, as it was he who first suggested an ethnohistorical investigation of some of the extinct and little-known native Indians of northern Mexico. Thanks go also to Dr. DiPeso and to Mr. and Mrs. George Chambers, of Tucson, Arizona, for making possible the microfilming of the Parral archives, and to Dr. Wm. C. Massey, recently of Texas Christian University, Fort Worth, Texas, for permission to use microfilm copies of documents from the Mexican National Archives. I am especially indebted to members of the staff of the Museum of Northern Arizona who lent their assistance in various ways, and particularly to Mr. Dale Carver, who prepared the map.

Many other persons donated their time or energies in one form or another, from general conversations and advice to specific suggestions during the course of research and data collecting. Unfortunately, space permits mention of only a few of these people. I want to thank Dr. Wigberto Jiménez Moreno, Director of the Instituto Nacional de Historia, México, D.F.; Dr. Philip W. Powell of the University of California at Santa Barbara; Dr. Woodrow Borah of the University of California at Berkeley; Sr. Francisco R. Almada of the Sociedad Chihuahuaense de Estudios Historicos, Chihuahua City, Chihuahua; and Professor Eugenio del Hoyo of the Instituto Tecnológico de Monterrey, Monterrey, N.L., México, for their most valuable ideas, hints, and suggestions; and Miss Nettie Lee Benson, Curator of the Latin American Collection at the University of Texas, and Srta. Gloria Grajales of the Universidad Nacional de México, for important bibliographical assistance during certain portions of the data collecting.

A great many residents of the state of Chihuahua assisted me in many ways and were always ready to offer their most gracious hospitality. While only a few of these persons can be mentioned, thanks are extended especially to Sres. William and Virginia Wallace and family of the Hacienda de Corralitos; Father José Guadalupe González, parish priest of Rosales; Father Salvador Velarde y Arce, then resident priest at Buenaventura; Sr. Manuel Ramírez, then *presidente* of the municipio of Julimes; Mr. David Spilsbury of Colonia Juárez; Mr. Gail Bluth and Mr. Oscar Bluth of Colonia Dublán; and the families of the latter four.

I am particularly grateful for the assistance of the office staff and members of the faculty of the Department of Anthropology at the University of Arizona, especially Dr. Edward H. Spicer, who directed the grant under which the initial research was done. I would also like to thank my dean at Northern Arizona University, Dr. Richard O. Davies, for his encouragement during the final stages of the manuscript. Appreciation is due to the University of Arizona Press for assistance in publishing this report. Last but certainly foremost, I cannot sufficiently express my indebtedness to my wife, Joyce, for her editorial help, for typing the final draft of the manuscript, and for her support and understanding during the preparation of the material.

W. B. G.

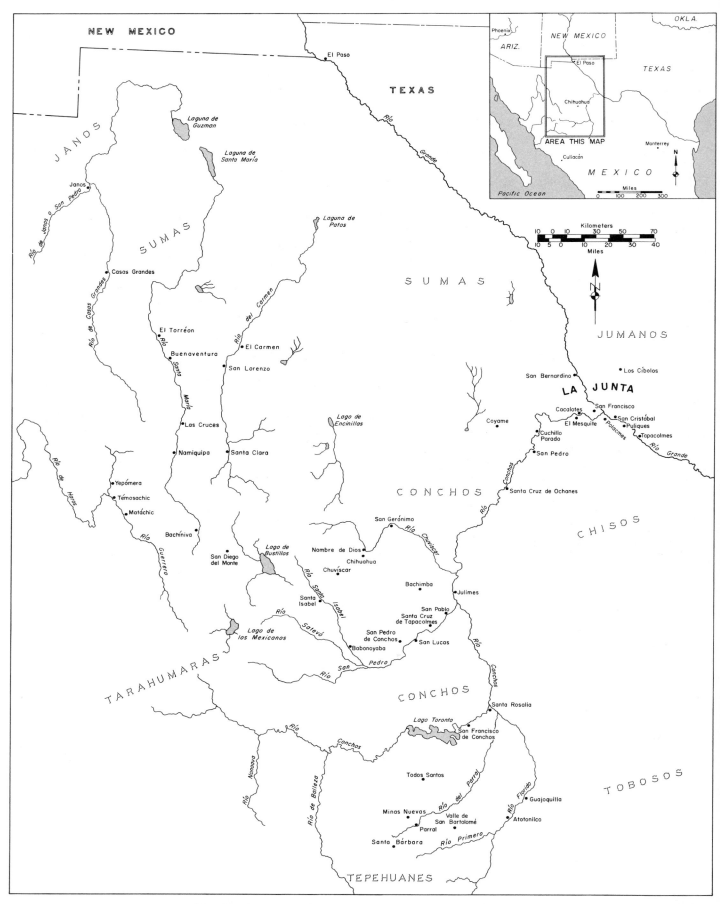

Map 1. The Conchería: Major Tribal Groups and Settlements.

1. INTRODUCTION

In the course of the penetration of Spanish civilization into different areas of the Americas, owing to factors of geography and natural resources, various districts, areas, or regions were established or developed. Some of these, especially the larger, were formalized into the Spanish political-administrative organization and given names such as Nueva Galicia or Nueva Vizcaya, and others, on a lesser scale, became townships or *corregimientos*. Still other regions became known by the names of the native peoples who inhabited them, such as the Pimería or the Tarahumara. Often these latter, in essence ethnographic or tribal areas, were administered in the Spanish system by a particular order of missionaries. This occurred, for example, in the provinces north of New Spain proper, with the Jesuits occupying the west coast of Cahitan, the mountain Tarahumara, and the desert Pima areas, and the Franciscans devoted to the Pueblo peoples of New Mexico.

One of these areas or regions − a segment of the political province of Nueva Vizcaya − occupied the central river valleys of the present-day Mexican state of Chihuahua (see Map 1). Beginning in the 1560s, the Spanish began to open up the northern frontier of New Spain in the southern portion of this province. At this early period, a number of different Indian tribal groups were described or at least mentioned. Within as short a time as something over 200 years, the nature of the Indian population had changed radically, and many of the earlier-cited aborigines were no longer on the scene, or the few who were left occupied a very unimportant position on the northern frontier. Indeed, by 1800 the Indian situation in Chihuahua was in many ways much more like what it is today, in the 1970s, than what it was only 150 years earlier, in 1650. By the 19th century, as now, the only Indian group of any consequence and size (with the exception of the warring-raiding intruder Apaches) was that of the Tarahumara, inhabiting essentially a "zone of refuge" (Aguirre Beltrán 1967) in the southwest corner of the state.

Geographically, the area we are concerned with is defined on the west by the highlands of the Western Sierra Madre and the country of the Tepehuan, Tarahumara, and Jova Indians, and on the east by the great deserts of the Bolsón de Mapimí, northeast Chihuahua, and Coahuila. Early Spanish settlement for the most part focused on the lower drainage of the Conchos River and on the drainages of the Florido, San Pedro, and Chuvíscar rivers and their tributaries, all of which join the Conchos to empty eventually into the Rio Grande. This central river valley region, in the last 30 years of the 1500s, was a small mining and ranching district, called Santa Bárbara after its first town. In the course of a century or so this district expanded northward to comprise all of the area up to El Paso; to the northeast it included the confluence of the Conchos and Rio Grande rivers, and to the northwest, Casas Grandes and its greater environs.

From the economic standpoint, this area can be considered a single unit − a mining area that spawned numerous ranches devoted to stock-raising and farming, and whose timber, salt, saltpeter, and other resources were exploited to support the mines. It possessed no specific name as a political unit, although later it formed the heartland of the province of Nueva Vizcaya. (The capital of this province was formally Durango; however, the governor, after the rich silver strikes of the 1630s, always resided in the more northern zone, at Parral or, later, in Chihuahua City.)

From the standpoint of native Indian ethnology, much of this region was considered by early Spaniards to be a single unit, and in the late 16th and 17th centuries it was dubbed the Conchería, after the Conchos Indians who dwelt to the north of the original mining district. Following the practice elsewhere, the Conchería, which soon included other tribal groups, was put under the religious administration of the Franciscans, who held the area until the end of the colonial period (Alessio Robles 1938: 1ff; Hackett 1926: 3-5; West 1949).

Although the boundaries of these units − the economic-exploitative and the religious-administrative areas of the Europeans, and the native tribal areas − did not correspond exactly, the region can be considered as a single whole. Here, during the course of the implantation of Spanish colonial society, certain types of Spanish-Indian contact led to particular patterns of Indian biological assimilation and cultural extinction. In other areas, some adjacent to this one, Spanish-Indian contact took somewhat different forms, which resulted in different patterns of assimilation and extinction.

The Santa Bárbara mines were founded in 1567, and farming in support of the mines was begun in Valle de San Bartolomé three years later. The opening up of the region, and the subsequent establishment of a number of different Spanish holdings − along the Río Florido in the 1570s, in the San Gregorio valley north of San Bartolomé in 1581, and in Todos Santos after 1590 − began the development of the Chihuahua central river valley area that was to continue for the next 150 to 200 years (Dunne 1948: 10-11; Jiménez Moreno 1958: 99-101; Saravia n.d.: 263; West 1949: 10-12).

Unfortunately, the events of this early contact history are, by and large, unknown. The Santa Bárbara-San Bartolomé district was in Tepehuan country, but the Indians in this immediate area apparently disappeared rather quickly under the pressure of Spanish demands for labor, judging from the lack of references to Tepehuanes in later sources. It was the need for workers on mines and ranches that soon turned the Spaniards farther north, to look for natives who lived along the Conchos, San Pedro, and other rivers. These people the Europeans called Conchos; their general native name for themselves was apparently *yolly* or *yolli*, probably meaning "the people" (Kroeber 1934: 13-4; West 1949: 11).

For the first 60 years or so, Spanish development of this Santa Bárbara district was rather slow, and was concentrated on Santa Bárbara, San Bartolomé, and the immediate environs. At least one man of the robe, the Franciscan de la Oliva, went farther north to work among the heathen Indians on the Conchos River. No doubt many other Spaniards were moving about and exploring the hinterland for deposits of metals, salts, and other resources, and for Indian laborers; slave raids were made as far north as the confluence of the Rio Grande and the Conchos River as early as the 1580s. The economic, political, and religious expansion and consolidation of the region continued into the 1600s, and this period is no doubt crucial for the understanding of the culture history of Spanish-Indian contact – but it is precisely this period on which the available documentary sources are silent, and the contact situation must be largely inferred from slightly later information (Hammond and Rey 1929: 54-5; Torquemada 1944: 345).

The Conchos and other Indians, dwelling to the north of this early area of settlement and playing an integral part in its development, are largely unknown ethnographically. The Conchos proper seem to have comprised a large group of people, considering the geographical extent of their territory, but no count or even estimate of their population or settlements seems to exist. The few statements available regarding their social and cultural characteristics are somewhat contradictory. They appear to have lived in small settlements (although even their type of dwelling is unknown) and to have practiced some agriculture. Early accounts play down their crop raising as something that scarcely existed, although these people dwelt in some of the choicest and best-watered country of the region, as Spanish settlement quickly demonstrated. One can only guess that Conchos were fairly sedentary, since their pattern of contact with Spaniards was noticeably different from that of their hunting and gathering neighbors.

By and large, Conchos (from the evidence available) rather easily became incorporated into the Spanish empire. In the 1600s they labored and fought for the Spaniards, who at this time often lauded them for their industry and constancy, despite earlier disparaging statements concerning their incapacities. Few Conchos ever developed the patterns of the nomadic desert-dwellers who maintained permanent hostilities toward the Spaniards. The two major revolts

against Spanish domination, in 1644 and again in 1684, were intense but short-lived affairs, after which the rebels (both Concho and Jumano speakers from farther north) returned to their places of work on Spanish holdings. In effect, the Conchos proper, whose territory the Europeans found most congenial for development, seem to have opted early to join the Spanish colonial system. Such a conclusion may be in error, however, since we know so little in detail concerning the impact of the Spanish system upon the first three or four generations of Conchos Indians (Alegre 1956: II, 37-9; DHM 1645).

In the march of European society northward, the Spaniards soon passed beyond the bounds of Concho country. The latter ran from just north of the Santa Bárbara district to the Suma-Jumano language border on the north (see Map 1). In the northeast, the line was immediately south of Cuchillo Parado, although it extended eastward to include a portion of the Rio Grande and Big Bend area. In the west, Concho country comprised part of the Santa María River valley, at least around Namiquipa and environs. From here, the boundary ran somewhat south and eastwards, along the Tarahumara, to a point west of San Francisco on the Conchos River. Spanish reports imply, but do not explicitly state, that throughout this vast region a single language was spoken, and more than one linguistic group may actually have been included.

Because of the need for auxiliary military forces and for laborers, Spaniards worked through local Indian leaders or caciques in the recruitment of troops and hands for farm and mine. Out of this practice seems to have developed the larger political-administrative unit of the Indian Conchería. The office of governor of the Conchería was instituted, and the Indian leader appointed to this post was issued a formal title by the Spanish governor of Nueva Vizcaya. For a considerable period the Indian governor served as one of the principal links between local Indian groups and the Europeans. When Spanish interests pushed beyond Concho country, the Conchería as an administrative entity was also extended to include non-Concho-speaking peoples. As a formal unit, then, the Conchería – which eventually was divided into eastern and western jurisdictions, each with its own Indian governor – served as one component in the contact structure between native and Spaniard in central northern Mexico.

By 1567, the year the Santa Bárbara mines were founded, Spaniards had been pressing forward, expanding the northern frontiers of New Spain, for more than four decades. Some 20 years earlier, silver had been discovered at Zacatecas and a veritable silver rush had taken place in that area. From Zacatecas, in the 1550s and 1560s, Spanish explorers then had pushed outward in a broad area to the east, west, and north. Durango was founded in 1563, only four years before Santa Bárbara. In 1564 and 1565, Francisco de Ibarra, the governor of Nueva Vizcaya, entered and explored Casas Grandes and vicinity, in the northwest of what later became a peripheral portion of the Conchería. Ibarra passed from the west coast through Opata country and the Sierra Madre on this expedition; it would be at least some 80 years before Spaniards moving along the eastern flank of the Sierra Madre through the Concheria proper would seriously begin to colonize and settle the Casas Grandes district. To the east of the Concheria, in the 1570s and 1580s, various settlements were established at Mazapil and in the Monterrey district, and by 1590 the Spaniards had sent an expedition into Texas (Alessio Robles 1938: 60, 89-93; Hammond and Rey 1928; Jiménez Moreno 1958: 99-100; Mecham 1927; Powell 1952: 10-4).

Franciscan missionaries moved out from the peripheries of Spanish settlement. In the 1550s and the following decades they worked among the Zacatecos Indians, penetrated the Laguna district, and explored Coahuila, and by the 1590s they were working among the Conchos Indians. In this same decade Jesuits entered the northern mission field, and by 1598 they had established their mission at Parras; in the next decade they began working among the Tepehuanes, and in 1611 they founded San Pablo Balleza, west of Santa Bárbara. By the 1640s both Jesuits and Franciscans were pushing their mission systems farther into the hinterland. At this time, the Black Robes founded their Lower Tarahumara mission district; 40 years later they did the same in the Upper Tarahumara. Franciscans continued to expand their system so that, by the 1660s, they had penetrated all the areas they would occupy during the colonial period, with the exception of La Junta (the area at the confluence of the Rio Grande and the Conchos River), which they would not enter for another 20 years (Alegre 1956: II, 41-2; Dunne 1944: 20ff; 1948: 13ff; Kelley 1952b; AHP 1641A).

By 1700 or so, the missionary expansion into the Concheria and adjacent areas was just about over, and during the next decade the last large mining strikes of Nueva Vizcaya were made in the vicinity of present-day Chihuahua City. The remainder of the colonial period was one of consolidating and, indeed, protecting the areas and holdings developed thus far.

As Spanish society was extended into new geographical areas, various reactions to conquest by the native peoples began to occur. In the case of some of the more settled Indians this response took the form of large and sometimes bloody revolts. These occurred in 1617-19 among the Tepehuanes, in 1644-45 among peoples of the Concheria, in 1648-52 among the Tarahumara, again in 1666 among some Conchos, and in 1648 among almost all the peoples of the Concheria – Sumas, Jumanos, and Conchos; finally, during the 1690s, the Tarahumara, with some Conchos, flared up in rebellion several times. Other natives, the more nomadic, developed patterns of reaction that led to almost constant warfare with the European-settled areas, much of it in the form of raiding. For these peoples, the Spaniards developed practices, if not policies, that aimed at extermination. Many bands of Coahuila, Toboso, Concho-speaking Chisos, Jumano-speaking Sumas, and Janos and Jocomes, to name the major ones, were eliminated from the scene, only to leave the way open for the eventual entrance of Apaches and Comanches.

Spanish defenses of Nueva Vizcaya, for much of the 17th century, were poorly developed. One presidio – that of Cerro Gordo – was built following the 1644 revolt. Military activities were carried out mainly on a local, fairly informal, and *ad hoc* basis until after 1685. At this date, in response to the hostilities of the previous year, the Spanish began in earnest to develop a frontier presidio system. From this time on into the following century, a chain of forts was developed all across the northern frontier (Hackett 1926: 17-8, 21-5, 296ff, 384; DHM 1748).

It was within this context of an expanding, conquering society that Concho- and Jumano-speaking Indians worked and fought for Spaniards. The Europeans uprooted many communities in order to bring the Indians closer to their places of work. In many, if not most, of the Spanish settlements where Indians lived, these natives were thrown together with many other kinds of people, both Indians and non-Indians. These more settled natives regularly joined Spanish forces – indeed they often formed the bulk of the troops – in military operations, especially during the 17th century. As these Indian groups dwindled in numbers, concomitantly with the development of the presidio system, the employment of Indian troops decreased greatly in the 1700s.

By the first decades of the 1700s, many of the aboriginal groups had become fairly well assimilated and acculturated. As the end of the colonial period drew nearer, Indians were more and more a minority, and were restricted to mission towns and to small areas of Spanish settlement. In these contexts, forced to give up many or most of their customs and to communicate in Spanish, they were rapidly assimilated into Spanish society. Finally, in the last 50 to 75 years before Independence, much of the mission, and probably some of the nonmission, Indian population was augmented by immigrants from outside the Concheria or from areas bordering the province. Examples of the latter were immigrant La Juntans, who remained as settled peoples at the sites where they were first found by the Europeans well into the 18th century, but who moved southward as individuals and small groups to the region of the Chihuahua and Parral mining districts, partly because of pressure they felt from the Apaches. From outside the Concheria came Tarahumaras, who, in the 1700s, were found in increasing numbers in the heartland of the central river valleys. Finally, as the La Junta settlements and the border settlements of the Tarahumara became depopulated of natives, the influx from these areas stopped or was reduced to a trickle. At the same time, Spanish society was developing more racial and cultural homogeneity, and the ranking system of the various social classes or *castas* – which included a slot or stratum called *indios* – was becoming simplified. The basic characteristics of the modern Mexican population of this area seem to have been fairly well formed by the time of Independence.

2. HISTORICAL SKETCH OF THE CONCHERIA

The history of the native peoples who originally inhabited the Concheria is essentially the history of the central river valley area in the 1600s. By the turn of the 18th century, owing to the infiltration of non-Indians and the acculturation and assimilation of the aboriginal population, the Concheria as a unit of native peoples was just about defunct. More and more, it was the peoples on the northern perimeter who, as free agents, had the most influence in major historical events – who could make decisions that would arouse segments of Spanish society to react in policy and with military force. This northern border population disappeared for the most part in the early years of the 18th century, to be replaced by outsiders – invading Apaches, who continued to be frontier warrior-raiders until the latter part of the 19th century. In the meantime, the remaining native Indian populations of the old Concheria became steadily smaller remnants, now functionally part of Spanish society.

This chapter, which is pieced together from the scanty data available, is an account of the major events in the history of the Indians of the Concheria. Some of this material has been published elsewhere, although much of what is presented here is new. For reasons of continuity and completeness, some of the information cited here is repeated in other parts of this paper.

THE EARLY YEARS

Spanish movements into and around the Santa Bárbara district, and on into the Concheria, are most obscure. Conchos Indians were first contacted in 1575, according to Miranda's report of this year, and the parties of Rodríguez and Espejo in 1581 and 1582 passed through their territory. While these two expeditions left excellent accounts of the portion of the Concheria they visited, for the next quarter of a century events of the contact between Spaniards and the natives dwelling around Santa Bárbara are largely unknown (Hammond and Rey 1927; 1929; Miranda 1871).

Sometime in the 1590s, Fray Alonzo de la Oliva began to work among the Conchos proper, who dwelt along the Conchos River. By 1604 he had established the first mission for these people (San Francisco de Conchos), and soon it was reported that he had some 4,000 neophytes in his flock (Jiménez Moreno 1958: 146-7; Torquemada 1944: 345; UTL 1619).

At this same time, Spaniards were also opening up some of the surrounding territories. Since the early 1590s the Jesuits had been working in newly discovered mission fields in the lowlands of the west coast, in the mountainous Sierra Madre – particularly among the Tepehuanes – and in the desert country southeast of the Concheria in the Laguna district (today, the area of Torreón and Parras). New Mexico was explored several times, and the province was finally established on a permanent basis by Juan de Oñate in 1608. In the next decade, Jesuits pushed their mission system as far north as the southern portion of the modern Mexican state of Sonora, establishing missions among the Mayo in 1614, among the Yaquis in 1617, and among the Lower Pima in 1619 (Spicer 1962: 25-9, 48, 87-8, 155-8).

During this period of expansion, Indians of the Concheria are not heard of again until the great Tepehuan revolt of 1617. On this occasion some Conchos as well as other non-Tepehuan Indians took up arms against the Spaniards, but the factors involved in their doing so are unknown. Two Spanish commanders operated against these rebels. One, a Captain Mosquera, campaigned in the salt flats (Las Salinas) area east of the Florido River, certainly seeking non-Conchos; he enjoyed little success and soon returned west to join Captain Medrano in the Santa Bárbara district. Here the Spanish troops fought several nations – Conchos, Tobosos, Nonojes, and Salineros. The Conchos were said to reside in the vicinity of Santa Bárbara and probably had been brought into the immediate area to work on local Spanish establishments. During the hostilities, the Indians burned a hacienda in the Santa Bárbara valley (Hackett 1926: 38, 98, 110; AGN 1617; 1618).

It seems that only a small group of Conchos was actually on the warpath at this time; certainly many were peaceful. In 1619, a Spanish commander, Gáspar de Albear, made a sally into Tepehuan country. He traveled northward through Concho territory, passing through Bamonoyaba (Babonoyaba) and a place called Tovolabaopa, and then turned southward again to attack the Tepehuanes and other rebels from behind. Albear stopped in Babonoyaba for three days; while there, he called together "all of the Conchos who, terrified by Tepehuanes and Tarahumaras, their constant enemies, were moving about through those hills (*montes*), seeking nourishment by hunting and fishing." Here Albear learned that some Conchos had joined the enemy Tepehuanes and had gone with them into Tarahumara country (UTL 1619).

Some of these Conchos, after the Spanish had pardoned them, offered to lead the Europeans to the great rebel leader Tucumudagui, but warned that more than 800 Tepehuanes were awaiting them with swords, lances, and arquebuses. The Spanish troops marched by way of the Valle de Aguila and Santo Domingo, in order that their presence would not be noticed. At a point some six leagues from a place named Cacalotichan, the Spaniards met the Indians in battle. Several captives were taken, and among them the friendly Conchos recognized the wife and daughter of Tucumudagui. Before the interrogation of these prisoners was completed, some 50 Indians arrived from Cacalotichan. One of the newcomers, a Concho chief named Cocle, tried to explain why he was in this backcountry. He finally pointed out to the Spaniards an Indian, a Concho, who had been captured quite young by the Tarahumara, and who could serve as an interpreter. The Spaniards were delighted because they did not yet have a good interpreter for the Tarahumara and Concho languages. Eventually the Europeans met the great chief or *tatuani* named Tucumudagui and were able to establish peace between the Conchos and Tepehuanes (UTL 1619).

In January of 1621, Tepehuanes from the Valle de San Pablo y San Ignacio, together with some Tarahumara Indians, rose and attacked some estancias in the Santa Bárbara region, looting, burning, and killing some Spaniards and friendly Indians. A Spanish force went out from Durango to San Pablo valley but by this time the rebels had taken refuge in Tarahumara country. This was on March 31, when Governor Mateo de Vesga arrived. The next day he dispatched Captain Francisco Montaño de la Cueva after the enemy with Spanish troops and 200 Indian auxiliaries. Montaño returned to San Pablo on April 18, bringing in 11 rebel Tarahumaras, including one Don Juan Cocle, who said he was king of all the Tarahumara nation, which consisted of 4,000 people. Peace was affirmed with Cocle and with two of his caciques, Don Pablo and Don Francisco, "heads" of Tarahumara rancherias (CPP 5: 126-31).

During this same year, a number of attacks were reported made on Spanish holdings and on friendly Concho rancherias, said to be loyal friends and considered under the protection of the Spanish Crown. On January 20, the enemy Indians attacked the haciendas of Alonso del Castillo, killing several people, including some Conchos Indians. On at least one occasion all of the Conchos of one rancheria were exterminated – reportedly more than 100 persons. Other assaults were also cited; in one, all of the Indians of Juan de Morales were killed (CPP 5: 75-118).

Some Concho Indians living deeper in the hinterland were also restive. Again, in this same year of 1621, a Concho cacique named Alonso was killed by some of these backcountry Conchos while he was on a labor-recruiting trip. The Spaniards considered this a rebellion, and sent a punitive expedition into Concho country in December under Captain Cristóbal Sánchez. About a league downriver from San Bartolomé the Spanish force was met by some 85 Conchos, including "caciques, governors, and captains." These men reportedly offered their services to the Spaniards as additional troops. This indicates that at least some Conchos were peaceful at this time; however, these people were from the mission of San Francisco de Conchos and probably had been requested by the Spanish administrators, or at least had been sent out by their missionary. A few skirmishes took place later with the rebels in the interior; some of the guilty were punished, and at least 10 Indians were taken to Durango, where eight were sold at public auction (Hackett 1926: 130-2; CPP 5: 137-42).

For approximately the next quarter of a century, Conchos Indians virtually disappear from the historical record. Until some time after Parral was founded, in 1631, the Spanish governor of the Nueva Vizcayan province resided in Durango, the center from which Spanish power emanated. During this period, backland warfare was waged with some of the less sedentary peoples of the region – Tepehuanes from around Mapimí, Salineros from the salt-flat country somewhat north and east of Mapimí, and Toboso and Chiso bands in the desert area east of Atotonilco and the Florido River. In 1635, it was reported that some Tepehuanes were still "delinquent" – these consisting of people who were left over and unpunished from past uprisings. An expedition was led out of Parral into Tepehuan-Tarahumara border country, including Las Ciénegas on the upper Conchos River, to pacify these rebels (Hackett 1926: 124, 126, 140-2, 158; CD [1671]; CPP 6: 291-409).

THE REVOLTS OF 1644 AND 1645

In the year 1644, and on into the last half of 1645, the general area to the north and east of the Parral district was aflame with Indian rebellions. While the causes of this outbreak are poorly understood, certain possible contributing factors can be outlined. Silver had been discovered in Parral more than a decade earlier, in 1631, and a few years later at San Diego de Minas Nuevas. As soon as word of these discoveries spread, large numbers of people rushed into the Santa Bárbara district. This influx of new people and the resulting development of Spanish society no doubt placed increased pressure upon the native population in the region. In addition, one source notes a five-year period of drought, accompanied by plague, that occurred immediately preceding the uprising. These combined events were possibly major factors in pushing the native population over the brink to the warpath (West 1949: 13; DHM 1645).

The biggest offenders during the hostilities seem to have been the Tobosos, Salineros, and other non-Concho desert dwellers. Indeed, the Conchos and their allies did not take up arms for the most part until the spring of 1645; when they did go to battle the Spaniards seem to have been either surprised or shocked. These Indians, in contrast to the more or less constantly raiding Tobosos, Salineros, and Cabezas, had been considered loyal subjects of the Spaniards. In fact, it was as late as December of 1644 that the Indian governor of the Conchería had returned to the Parral district with 80 Conchos following a campaign against the Tobosos, Cabezas, and other desert enemies. By August of 1645, most of the Conchería peoples had surrendered, and the remainder of Spanish action was focused upon bringing the rebels living to the east and south to peace, a task that was eventually accomplished by early 1646 (Alegre 1956: II, 37-9; AHP 1645Aa; CD 1644; 1650a; DHM 1645).

When, by the spring (April) of 1645, the Conchos had gone to battle, a rather large group of individual nations were reported to have joined them in the fracas. The Spanish governor, Francisco Montaño de la Cueva, wrote that the confederation included Conchos, Mamites, Julimes, Olozasmes (Olhasmas), Oposmes, Xiximbles, Tocones, Mosnales, Bachichilmes, Tapacolomes (Tapacolmes), Hovomes, Zabasopalmes, Bacabaplames, Ayozomes, Zolomes (Cholomes), and Nababayoguames.* These, he reported, had joined the nations of the Rio Grande (at La Junta); however, some of these were clearly La Junta nations. Other sources also mention the Chisos and Tatamastes as among the rebels. At one time or another, "Conchos" (that is, the various member groups of the confederation) were said to be in league with the rebel bands located farther south, such as Tobosos, Cabezas, Salineros, and Colorados; however, while there was no doubt communication among these peoples, the existence of such a league is poorly borne out by the documentary evidence regarding specific alliances (Alegre 1959: III, 37; CD 1650a; DHM 1645: AHP 1645Aa).

The first hostilities broke out in the area south of the Conchería, but the sources do not clearly indicate just where this general revolt began. Alegre describes it as having started in the area of the missions of Tizonazo (Jesuit) and San Francisco del Mesquital (Franciscan). From the Salineros in this region, the conflagration spread to Tobosos and then to the members of what was later the Concho confederation. Another writer of the period, Nicolás de Zepeda, stated that the Tobosos started it. In either case, general information indicates that a number of these bands – Tobosos, Salineros, and Cabezas – who dwelt in the desert backlands were in perpetual hostilities with the Europeans, because of their raiding activities (Alegre 1959: III, 23-24; DHM 1645).

The Indians of the Conchería apparently began their part in the revolt when the inhabitants of the Concho settlements of the San Bartolomé Valley rose up, killed two people, and stole numerous cattle. From San Bartolomé the Indians moved northward. They first attacked the mission of San Francisco de Conchos, killing the two missionaries

there and profaning the church. They also murdered another Spaniard, named Lorenzo Sotelo Montezuma, and a number of Indians who had remained loyal to the Spanish side (including the Concho governor Joseph Juan, one of his sons, his uncle, and several others). The rebels then continued to the mission of San Pedro de Conchos, where they burned the church and repeated the destruction of church objects. They assaulted the hacienda of Captain Baltazar de Ontiveros, putting to death three Indian workers and carrying off two mulatto girls and most of the livestock. During these hostilities they also attacked Atotonilco and San Luis Mascomalhua (Alegre 1959: III, 39; AHP 1645a; CD 1650a; DHM 1645).

Governor Montaño de la Cueva went after the rebels with a large force, consisting of 90 Spanish horse and 286 Indian auxiliaries as infantry. This contingent penetrated 80 leagues (approximately 240 miles) into the hinterland, to a place called Bamoelchiquipa in the Concho tongue, some 10 leagues from the Rio Grande, and almost certainly on or very near the Conchos River. Here they attacked the Indians on Sunday, July 16, 1645. Some 20 persons were killed, including two Mamite chiefs, and 10 men and 35 women and children were taken prisoner. Another 19 (apparently) were also caught and hung, including the reputed leader of the group. Many of the Indians saved themselves by fleeing across the river to the far side (Alegre 1959: III, 37; CD 1650a).

Montaño then sent messengers to those who had escaped, telling them to come to the Spanish camp to make peace. The chief of the Mamites was the first to surrender, which he did not only in the name of his own group but also for the Olozasmes. About an hour later, one Simón Guajacole, the son of the chief of the La Junta pueblos, also cemented friendship with the Spaniards at a place called San Nicolás. In a later summing-up, Montaño stated that there had been 22 gentile (that is, not yet missionized) nations from the Rio Grande in the rebellion, aside from a number of Christian Concho groups (CD 1650a).

Whatever peoples did not make peace at this time had done so, however, by the beginning of September. Seven bands surrendered to Montaño by sending him a piece of paper with six lines (*rayas*) and two crosses drawn on it. The Julimes, who together with the Mamites had been the prime movers of the rebellion, were some of the last to surrender. Montaño wrote that the most acculturated (*ladinos*) of the Conchos Indians had been with the Julimes (CD 1650a; DHM 1645).

On his return home, sometime before October 11, Montaño settled 170 persons at San Pedro and 100 at San Francisco de Conchos. Following this, he sent another 73 persons of "all nations," plus 40 Mamites, to the pueblos of San Marcos and San Luis (Mascomalhua) and to other places that had been abandoned during the rebellion. He then reported that more Indians from the hinterland were also

---

*Spanish renderings of ethnic and band names vary widely in the written sources. For purposes of accuracy, especially for future researchers, I have spelled these names in the text as they occur in the documents. In the section on band and group names in Chapter 3 I have listed almost all of the names of Conchería peoples, and their variants, that have shown up in the course of research for this paper.

waiting to settle at these places. At the same time, more than 200 Indian workers from the haciendas and other Spanish holdings of the San Bartolomé Valley were returned to their places of work (CD 1650a).

More interesting, however, is some of the information concerning the nature of the rebellion. In fact, some of the features of the uprising indicate that it was a genuine nativistically oriented revitalization movement, similar to the movement a number of years later in 1684 (see below). The leader Bautista, according to Montaño's accounts, preached a strong anti-Spanish-culture doctrine. He told his followers that there was to be no more God, king, priests, or Spaniards. The name of Jesus was not to be mentioned, nor that of Holy Mary; anyone who said such words would die. Rosaries, medallions, and images were not to be worn or carried, and Christian baptismal names were no longer to be used, only native personal names. Bautista exhorted the Indians to kill all Spaniards, to make slaves of their children, and to make use of Spanish women as they wished (CD 1650a; DHM 1654).

In another place, however, Montaño mentioned a certain Thomás, in whom, he said, all the Indians "had placed their hopes." Thomás had begun the rebellion and had been the cause of the death of one Joseph, his father-in-law, possibly the Concho governor Juan Joseph at San Francisco de Conchos (CD 1650a). Father Nicolás de Zepeda noted in his general account of the 1644 revolt that when the Conchos, Julimes, and Mamites had first gone on the warpath, it was reported that the rebels did not have to fear death because the "devil" had told them they would be resurrected in three days (DHM 1645).

THE 1650s TO THE 1680s

The expansion of the Spanish holdings in Nueva Vizcaya made considerable progress during the last half of the 17th century. In the 1650s, new mining discoveries were made in the Parral district, most notably at San Francisco del Oro, northwest of Santa Bárbara some five miles, and at Monserrate, a somewhat shorter distance south of San Diego de Minas Nuevas (West 1949: 13-4). In the missionary field, the Franciscans opened up much new area in the 1650s and 1660s, penetrating along the eastern skirt of the Sierra Madre as far northwest as Casas Grandes and Carretas. Aside from mission personnel, a number of civilians also were entering the region (see Chapter 6: *Conditions at the Missions*).

In the years from 1648 to 1652, the Europeans were occupied with the several Tarahumara rebellions in the area to the west and north of the Parral district, as well as with the more or less constantly raiding desert dwellers to the east. For the most part, the Indians of the Conchería had little part in these uprisings and battles, except that when various Concho settlements were raided by the hostiles, many Concho auxiliaries assisted the Spanish troops against their common enemy (Spicer 1962: 30, 32; AHP 1646Ab;

1653Aa; CD 1646). However, Conchos were occasionally implicated as hostiles. For example, in 1650, it was reported that some of them had joined the Tarahumara to attack the town of Villa de Aguilar in Tarahumara country (BL 1649-1700). It is also known that some Conchos, at least individuals, operated fairly closely with the raiding Tobosos, who were very active in the 1650s, and Conchos and other Indian hacienda workers often joined together for quick raids and other acts of banditry (AHP 1654Aa; 1654Ab; 1655A; 1657B).

In the spring of 1653, the Jesuit José Pascual wrote that the Conchos from Namiquipa had sent a messenger to the Tarahumara to say that they would ally with them against the Spaniards. Conchos, apparently, had also been responsible for some raiding in the area of Pascual's mission of San Felipe during the previous month. The Indian governor of Santa Isabel had reported that a Concho by the name of Jusepe was in revolt and had stolen some cattle from around Santa Cruz and "other places." Jusepe's group had then gone to the vicinity of Namiquipa and had tried to arouse the rancherias in this region. Various reports confirmed, however, that the natives of San Pedro, Chubisca, Santa Isabel, and Babonoyaba were quiet, as were those of Mulatos, Yaguna, and other areas of the Tarahumara (AHP 1653Bb).

Other sources continued to indicate a certain amount of trouble with some of the Conchos, apparently mainly those who lived in the western area. Several Tarahumara in this same year (1653) reported that they had battled a group of Conchos that included several Julimes. Fray Hernando de Urbaneja from the Babonoyoba mission wrote in July and again in August citing incidents that had occurred among the Conchos. The Indians of Batnamiquipa (Namiquipa) had killed two horses they had stolen from a Tarahumara from San Andrés, and three Conchos had killed a horse near Babonoyaba. Seemingly, much of this activity consisted simply of Indians raiding each other. Some Conchos took five horses and some women from the Tarahumaras of Yaguna, because these Tarahumaras had done the same to them. Nevertheless, there is no evidence of any kind of Concho uprising at this time, although a number of these Indians were objecting to having to work for the Spaniards at harvest time. Finally the Spanish sent Juan Sánchez Rico into the region to investigate the situation. Sánchez Rico reported back that aside from a few troublesome Indians, he found the Conchos quite obedient (AHP 1653Bc).

The tension along the Concho-Tarahumara border seems to have continued for the next three or four years. Raids occurred in the area on a number of settlements, both Indian and Spanish. Father Pascual of San Felipe claimed that the attacks made in the region were carried out by Conchos, while the Franciscan Urbaneja at Babonoyaba maintained that much of this raiding was done by Tobosos and other non-Conchos. Reports came in from the several areas to the effect that the raiders spoke Concho, Toboso, Tarahumara, and Tepehuan. Certainly, Conchos were often guilty. In one case, for example, Conchos from Alabachi under Chief Chichipo were reported to have carried out an attack in the Parral area, taking both clothing and animals. It was also said that Conchos got together at San Pedro to send out squads for raiding (AHP 1655A; 1656A).

By 1656, the situation in the Western Conchería had deteriorated to the extent that, at least in the minds of some people, there existed the possibility of a large-scale war between the Tarahumaras and Conchos. Missionaries, and apparently some of the Indians, thought something should be done about the threat. The Spanish government eventually called Concho and Tarahumara chieftains to Parral to establish some kind of peaceful relations among the settlements of the two groups. Concho caciques denied charges made against them, and later the Western Conchería governor sent his captain, a Don Martín, to the Jesuit mission of Father Vijilio Máez to aid in cementing peace. Eventually this entire affair was quieted down. The Spanish captain, Juan Gutiérrez Tamayo, made an inspection tour of the Tarahumara and Concho towns involved, obtaining formal commitments to peace from their officials (AHP 1656A).

While, as noted previously, the Eastern Conchería during these years was for the most part quiet, one group belonging to this jurisdiction, the Chisos, was apparently often active in raiding Spanish settlements. These desert-dwelling Concho speakers were frequently allied with other nomadic groups of the eastern area, and, judging from the documentary sources, Spanish contact with them seems to have been somewhat sporadic.

The term "Chiso" occurs in accounts of the 1644 and 1645 hostilities, but no other information is available on these people at this time, and it is not certain whether the word is used specifically or generically (AHP 1645Aa; CD 1650a; DHM 1645). In the next decade, the Chisos were said to be a large nation that dwelt behind the Tobosos (AHP 1653Ac).

Often during the 1650s, and then occasionally until the 1684 revolt, Chisos were reported to be in a state of war with Conchos, Julimes, Mamites, and other more or less settled groups, as well as with the Europeans. The Eastern Conchería governor during this period, Hernando de Obregón, is known to have made a number of trips and sallies into Chiso country either to punish them or to investigate disturbances; Chiso bands were often said to be in league with Tobosos. No doubt because of the more hostile attitude of these people, it seems to have been customary for the Spanish, when they were in contact with Chisos, to admonish them to be peaceful toward Spanish settlements and to fight the Tobosos (AHP 1653Aa; 1653Ac; 1653Bb; 1653Bd; 1654Aa; 1655A; 1656A; 1658Aa).

Occasionally Chisos requested settlement with the Spaniards, but this type of contact occurred on occasion with all of the desert raiding groups. For example, in 1673 a large number of Chisos arrived at San Francisco de Conchos, stating that they wanted to settle down and embrace the Catholic faith. Spanish authorities, however, saw too many difficulties in having all these Chisos in one place, so they decided to distribute the Indians among several places of work in the Parral district. It is unknown what the outcome of this decision was (AHP 1673A).

THE UPRISING OF 1666

After 1656, there is little information on the Conchos for about a decade. Probably the situation in the general region of the Conchería continued approximately as it had since the major uprisings of the mid-1640s. The people of the Eastern Conchería remained essentially at peace, either living on Spanish haciendas or living in their own towns while they worked for the Spaniards. From later events it seems that the Western Conchería peoples may have continued to have their troubles. Some of these were with the Tarahumara; others, with the Europeans, resulted from the pressure of missions and settlers in the area; and the Indians continued to resist to some extent the obligation to work for the Spaniards.

The years 1666–67 saw flare-ups of Indian troubles on the frontier. In 1666 some of the western Conchos in the areas of recent Spanish contact were reported to be in rebellion, but the incident turned out to be rather minor. Precise details regarding the events of this uprising are lacking, but records indicate that a drought occurred about this time, followed by a famine and a plague. In 1667, Tobosos, Cabezas, and Salineros went on the warpath, and accounts indicate that Conchos were in communication with these rebels (Anonymous 1954: 30; Hackett 1926: 188–92; BL 1649–1700; DHM 1667a; 1667b; 1669).

In the spring (March) of 1667, the Nueva Vizcayan governor, Antonio de Oca Sarmiento, wrote that the Conchos (but only some of them) had attempted an uprising "in imitation" of the desert-dwelling Tobosos and Salineros, who maintained themselves in open defiance of Spanish authority. In a later piece of correspondence he made note of the miraculous success of the Spaniards in putting down the movement (Hackett 1926: 188; CPP 9: 463–83; 15: 527–34; DHM 1667a; UTD 1671–1685).

It is unknown how or when the rebellion began. However, once Spanish authorities learned of it they made a punitive expedition into what Oca Sarmiento called the greatest part of the Concho province, getting as far northwest as Amiquipa (Namiquipa) (BL 1649–1700).

When troops reached San Pedro de Conchos, the Western Concho governor, Don Constantino, and the Eastern Concho governor, Don Hernando de Obregón, were questioned. These men had some Concho chiefs brought before the Spaniards, and it was learned that four rancherias of Conchos, belonging to different bands (*parcialidades*), were the ones who were actually up in arms. Under one Matías, from the hacienda of the Sáenz family, these groups were attempting to attract to their cause the rest of the Conchos, some wild Indians (*bozales* – of unstated affiliation), and the people of Casas Grandes (Sumas?). The specific complaint registered was that they did not want to go to work on the harvest on Spanish holdings (BL 1649–1700; DHM 1669).

After sending messages to the Indians from the Sáenz hacienda to return to their lands in peace from the mountain to which the Indians had fled, the Spanish group moved northward from San Pedro to Santiago de Babonoyaba, then through La Cieneguilla, the Santa Isabel mission, and San Andrés, to Santa Cathalina de Namiquipa. Here they arrived on November 24, 1666. Along the way they had sent messengers to Conchos living along the Tarahumara border and to the rancherias north of Namiquipa, in the direction of Casas Grandes. Oca Sarmiento made his headquarters at Namiquipa, where there were several Concho settlements; from here he sent forth contingents and eventually located the chiefs of the rebellion. Some of the Concho leaders were chastized and new officials were appointed for their settlements. The Spanish force then marched back home, after sending word of the state of the situation to Captain Andrés de Gracia at Casas Grandes (BL 1649–1700).

Despite the success of the Spanish authorities in putting down the most rebellious of the Concho rancherias at this time, a few years later, in 1669, when the Bishop of Durango made an inspection trip into the region, he reported that the natives were still in turmoil, and for the same reasons given on previous occasions – they objected to the harsh conditions under which they were forced to work at Spanish holdings (CPP 315–32). However, no widespread, open revolt of the peoples of the Conchería occurred for another 15 years.

THE 1684 REVOLT

In the middle of the year 1684, four years after the great Pueblo revolt in New Mexico, the tribes of northern Mexico, from the Sierra Madre into the desert country to the east, rose up against Spanish authority.* At one time or another almost all of the peoples of the region were involved – Conchos; Julimes; La Juntans; Sumas from Casas Grandes, the Rio Grande, and the intervening desert area; and many other peoples. The only exception was the Tarahumaras, who, however, were reported to be "restless" on occasion during this period (AGN 1684).

In the early phases, this rebellion was generalized over a broad area and the Spaniards tended to view the various uprisings as some kind of conspiracy. However, as events developed, something of the underlying regional disunity of the area began to show through what initially appeared to

be homogeneity; also, the lack of ability to maintain continuous, coordinated effort, especially on the part of the more settled Indian groups, became quite evident.

No doubt there was communication among the several tribal groups, and this included, of course, contact with people from New Mexico. However, it is impossible to document very thoroughly the amount of contact and the kinds of alliances that actually took place. Whatever impetus the New Mexican situation may have given to the trouble in 1684, sustained and coordinated effort seems to have occurred only at the beginning.

For ease of presentation, the general area can be divided into three parts – the northwest, the central valleys and northeast, and the eastern desert – and to some extent this division is supported by the course of events during and after the uprising. In the west, including part of the central desert area, Sumas, Janos, Jocomes, Mansos, Chinarras, and Conchos took part. After a period of Spanish retaliation these people were more or less pacified, although trouble between them and the Spaniards continued to broil for many years afterward. Indeed, as Spicer has noted, this was a border area involving several different tribal groups – apparently a recent situation – and the relations among these different ethnic entities were not yet well worked out, or were having to be reworked because of the new contact conditions. It is immediately after this period that the Apaches emerge as the dominant people, with a way of life adjusted to the new conditions in this area of the frontier (Spicer 1962: 230–2).

Farther to the east, along the valleys of the rivers that eventually empty into the Rio Grande, and down to La Junta proper, the rebellion took a somewhat different course. Again, as in the 1640s, the hostilities carried out by these people were short-lived; in part they were supported by a leader who arose to preach a fairly clear-cut, anti-Spanish-culture doctrine, but his message apparently failed rather quickly to satisfy his followers. After about six months, all or most of the river-dwelling Indians returned to the Spanish fold and resumed their work on haciendas and ranches and in mines (Hackett 1926: 218–24; AHP 1684Aa).

In the eastern desert country, from the Big Bend to the Parras-Laguna district, the pattern was again different. These peoples – Toboso, Salinero-Cabeza, and Coahuila groups, and at least some Chisos – had been raiding for decades, and the practice was now fairly well integrated into their respective ways of life. It would appear that the period around 1684 was simply a high point in what had become their normal pattern of activities (Hackett 1926: 218–24; AHP 1684A; Griffen 1969).

What might be called the "causes" of this particular revolt are not clear. While many Spaniards felt that these hostilities were carried out in imitation of or at the instigation of New Mexican Indians, certainly local conditions in northern Mexico played a significant part, and an adequate account of the factors behind the uprising will have

---

*This revolt and various aspects of it have been written up elsewhere (see, for example, Forbes 1960; Hughes 1914; Spicer 1962). Only a brief summary will be presented here, focusing upon the interaction and movement of local peoples of the Conchería, and emphasizing the sources in the Parral Archives.

to await new evidence. One source refers to a great drought (*la seca tan grande*) in the Casas Grandes district; otherwise it is unclear whether harvests had been poor in the years immediately preceding the trouble, whether plagues and sickness had increased, or whether other factors of this nature were in operation, adding to the tension felt by local Indians in this culture-contact situation (AHP 1684Ab; 1684Db).

One factor that certainly would have increased tension was the arrival of the many New Mexican settlers who eventually moved on into Nueva Vizcaya after the Spaniards had been driven out of New Mexico to El Paso. New Mexicans are reported to have resettled in the northwest in Casas Grandes, Santa Ana del Torreón (in the San Buenaventura valley area), and Namiquipa; south of the latter in the Papigochi Valley in the Tarahumara and in the region of Babonoyaba, and at San Juan de la Concepción; and at Nombre de Dios (in the vicinity of present-day Chihuahua City), north of the latter up the Sacramento River, and east and south to Julimes. A number of complaints had been registered against these New Mexicans by both Tarahumara and Concho Indians, and these complaints were said to be particularly heavy in the area between Casas Grandes and Namiquipa. At one time the Spanish governor, Joseph Neira y Quiroga, noting the great friction between these settlers and the Indians, ordered the New Mexicans to appear before him within 20 days, the penalty for noncompliance being either deportation from Nueva Vizcaya or death (AHP 1684Db; 1684Dc; AGN 1684).

This influx of people into the area, putting increased pressure upon the land, food, and natural resources in general, was probably an important contributing factor in triggering off the revolt. Indeed, the Spanish commander at Casas Grandes, Francisco Ramírez, wrote to General Juan de Retana to this very effect. The New Mexicans seemingly had usurped Indian lands as they saw fit, and he noted that the Spaniards at Casas Grandes had not only planted on Indian lands but had also moved into the Indians' houses. However, Ramírez did not place the entire blame for the uprising upon the colonists but added that such people as traders from Parral and Sonora, and even the missions of the region, had played their part in the Indian unrest. In another statement Ramírez put the blame on the Mansos at El Paso for inciting the natives in the Casas Grandes area (AHP 1684Ac; CPP 23: 10–13).

The Northwest

In early May, what are considered the first hostilities of the 1684 rebellion broke out in the Casas Grandes district; however, restlessness had been noted among the Mansos at El Paso as early as 1681, and Chisos, Tobosos, and others had already been causing trouble. Shortly after this, Indians began to leave the San Bartolomé Valley and the Spanish holdings in the Parral district to join the rebels (AHP 1684Ab;

1684Db). (See DiPeso 1974: 866–75 passim for many more details on the hostilities and their archaeological context in the Casas Grandes area.)

North of Casas Grandes, on May 6, a combined group of Sumas and Janos Indians attacked the mission of Nuestra Señora de la Soledad at Janos, killing the lay brother, Fray Manuel Beltrán, and carrying off alive four Spanish women and three children. A *mozo* at the mission escaped to warn the people at Casas Grandes. A week later, on May 12 or 13 (or both), the Indians attacked the Casas Grandes settlement. By the time the Spanish military, consisting of about six men under Ramírez, could reach the mission itself, the Indians settled there had already joined the rebels and the Spaniards found Fray Juan de Porras there alone (AHP 1684Db; CPP 23: 5–16).

Hostilities lasted in this northwestern area for several months. Many Christian Sumas and Janos had gathered at Carretas, which place they eventually destroyed. Conchos who had lived south of Casas Grandes reportedly joined Sumas from El Ojito de Samalayuca and razed the mission of Santa Gertrudis. Sumas and Mansos of the El Paso district also went on the warpath (Forbes 1960: 201–2; AHP 1684Db; CPP 14: 98–102; 23: 5–16).

The Spaniards at Casas Grandes pursued the rebels, eventually cornering them at a mountain called El Peñol del Diablo. On June 2 (or possibly the day before) the Spanish forces engaged in a pitched battle with the rebels, and were beaten off. The Spanish commander, Ramírez de Salazar, estimated the enemy to be about 2,000 strong and to include the Sumas, Jocomes, Janos, Chinarras, Mansos, Conchos, "and other unknown nations." A report from Francisco Cuervo y Valdez characterized the rebel nations as being the Sumas, Janos, Jocomes, Chinarras, Mansos, part of the Conchos, "and other nations from the sand dunes of the Río del Norte. . ." (Forbes 1960: 203; AHP 1684Ab; 1684Ac; CPP 14: 98–102; 23: 5–16).

In September, Janos, Sumas and other raiders attacked and sacked Casas Grandes, burning buildings and driving off many animals. Attacks and assaults in the general area continued for the next couple of months. By December, with the help of a number of reinforcements, Ramírez established what turned out to be a somewhat precarious peace with the northwestern rebels. By this time, many settlements and homesteads had been assaulted and animals stolen or killed. Several missions had also been destroyed, including Janos and Carretas, and apparently also El Torreón (Forbes 1960: 204–5; AHP 1684Da; 1684Db).

In the meantime, before peace was established with the northwestern bands, many other attacks and hostilities took place in the central desert and northwest portion of the Conchería. Sometime after May 20, a large Spanish wagon train, en route by way of the Laguna de San Martín to the northern salt flats (Las Salinas) and to El Paso with supplies, was stopped at Las Encinillas by a large contingent of rebel

Indians. These were all or mainly Sumas; while they had the wagons surrounded some Conchos arrived and offered the Sumas clothing, horses, and deerskins. Finally, the Suma chief told the Spaniards that he and his men were off to Agua Nueva, about three leagues away, for a large meeting or gathering of Indians, apparently including Conchos, Chinarras, Julimes, and "other nations." These rebel Indians, the chief said, were also in league with the people of Sonora and with the Tobosos; however, all the men who would be needed to attack the settlement of El Paso would be at the junta at Agua Nueva (AHP 1684Ab).

Three other large gatherings or juntas of Indians were reported about this same time. One was at La Cieneguilla, in the area of Agua Nueva and Las Encinillas, one on the Rio Grande, and one at Nombre de Dios. Captain Pedro Márquez at Nombre de Dios gave an account saying that the Spaniards there (some seven or eight men) had been living day and night with their weapons in their hands. This he wrote on May 24, stating that for more than 12 days Indians had been coming in from other places. One squad had arrived on May 22 from Santa Clara and the Casas Grandes area. All the Indians had then held a large dance that night, and Márquez stated that the Spaniards assumed that the natives had probably brought scalps with them from some of the people they had killed at Casas Grandes (AHP 1684Ab).

Later, the Indians from the gatherings at Agua Nueva and Las Encinillas assaulted Los Sauces (nearby, and consisting only of a few Spanish huts), and then attacked various places around Nombre de Dios, including an estancia called San Lorenzo, stealing a number of horses and cattle. It was reported that they were also planning to descend on El Valle – probably El Valle de San Bartolomé. Still later, on July 20 or 21, a hacienda at Tabalaopa was hit and on July 27, off to the northwest, the Janos and Chinarras raided the settlement of Santa Clara, where some Spaniards had apparently settled. A number of isolated Spanish homesteads were also attacked and destroyed (AHP 1684Ab; 1684Da; 1684Db).

The Central Valleys and the Northeast

For the peoples of the Conchos River and La Junta areas, the immediate circumstances before the uprising were somewhat different from those in the Casas Grandes and general western area. Particularly for the La Junta region this period was, at least superficially, one of increased contact with the Spanish empire, although this did not involve immigrant settlers from the outside. Rather the contact was with missionaries and an expedition into the area. In October of 1683, Juan Sabeata, a Jumano chief, and several other native *principales* testified in El Paso that the Indians wanted missionaries sent to them at La Junta, but that similar requests had been turned down in Parral.

The Franciscan Nicolás López took interest in this new possibility for conversions, and he informed the Indians that

before missionaries would be sent to them they first would have to build churches. Shortly afterwards, when López arrived at La Junta with his two companions, Fray Juan de Zavaleta and Fray Antonio de Acevedo, they found that two churches had already been built, and seven more were soon put up (apparently all of reeds and similar material). Soon after this Maestre de Campo Juan Domínguez de Mendoza arrived at La Junta on his way into the interior of Texas. López and Zavaleta joined his group, leaving Acevedo in charge of the La Junta missions. Good progress in missionization was reported while Acevedo was alone at La Junta (Bolton 1911; 1912; Hackett 1934: 349-53; Hughes 1914: 332-3; Kelley 1952b; 1955; DHM 18th).

In June of 1684, when López and Domínguez were about to return to El Paso, the La Juntans asked that another six missionaries be sent to them, possibly indicating a genuine desire for more intense contact with the Spanish way of life. However, by this time the peoples in the desert country between La Junta and Casas Grandes were already on the warpath (Hughes 1914: 333, 358; AHP 1684Ab; 1684Db).

Slightly before this time, apparently by May 25 (letter from Juan de Retana, May 28, 1684, cited by Forbes 1960: 202), the Conchos River and La Juntan Indian laborers who worked in the Parral district were leaving to join the rebel forces to the north, and some Conchos had been active even as early as May 20 (AHP 1684Ab; 1684Db; 1685Db).

There is little information on the actual participation of these peoples in the general uprising. In July, testimonies taken at Parral indicated that the Concho governor Hernando de Obregón and two other leaders, Don Juan de Salaices and Don Diego, were at La Junta with a large group of Indians who were making preparations to attack the Spaniards. Salaices, whose name is otherwise given little importance in the documentary sources, seems to have figured most importantly as a leader in these plans. His "rancheria" was the site of the San Cristóbal church, and a place where many of the rebel Indians congregated at one time or another (AHP 1684Aa; 1685Db).

Some 18 Indians were executed at Parral around this time (summer) for inciting rebellion. This may only have antagonized the natives, although apparently some groups remained more or less faithful to the Spanish throughout the trouble. Obregón declared later that the reason for the Indians' withdrawal from the haciendas to take part in the revolt had been the recent imprisonments of natives by the Spanish authorities. This statement probably refers to some trouble earlier that spring, around March and April, that involved Chisos in particular, although some Conchos had also been implicated (Hughes 1914: 358; AHP 1684Aa; 1684Db).

Late this same spring, General Juan de Retana, commander of the San Francisco presidio, made an entrada down the Conchos River, getting at least as far as La Junta. Apparently the Concho governor, Obregón, and the Franciscan Fray Juan de Sumesta were also along (AHP 1685Db).

The river dwellers were active only for six months or so; by February of 1685 most had come in to make peace with the Spaniards. Among the returning Indians was a Concho called variously Domingo, Taagua, or Montezuma, and there were a number of stories being circulated concerning his supernatural power. Some of the Indians said he was evil by nature and in the deeds he performed – for instance, he had given the Indians to understand that he could fathom all the thoughts and designs of the Spaniards. It was he, so the rumor had it, who had been the instigator behind the general withdrawal from the Spanish settlements at the start of the revolt (AHP 1685Db).

From testimonies taken shortly thereafter by the Spaniards when they learned of these reports, this individual was clearly the leader of a nativistic movement, and his doctrine gave a number of the local peoples an ideological support for the rebellion. Unfortunately, the factors leading up to Taagua's formulation of the code he finally presented to his followers can only be guessed at (see Wallace 1956; AHP 1685Db).

Several Indians, including the leader himself, testified regarding the movement and the doctrine preached. These witnesses, in order, were: Lucas Tamo, a Tapacolme who was described as a hacienda worker for one Lope de Hierro, apparently in the San Bartolomé Valley; Antón Auchi, also a Tapacolme who worked for Hierro, but who said he lived at San Pedro de Conchos; Hernando Casuela, a Concho who worked for Juan de Navarrete; and Gaspar de los Reyes, alias El Gasmunio ("the hypocrite"), also a Concho and a servant on the Muñoz de Rivera hacienda. These two Conchos reportedly spoke Spanish fluently. The leader, Taagua, who also gave his confession at this time, was a Concho, estimated to be about 30 years of age, and his native name was said to translate into Spanish as Montezuma (AHP 1685Db).

Taken together, the statements of these "witnesses" afford a fair picture of the movement. Much of what follows is taken from Taagua's confession, in which he admitted everything that the others said about him except one point, as noted below. It seems that some six years previously he had fled from the hacienda of Domingo de Apresa, and that the time of this questioning was the first occasion on which he had actually been back in the immediate Parral district. One of the witnesses, however, stated that for about two years before the revolt he had heard of Taagua's reputation, and another said that he knew Taagua had been at Tabalaopa, San Pedro de Conchos, and San Marcos trying to get up some dances and mitotes. As might be expected, then, Taagua was already a religious or ceremonial leader of some note among the Indians of the area (AHP 1685Db).

Taagua stated that before the revolt he had been on his way back to Domingo de Apresa's place. However, when he arrived at Todos Santos he learned that many Indians were being hung in Parral (possibly a reference to the execution of 18 Indians noted above, a result of the earlier spring investigation that the Spaniards had carried out). With this news, out of fear he turned back and went to San Pedro, and then on to Bachimba. Apparently he had been spreading his message at this time, because he confessed that he had spent two days at Bachimba waiting for the Indians from the haciendas. They all finally congregated at San Antonio (de Julimes), and Taagua mentioned specifically that "Julimes, Mamites, Conchos and other nations" marched with him to the pueblo of San Cristóbal at La Junta (AHP 1685Db).

Casuela, the Concho, reported that he was already at La Junta when Taagua arrived. When the leader was a short distance away, the people had gone out to meet him with lighted cigarettes, so that they could give him some, and then they could all come to the gathering place joyfully and smoking contentedly over his arrival (AHP 1685Db).

At La Junta, Taagua went to the rancheria of the Indian chief Don Juan de Salaices, where he appropriated the newly constructed church of San Cristóbal. Somewhat later, a large dance was held at this settlement (AHP 1685Db).

Witnesses stated that Taagua often sat at the foot of the altar inside the church. From here he would talk to another man standing close by who relayed Taagua's statements to the crowd in a loud voice. Taagua's message was that his Indian followers should be of good spirit and have courage, because the supernatural had communicated power to him, power to help the Indians overcome the Spaniards (AHP 1685Db).

With this power, Taagua claimed he could magically remove the long bone or wrist bone (*canilla*) from the arms of the Spaniards while at the same time stuffing them with grass (*sacate*). This would leave the Europeans maimed so that they could not fire their arquebuses, use their swords, or fight in any other manner. One witness said that the weapons of the Spanish would fall to pieces, their horses would be immobilized, and the Spaniards themselves would drop dead. Furthermore, if the Indians would go to battle with the proper spirit (*animo*), they would not have to use their bows and arrows, but simply go up to the dead Spaniards and take what booty they wanted from their bodies (AHP 1685Db).

According to the testimony, while the rebelling Indians were congregated at La Junta, General Juan Fernández de Retana arrived with his punitive forces. It is not certain whether any fighting actually took place, but Taagua, of course, preached that the natives could easily overcome Retana's men. After the Spanish troops were subdued, he had preached, he and his followers would march on Parral; he would send for wind or a flood, or, failing this, a large cloud of stones, which would come and destroy everything, knock down the buildings, and kill all of the Spaniards and (in one statement) their Indian allies. One witness added that with the destruction of Parral the Indians were going to move on to where the king lived and, the implication was, finish him off too (AHP 1685Db).

Such was Taagua's message, and witnesses testified that

all of the Indians were afraid of him, which was why they had fled from the haciendas. One man testified that Taagua's power had come from the saint, Santiago, who had communicated to him from heaven. Taagua confessed, however, that he had received this message and power from his father, whom he named as Don Lázaro (he did not mention Santiago); Don Lázaro had communicated through his messenger Gabriel, and had commanded that all of the Indians obey his son. One man stated that Taagua had claimed that he himself was God, but this statement may have been made for its effect upon the Spaniards (AHP 1685Db).

Other aspects of Taagua's leadership behavior were described by the declarants. Taagua would seat himself in church, holding a cane (*baston*) or painted stick in his left hand. On three occasions – once inside the church of San Cristóbal, another time outside this same church when sitting on some buffalo hides, and the third time at San Antonio where the Indians first gathered to meet him – Taagua had received formal obedience from his followers. They would come up in turn, kneel before him three times, and kiss his left hand; Taagua would then bless them as the priests did (AHP 1685Db).

Two of the witnesses, Auchi and Cazuela, stated that they had heard among the Indians gathered at La Junta that Taagua never ate food, but only smoked (*chupaba*). Both went on to say, however, that they later saw him consume rather large meals (judging from the menus they cited) (AHP 1685Db).

Lucas Tamo reported having heard from among the people that Taagua had claimed that the marriages the Franciscans had performed were not legitimate because the Fathers had never returned to La Junta; consequently, the men and women could associate with whomever they wished because there would be no Spaniards around to reprimand them. Taagua denied this, but admitted that there had been a rumor going around to the effect that "there would no longer be any compadrazgos [that is, Church rites of baptism, marriage, etc.] because God has passed on and there was now another way of living" (AHP 1685Db).

As mentioned above, not all of the Indian nations became hostile to the Spaniards during this revolt, and one of the persons testifying in Taagua's case made note of this. Witnesses estimated that the Indians at La Junta ran between 1,000 and 2,000 persons. Tamo stated that those who had joined Taagua were the Pusalmes, Polalmes (Polacmes), Cacalotes, Conejos, Cholomes, and Conchos, and a number of other groups that he was "unfamiliar with." Other nations – such as the Oposmes, Pulicas, Auchanes, and Tapacolmes – had claimed they were not angry with the Europeans. This had infuriated Taagua, who threatened them with his power, fearing that they would try to make peace with the Spaniards; he accused them of having freed a certain Matías del Hierro who had been with Retana's expedition when the latter had gone to talk to the rebels (AHP 1685Db).

Once apprehended, Taagua readily confessed to every-thing, with the one exception already noted. He stated that he had acted as the witnesses testified because he had been "deceived by the devil." Interestingly, one witness had previously reported that while they were all on the road on their way back to the Spanish settlements, the Julimes Indians (Taagua actually may have been a Julime) had said that Taagua was among them but that no one should mention it – he would simply take up work on a hacienda and no one would be the wiser. Taagua had replied to this, however, stating that it made no difference if the Spanish apprehended him because he had done everything under the orders of his "father." The Spanish authorities in Parral apparently did not feel that Taagua's role in the revolt had been very serious, for they merely sentenced him to four years of personal service on a hacienda (AHP 1685Db).

The Eastern Desert

Finally, the peoples of the desert region east of the Conchería proper were also considered to have been a part of the 1684 revolt. As noted earlier, warfare and raiding were generally endemic among these nomadic peoples; for several months before the Suma and their allies took up arms in the Casas Grandes district, the Spaniards had been investigating their hostile activities (AHP 1684Aa).

Raids on Spanish settlements and wagon trains had been carried on as far south as Las Bocas. Chisos in particular – Chichitames, Osatayoliclas, and Guesecpayoliclas, as well as others – were involved, and they were sometimes reported to be in close alliance with Tobosos in these activities. In some of the testimonies, "Chisos" were reported to be intending to kill not only Spaniards, but Conchos, Julimes, and Mamites as well, apparently because these Indians were considered to be friends of the Europeans. However, some Conchos also were definitely involved in the hostilities, and the long-time Concho governor, Don Hernando de Obregón, was implicated and brought before the Spaniards to testify. Several places, including the town of San Antonio (apparently the later Julimes, and the permanent residence of Obregón), were cited as locations where the Indians would congregate for their raiding activities (Hackett 1926: 218–24; AHP 1684Aa).

THE FINAL STAGES OF CONCHERIA HISTORY

In the period of the half-century or so after the 1684 uprisings, the region of the Conchería underwent a number of changes, and by the end of the century, results of the many contacts between Spaniards and Indians were contributing toward the development of a rather different frontier situation. In the Conchería during the 17th century, Spaniards very often dealt with the many Indian communities as units, working through the various native leaders; on occasion the relations between Spaniards and Indians were intensified by large-scale outbreaks of native revolts, when the various Indian rancherias would temporarily join together. As time went on, many of these Indian communities ceased to exist, and during the 18th century those that remained became increasingly subordinate to Spanish settlements. Consequently, there were no more native uprisings within the heartland of the Conchería, and the focus of Spanish-Indian conflict receded to the peripheries of the Concho province, where outlying groups engaged in continuous, small-scale fighting and raiding.

This period was also marked, especially in the early years, by expansion and changes in Spanish society. Indeed, this was the time of the last great push of the Spaniards in the development of frontier settlements. In the 1680s, the Jesuits opened up their Upper Tarahumara mission district. Farther away from the Conchería, in the west coast area, the Jesuits also founded the Upper Pima mission district in 1687; 10 years later these Black Robes began the missionization of Lower California. In the north, by 1692, Spaniards were definitely moving back into New Mexico, after their expulsion from that province 12 years earlier by the revolting Pueblo Indians (Spicer 1962: 33-5, 105, 118-9, 162).

Within the Conchería in 1694, a decade after an abortive attempt to missionize La Junta, the Franciscans reorganized and made a major step in the development of their mission holdings all over the province. In 1714-1715, the men of this order began to have a more lasting effect on the La Juntans, and they maintained missions for most of the next 50 or so years at the Conchos-Rio Grande confluence. Finally, in 1707 at Santa Eulalia, and in 1709 at San Francisco de Cuéllar (later to become San Felipe el Real de Chihuahua) – both in the area of present-day Chihuahua City – new mines were opened up. These developments, preceded by a short but intensive silver rush at Cusihuiriachic in 1685, produced fundamental shifts in the locus of Spanish population and power in the years following (Almada and others 1959: 1-5; Massey 1949; AHP 1715Ac).

Without much question, the native Indian population of the Conchería felt the burden of this increased contact with Spanish society. The peoples in the heart of the province seemingly submitted to this pressure and became more a part of Spanish society. The 1684 revolt was the last time the Conchos in the eastern area acted as any kind of a unit, with the exception of the peoples living at La Junta; the Conchos who lived in the west ceased to be any kind of a unit soon after 1697, the time of their last attempted rebellion. Indeed, from the turn of the 18th century, references to these people as a group or nation virtually cease; the position of governor is not cited for the Eastern Conchería after the 1680s, nor for the Western Conchería after the 1690s.

By the 1690s, the Tarahumara on the western edge of the Conchería were feeling the increased pressure of Spanish expansion. The Upper Tarahumara rose up some three times during this decade, although following the last hostilities, in 1697, they remained essentially quiet in their mountain-

ous refuge for the remainder of the colonial period. These Tarahumara troubles did, however, affect some of the Concho population of the northwest part of the Conchería during the 1690s.

To the east of the Conchería, in the desert region of the greater Bolsón de Mapimí, other events were taking place that also had some effects upon the peoples of the Conchería proper. At this time the Cabezas Indians were a fairly good-sized raiding band that had been operating in the more southerly portions of Nueva Vizcaya and western Coahuila – Mapimí, Parras, Cuatro Ciénagas, and Monclova – but who occasionally extended their raiding operations farther south. Around 1690 they made peace with the Spaniards and settled permanently at the town of Parras.

The capitulation of these Cabezas left a niche open for the remaining nomadic-raiding Indians, such as Tobosos and some of the other Coahuila groups. The Tobosos dwelt just east of the Parral district and often were in league with Coahuila groups as well as with Chisos to the north. They suffered considerable losses at the hands of the Spaniards – both by the sword and by deportation – during this turn-of-the-century transition period. Finally, in the mid-1720s, the last of the Toboso bands were deported from the province, together with a number of Coahuilans.

The demise of the Tobosos and of a portion of the Coahuilan population left, in turn, a new opening to be occupied by the few remaining Chisos and other Coahuilans, and some of the more desert-nomadic peoples in the area around La Junta, such as Cholomes and Sumas. By 1740 Apaches from the north were also moving across the Rio Grande, as Chisos had been doing before them; indeed, pressure from Apaches had been felt by some of the Rio Grande peoples since the 1680s (Bolton 1930: 321ff; Griffen 1969).

As Apaches and others from the north extended their zones of exploitation south of the Rio Grande, the peoples such as the La Juntans, who were already inhabiting the region, were confronted with a new and rather different type of contact situation. This was even true for the more nomadic Sumas and Cholomes, some of whom were doing considerable raiding in the 1740s and 1750s. The end result was that La Juntans as well as other original inhabitants of the region were forced eventually to move closer to or to join Spanish settlements as the Apaches became more entrenched in the area.*

In the western portion of the Conchería, a very similar process took place. Raiding bands of Indians developed, relying heavily upon Spanish settlements for much of their sustenance; eventually these groups were dominated and then taken over by the Apaches. As in the east, these no-

---

*I agree with Kelley (1952a) that the pressure from the Apaches supposedly felt by the La Juntans may be quite overrated. It is to be hoped that additional research in this region, possibly of an ecological nature, will uncover some of the other factors in the population shifts that took place in the 17th and 18th centuries.

madic raiders were indiscriminate in their attacks – any settled communities were fair game, Indian or Spanish – and the more sedentary natives were eventually forced to move in with the Spaniards. The Spanish reaction to this change in the Indian scene was to increase their own organization of frontier defense. From 1685 on into the next century, they developed their presidio system in an ineffectual attempt to combat the now quite efficient raiding specialists inhabiting the backlands.

In summary, the history of the Conchería and its original native population all but ceases after the early 1700s, except for the area of La Junta, whose peoples continue to be documented well past mid–century. The outstanding episodes more and more concern the warring-raiding groups; the more settled Indians were turning into remnant populations, occupying a lower-ranking status in Spanish society and becoming at least partly acculturated and assimilated, with little power in the determination of events.

The Northeast Conchería

In the last half of the 1680s and well into the 1700s, raids and attacks by Chisos and others continued in the general northeastern area. Indeed, the termination of the 1684 revolt among the Conchos proper seems to have involved little, if any, cessation of hostilities on the part of the more nomadic peoples. In 1686 and again in 1688, Chisos and Chichitames, together with Cholomes and Tobosos, were on the warpath. Such activity, of course, only evoked punitive action from the Spaniards. In late 1688 or 1689, General Juan de Retana, the commander of the presidio of San Francisco de Conchos, made an expedition into the La Junta region (Hackett 1926: 248–56; UTD 1683-1697).

Whatever effect Retana's action had, it seems to have been rather ephemeral, and the Chisos and their allies continued to commit depredations. In 1691, it was learned that seven nations were banded together; six of these were cited as the Satayolilas (Osapayoliglas), Chichitames, Guasipayoles (Guesecpayoliclas), Hijos de la Tierra, Hijos de las Piedras, and Cocoyomes; the first three were Chiso bands, the last three Tobosos. It is unknown what the seventh nation was; however, the Suninolilas (Seuliyoliclas) and the Sisimbles were also reported to be active at this time (BL 1693b).

On October 23, 1691, Retana reported that he had received a message from Julimes from Don Nicolás, Indian governor of the "nations of the north"; Nicolás was on his way to Conchos with the Suninolila chief and four warriors. For some undetermined reason, about six leagues from the presidio, the Suninolilas fled. The governor, however, continued on to report the incident, stating he knew of no reason for these men to have turned back since the northeastern bands were now ready to talk peace. Retana then dispatched four Indian messengers to the northern nations (unspecified). At the same time, to the head chief of the Cisinbles (Sisimbles) he sent a banner (*bandera*), a hat, and other gifts. He

did this, he recounted, because the Sisimble chief was the cacique whom all the other nations in the area respected (BL 1693b).

In 1692 and into the following year, Chisos, including the Batayolilas, Solinyolicuas (Seuliyoliclas), and Chichitames, together with Cholomes and Cíbolos, were reported to be still at war with Spanish settlements, and this included some raiding of the La Junta pueblos. Because of the refusal of these peoples to make and to keep the peace, Retana found it necessary, in 1693, to carry out another campaign to La Junta in an attempt at pacification. After this expedition all of these nations, except for the Sisimbles, were said to have been reduced to peace by Retana. Later this same year Chichitames, Osatayoliclas, Guesecpayoliclas, and Sisimbles settled at San Francisco de Conchos for a short period. Indeed, the Suninoliglas and Batayoliglas appeared before Retana while he was at La Junta, and they were granted the old Tapacolme site on the Rio Grande for a settlement. The population of the two groups together was counted at 300 persons. During this same period, considerable communication took place between the Spaniards and the Cíbolos and Jumanos, through their governor, Don Juan Xaviata (Hackett 1926: 248-54, 260, 280-7, 328-58, 396-8; AHP 1722Bb; BL 1693b; 1695a).

Hostilities apparently continued in this northeastern region, but the documentary sources are quite incomplete. Tobosos were constant troublemakers and Chisos were often said to be in league with them (AHP 1704Aa). In 1710, Chinarras, although supposedly at peace, were raiding in the area of Chihuahua City (San Francisco Cuéllar). About two years later, Cholomes attacked the towns and environs of San Antonio de Julimes and San Pablo, and carried away some 40 head of cattle from these settlements. This was, however, no mere hit-and-run raid, for these Cholomes had previously spent more than a month in the town of Julimes trading and selling deerskins before they drove off their booty. Unfortunately, further information on this assault is not available, except for a note that a contingent from Julimes took out after the raiders. They managed to capture a horse belonging to the attacking squad, and the animal was definitely from the Coyame ranchería. One of the enemy was also taken prisoner. Three Indian governors – one from the Cholomes, and one each from the towns of San Pedro and Santa Cruz – managed to retrieve him, but almost immediately the Julimes contingent (six Indians and two Spaniards) recaptured the man. The Indian governors of the two towns were later picked up, but it is unknown what, if any, punishment was meted out to them. The Spaniards were well aware that the hostility of these northern people was quite serious, and dangerous, at this time (BL 1709-1715).

The following year, in 1713, Chiso band names occur again among the hostile groups. These were Batayolilas, Sinayoliglas or Suniyoliglas (Seuliyoliclas), Sisimbles, and Chisos. It is unclear what part the various Chiso groups played in the current or later border hostilities; there is practically no further reference to specific Chiso groups, other than to Sisimbles, after this time (BL 1709-1715). However, in 1715 and 1718, Chisos and Sisimbles were reported to be in alliance with Cocoyomes and Acoclames, both Toboso bands (AHP 1715Aa; 1718Aa; 1718Ad).

Also, in 1717, gentile Sumas in the Rio Grande area downriver from El Paso were "mixed up" with other various (unidentified) peoples, and Chinarras, Otames, and Apaches were referred to as inhabiting the region between the Rio Grande and Santa Ana de Chinarras (CPP 24: 219-58).

This period marks a significant point in the transition of the ethnic identity of the more nomadic of the Chihuahua peoples. The tribal groups that had been in this northeast region since the arrival of the first Europeans were rapidly giving up their place to newcomers who, eventually, turned out to be Athapaskan-speaking Apaches. The last phases of the disappearance of the original inhabitants can be noted in the 1720s. After 1723 and the large deportations of the Toboso band and many Coahuilans from the Nueva Vizcayan province, Chisos and especially Sisimbles absorbed many of the refugees from both groups; in 1725, for instance, Sisimbles and a few Cocoyomes and Coahuilas were found together, and the name "Chiso" appears no more after this time (Griffen 1969).

A glimpse of the process of the arrival of the Apaches is given in one account of 1724. In this year the Sisimbles clashed with some Apaches who had gone to La Junta to trade. There, the Sisimbles stole the Apaches' horses and took off down the Rio Grande; the Apaches went in pursuit and located the Sisimbles camped on the river in front of the mountain named Chocamueca. If the Apaches' account of this can be believed, the Sisimbles at this time were rather formidable adversaries. The Apaches were afraid to attack because the Sisimbles were so numerous (they probably included the above-mentioned refugees) and had a great number of horses and mules with them (AHP 1722Bb). However, within another quarter of a century the Sisimbles were just about extinct; in the year 1748 the last band of Sisimbles, consisting of some 16 persons, was finally captured by the Europeans (AHP 1725Aa; 1725B; 1727Aa; BL 1748; 1751a).

The communities of La Junta, with the possible exception of the Cholome rancherias up the Conchos River, followed a somewhat different course. A strong effort at missionization was made in 1715-16. However, because of "restlessness" (*inquietud*) and hostile acts on the part of the Indians, the missionaries were forced to flee from their missions on several occasions. This was a common enough occurrence that both Fray Juan Miguel Menchero, the Franciscan *procurador* who stayed in the area until 1725, and José de Berroterán, commander of the presidio of San Francisco de Conchos in 1729, reported that the Franciscans adopted the practice, in 1720 or shortly thereafter, of staying at La Junta only part of each year; the remainder of

their time they spent in Chihuahua City (DHM 1748; UTD 1720-1799; AHP 1730Cc).

The first rebellion of the La Juntans after their 1715 missionization occurred in 1718; according to Fray Andrés Varo, writing a few years later, it was followed by a military expedition to the area by Martín de Alday. Again in 1720, the Europeans found it necessary to send a punitive force into the region. This was commanded by Captain Juan Bautista de Lizáola, whose troops consisted of 140 to 160 soldiers and Indian auxiliaries. While this occasion was dubbed by some an "uprising," opinions of some of the citizens of Parral were that these were generally obedient Indians and that whatever had taken place must have involved a rather minor incident (Hackett 1937: 408-9; DHM 1748; AHP 1720A; 1722Bb).

In 1724, while the missionaries were at La Junta, Fray Andrés Varo, the vice-custodian of the La Junta missions, reported that the natives were again planning a rebellion. According to Varo, who noted considerable damage done to the church ornaments on a previous occasion (1720?), there were two principal persons behind this movement: the Cholome general, Juan Cíbola, and one Don Alonso, said to be a harsh enemy of the holy Catholic religion. Earlier, as soon as Alonso had been elected as a leader, he had gotten all of the people of the mission together and tried to get them to rise up when the Spaniards entered the region (AHP 1722Bb; 1730Cc).

Because of the past trouble in this area, Spanish authorities began an investigation of Varo's report. Several Spanish citizens were questioned, including another friar, Pedro Sanches, and two Indian governors, Luis Caburraja of Julimes, and Antonio Martín from Santa Cruz de Tapacolmes. The general opinion was that the La Juntans would not go to war; they were generally faithful to the Spaniards and had assisted them in fighting the wild Indians, and they were knowledgeable about the Spanish way of doing things. In October, after this questioning, the major caciques of the La Junta pueblos reaffirmed the peace with the Spanish governor, and no rebellion actually occurred (AHP 1722Bb; 1730Cc).

Again, some two years later, in the spring of 1726, several different peoples from this general northeastern area went on the warpath. These included a few Apaches, Cholomes, Sumas, Cíbolos, and the people under the chiefs El Venado ("the deer") and El Pescado ("the fish"). El Venado lived about 12 leagues up the Rio Grande toward El Paso with his people, and El Pescado and his group were located some two leagues downriver from the Venados. These rebels together sacked the mission of Coyame and carried off the saints, cattle, horses, and oxen of the mission; they killed two people and captured both missionaries there – Fray Andrés Varo and Fray Antonio de Aparicio. The two priests were rescued and taken to the town of San Francisco by Norteños ("northerners," the general term used at this time for the La Juntan peoples). Fighting broke out between the

La Juntans and the insurgents, and Captain José de Aguirre made two expeditions into the area, bringing out the missionaries and taking captive a number of the leaders of the revolt (DHM 1748; UTD 1710-1738a).

On Aguirre's second entry, in April of 1726, the party went to the town of San Francisco. Here, they found that the people from the pueblos of San Juan, Guadalupe, San Cristóbal, and Mesquites had congregated to defend themselves against the enemy. The Spaniards then learned that the peoples under El Tecolote ("the owl") and El Barrigón ("big stomach") – Cholomes, but related (*emparentado*) to the Norteños and dwelling to the north of La Junta – were on the side of the La Juntans. Messages were sent for these people to go to La Junta for their own safety; this they did, and the Europeans designated a spot about one league from the town of San Francisco where they could settle (UTD 1710-1738a).

The Spanish commander then called for the rebel chiefs, El Venado and El Pescado, who were supposedly 10 to 12 leagues up the Rio Grande. However, these men showed up almost immediately, in the company of the Suma general Bartolomé and a gentile cacique subordinate to him named El Cuchillo ("the knife"). With this, and partly because the Venado and Pescado chiefs had arrived at San Francisco so quickly, the Europeans saw that these people were indeed ready to invade the La Junta towns. The rebels, with the Coyames (Cholomes) and the Cíbolos, numbered around 3,000 persons, according to the Norteños (DHM 1748; UTD 1710-1738a).

The Spaniards then made prisoners of many of the leaders – Don Juan of the Cíbolos; his interpreter, Nicolás; the Suma general and El Cuchillo; the Pescado and Venado chiefs; the governors of the Cholomes of Coyame and San Pedro de Alcántara, Diego and Lucas; another Cholome cacique; one Cayetano (probably a Cholome); and two Cholome brothers called Los Toritos ("the little bulls"), who had been very instrumental in the trouble. With this, Cholome leadership seems to have been severely disrupted and an end was put to these hostilities. According to Commander de Berroterán, the enmity created at this time between the Norteños at La Junta and the Cholomes and the others had continued down to the time of his writing in the mid-18th century (DHM 1748; UTD 1710-1738a).

In the meantime, Don Pedro El Coyame, the general of the Cholomes, with some 40 Cholome families, had escaped the Spaniards. About the time of (or slightly before) Aguirre's second expedition in the early part of April 1726, Don Pedro and his party were seen and spoken to at the town of Santa Ana de Chinarras on their way to Tabalaopa and San Pedro (de Conchos). El Coyame recounted that on Aguirre's first entrada, as soon as the Spanish troops had left the Ciénega del Coyame, the home of these Cholomes, he and his rancheria had returned. On their arrival at the Ciénega they had been stricken with terror by the heads of two Indians they had discovered stuck on two poles, left for them by the

Europeans as a warning against further rebellion. With this, El Coyame and his people decided to move southward to join the Spaniards, and thereby missed the events of Aguirre's second punitive expedition. Later, the Bishop, Don Benito Crespo, resettled them at the Franciscan convent at Chihuahua City, where they apparently remained (Arlegui 1851: 90-1, 100; UTD 1710-1738a).

In 1729, Commander José de Berroterán led an expedition from the presidio of San Francisco de Conchos to the north of the Rio Grande, reconnoitering for the possibility of establishing a presidio in that area. He reported that Apaches, Pelones, and Jumanes were the enemies of the Spaniards; a year later, Apaches and Cholomes were said to be together, although all of these people apparently got along with the La Juntans (BL 1729).

The remainder of the history of the La Junta peoples is extremely sketchy. These Indians continued to work for Spaniards and to have other contacts with Spanish society; they also maintained some peaceful contacts with a number of native groups that dwelt in the surrounding region, including Apaches.

Missionaries resided here only sporadically, as was noted by Menchero and Berroterán; it seems to have been around mid-century that missionary contact was the most regular. Despite missionization activity from 1715 on, in 1731 the officials of the La Junta towns requested missionaries, apparently having been without them since the last uprising in the area. Moreover, Fray Menchero underscored the need for religious men to administer the area about this time, noting that missionization had not yet proceeded very far (AHP 1730Cc; AGN 1730; DHM 1748; UTD 1720-1799).

In any event, contact with Spanish society seems to have been increasing during this period, at least in some ways, while the La Junta population was decreasing. Around the mid-1700s, the Spaniards sent several expeditions into the area to determine the feasibility of erecting a presidio at La Junta because of the increase in Indian (non-La Juntan) hostilities as far south as Chihuahua City and the Tarahumara villages (BL 1746; DHM 1748).

The division between the La Junta pueblos and the natives in the surrounding area may have been growing at this time. While the events around 1726 were said to have caused a rift between the town-dwelling Norteños and such people as the Cholomes, as noted above, it may well have been that the difference in the nature of the contacts the two groups had with Spanish society was helping to widen whatever gulf had existed before. The priests at La Junta in 1748 described the Cholomes at Santa Cruz de Ochanes (in contrast to the La Juntans proper) as haughty, uncontrollable people (*unos altaneros sin sujecion*). To be sure, at this date it seems to have been the Cholomes and the related Sumas, and a few Apaches, who were the principal troublemakers (AGN 1730; BL 1729; 1746; UTD 1710-1738b).

The La Juntans in 1748 reported that there were three rancherias of Apaches with whom they were at peace and carried on trade. (Presumably the hostile Apaches referred to above belonged to other bands, though this may not necessarily have been the case, given the quality of reports about themselves and other Indians that the natives often gave to the Spaniards.) One friendly band was under chief El Ligero ("the swift one," or "speedy") and consisted of about 100 families; these people often visited La Junta but would stay only two or three days at a stretch. Another group was named *de Natafe (Natagee)* because of their particular hair style – the style of the friars. The third was the rancheria of Don Pascual, who was known to have traveled across the river into the Chihuahua area on various occasions – into the Bolsón de Mapimí and to the Conchos presidio (BL 1746).

Other, presumably less friendly Apaches lived upriver from La Junta, in the direction of El Paso, in the company of Sumas and some Cholomes. In 1746, Fray Menchero noted that Apaches and Sumas lived along the Rio Grande in this region. Information collected in 1748 and 1749 gave evidence that Sumas, Cholomes, Pescados and Venados, and several groups of Apaches were allied together. In 1749 they were reported to be raiding the area of Chihuahua City. Three Suma bands were involved, living between El Paso and El Cajón, downriver: one was under El Chamiso, one was from Piedra Abajo, and the third was from Palo Clavado. The Cholomes maintained their rancheria at a place called Cola de Aguila. Of these peoples, the Sumas and Apaches together were reported to total 106 persons, and this small figure may be an indication of the impending extinction of both groups. Exactly how many Apaches were allied with these Sumas (as well as with the Cholomes and others) was left unstated. On one occasion it was mentioned that Chinarras lived downriver from the aforementioned peoples, but otherwise this group was seldom cited. In 1754 Sumas, Pescados or Venados, Cholomes, and Apaches were again reported to be raiding the area of Chihuahua City and other parts of the northern frontier zone (BL 1746; 1749-1750; CPP 35: 342-51; 36: 41-3, 475-9; UTD 1749b).

In the La Juntans' 1748 account, it was this latter combined group that raided the La Junta pueblos and then raided southward and committed depradations in the Chihuahua area; they may also have been the same people who were reported to have raided the Cholomes at Santa Cruz de Ochanes. Sometimes this confederation seems to have consisted of two rancherias of people – apparently the Sumas-Cholomes were referred to as one group and the Apaches the other. At least once, after a raid on the La Junta towns, the Norteños themselves sent out a punitive expedition after the attackers (BL 1746; DHM 1748).

While it was suggested at least as early as 1718 that a presidio be established at La Junta, and Berroterán in 1729 reconnoitered the Rio Grande area for this purpose, such a proposal was not actually carried out until 1759-60. The erection of this presidio was reportedly the cause of considerable upset among the native population; it is possible that at this time the tempo of exodus southward from the area

was increased, judging from the somewhat more rapid decrease in population at this time. Indeed, the La Juntans were reported to have become quite disturbed in 1748, when they learned of Idoyaga's expedition to investigate the possibilities of putting up a presidio; consequently, it is not difficult to understand how the actual establishment of a presidio a few years later triggered hostile reactions in the natives. It was soon after this, in 1754, that a group of Indians who said they were from the Nueva Vizcayan missions of San Cristóbal, Guadalupe, and Julima (Julimes) asked to be settled at a mission in Coahuila; this was accomplished at the place of San Ildefonso (Hackett 1937: 409; Portillo 1887: 317-8; DHM 1748).

By 1767, the presidio, founded in 1759-60, was removed to Julimes; however, by 1773, it had been reestablished at La Junta. It is during this period that the La Junta pueblos drop from history and that various bands of more nomadic peoples, the Apaches excepted, disappear from the scene in the general area of northern Nueva Vizcaya (Kelley 1952; 1953; Kinnaird 1958: 73; AHP 1730Cc; BL 1746).

The Northwest Conchería

In the northwest of the Conchería a different series of events was unfolding. The nature of early Spanish contact is uncertain, and what actually happened here can only be guessed at. Francisco de Ibarra visited Casas Grandes in the early 1560s; after this the region apparently remained for the most part free of Spanish contact until the 1640s or after. While most dates concerning the founding of the Casas Grandes mission seem to indicate a date in the 1660s, Arlegui gives the establishment of this mission as 1640. Certainly there was some Franciscan activity in the area around this time – by 1649, the Franciscans had moved westward across the Sierra Madre into Sonora and had established a mission for the Opata at Teuricatzi, although these men were replaced by Jesuits after 1651 (Spicer 1962: 232).

From the mid-1600s on, the native population of this general region was beginning to feel the pressure of contact with the Europeans. Some of the peoples of the area – those who inhabited the river valleys – were more settled than those who dwelt in the less well watered retreats of the mountains and deserts. Again the history of the contact processes tends to divide along these ethnographic-geographic lines, as in the eastern part of the Conchería. Most of the Conchos (perhaps all) and some of the Suma, and the Opata of Sonora, fell into the category of more settled groups; the more nomadic peoples were the Sumas, Janos, Jocomes, and Chinarras. The former eventually ended up in the midst of Spanish settlement, and on the "Spanish side" against the latter, who developed a raiding pattern of reliance on Spanish holdings but remained essentially outside the Spanish fold and out of Spanish control.

While the settled peoples were missionized rather peaceably during this period of the 17th century, the more nomadic groups were reported to be giving considerable trouble.

From the 1650s on, "wild" Sumas kept Opata missions in the Teuricatzi region in unrest, and they were the subject of complaints by both Franciscans and Jesuits. Jesuits in the 1650s managed to settle some 100 Sumas at Teras on the Moctezuma River; however, these people were not very tractable to mission life and soon returned to their backland haunts (Bannon 1955: 87, 101, 103-5, 134, 141; Sauer 1934: 70-4; Spicer 1962: 232).

As was noted earlier, a number of these peoples, Sumas in particular, were major participants in the 1684 revolt in Casas Grandes. No sooner was this uprising put down than rumblings of unrest and rebellion were again heard – and the Spaniards were to have trouble with the native population of the area for many years to come. However, as will be seen below, the Conchos were to follow a pattern different from that of the more nomadic Sumas, Janos, and Jocomes. The result, for all Indians, was biological extermination, emigration from the province, or assimilation either into Spanish society or into Apache groups who moved in from the north (Spicer 1962: 233).

During the latter part of 1685, a number of months after the Suma and other nations of the area had been pacified, the rumblings of revolt were again heard. A number of incidents had occurred, and the Spanish authorities began to collect testimonies from various persons. The results of this questioning indicated that the Sumas and others were planning to rise up again (the Spanish captain, Francisco de Archuleta, stated that they had already rebelled three times, and each time had been pardoned) (AHP 1685Dc).

The information gathered reveals some of the complexities of ethnic groupings and alignments at this time. While Conchos were implicated, it is not clear where they, or Chinarras, stood in the matter. Some of the conspiring Indians declared that Conchos could not be trusted, or that they were part of the enemy because they were friendly to the Spaniards – who in turn thought rather highly of the Conchos (AHP 1685Dc).

Among those brought in to testify during the first round of questioning were a Piro, a Chinarra, a Suma, and a Jumano, plus several others, apparently mostly non-Indians. Then a number of Indian men, considered to be more directly involved with the trouble, were questioned. These included a Suma, Juan Isidro, and one Antón Zuamichi (Suma?) from the town of Carretas; Juan el Estudiante, a Suma, Antonuelo Paaguizi, and another Antonuelo, all from the mission of Nuestra Señora de la Soledad at Janos, as well as Francisco, a Suma, who was an ex-governor of this mission; Sebastián Nauquizhariqui and Sebastián Mayizuga, both from Casas Grandes; Hernando Cafueminaaucu from the mission of San Buenaventura; and three men whose residence was not stated: Francisco Chaya, Martín Phacozhaca, and Bernando Caacoie (AHP 1685Dc).

As information accumulated, it turned out that there were several occasions when the would-be rebels had planned or were planning to rise up. The peoples involved in these machinations were the same who had just returned from the warpath, and the confessions of some of the culprits include the names of "nations" or groups not encountered in other sources. The Sumas included several groups: the Sumas of Casas Grandes (or at least from the "jurisdiction" of Casas Grandes, which comprised Janos and Carretas), who seem to have been the leaders; Sumas from Los Médanos ("the dunes") and from El Ojito ("the small spring"); Janos; Jocomes; some Mansos; and the unfamiliar groups called the Ziquipinas, Amochimisquina, Amjiqui, and Otames (see Chapter 3). Occasionally it was stated that the Julimes or other nations to the east were also ready to join the Sumas (AHP 1685Dc).

Apparently, in the several incidents that came out, the Suma had simply been acting hostile. On one occasion, a Sunday, September 16, the missionary at Casas Grandes discovered that many Suma had not shown up for mass, and he began to speak to those who were present, castigating the absentees for not attending the service. One of the Suma men who was there was reported to have said (in several versions), "Toss that Father outside to me, since he is so brave; I'll cut his throat" (AHP 1685Dc).

Several times Sumas were reported to have said, in effect, that they were going to kill Spaniards to avenge the deaths of relatives they had killed, and because everything around Casas Grandes belonged to the Indians – the horses, cattle, sheep, and corn – for the Spaniards actually possessed nothing. The Sumas should be eating what the Spaniards had and the crows and buzzards should eat the Spaniards (AHP 1685Dc).

Sumas were also heard bragging that they were very manly because they had burned all of the buildings, wheat, and corn, and had carried off all the horses in the vicinity. Later, declarants stated that the Sumas of Casas Grandes were trying to be the first to start the war again so that the other bands would think they were very brave and valiant (AHP 1685Dc).

Finally, when the conspirators were brought in to take the stand, they confessed to several plots to kill the Spaniards. For various reasons, these plans had not yet been executed. For example, the first attempt, which had been planned immediately after the peace had been made, was scheduled for a time when Conchos and Sumas were to have a racing contest. The Sumas were going to attack the Spaniards (and the Conchos, according to some declarants; one, however, said that Conchos were to assist the Sumas at this time). Several reasons were given for the failure to make the attack – that the Janos who were going to join the Sumas had backed down; that the Conchos had advised against an attack at this time; and that the Conchos had too quickly beaten the Sumas at racing (AHP 1685Dc).

Some time after the race, when a priest was scheduled to arrive at Casas Grandes from Parral, the Sumas were planning to attack the Spaniards, but they desisted because it had begun to rain. Around September 30, two weeks after the incident at church, the Suma were again ready to kill the Spaniards, this time about the hour of mass, but a platoon of some 12 men from El Paso under Maestre de Campo Alonzo García had arrived in town, upsetting the Sumas' plan. Now, however, at the time of these confessions in early October, the Indians of "all the nations" were planning to go to war at the next full moon. All the tribes of the area, east to Julimes and north to the Toma of the Rio Grande (near El Paso), were reported to be willing to join the revolt; the only peoples not yet contacted for the rebellion were Apaches and Piros. Many of the nations farther to the west (such as the Janos, the Jocomes, and their allies) were already gathering at the mountain where the Indians had last fought the Spaniards (El Peñol del Diablo?) (DiPeso 1974: 908; AHP 1685Dc).

Thus informed, the Spaniards proceeded to punish the conspirators. By December, 77 Suma men had been put to the sword – 52 in Casas Grandes, 15 in Teuricatzi, 5 in San Miguel Babispe, and the remaining 5 at Santa María (Baserac). By this action, the Spaniards quite effectively destroyed the dominance that the Suma had been enjoying in this western area and unintentionally gave the leadership of the unsubjugated Indians to the Janos and Jocomes for the next few years. Unfortunately, it is not known what became of the wives and children of the men who were executed. For a while at least, those from Casas Grandes remained at this mission. However, many of those who had been apprehended in Sonora were sold into slavery; even the soldiers of the Sinaloa presidio were reported to have some of the families that had belonged to the Casas Grandes mission (Spicer 1962: 233; AHP 1685Dc).

During this period, warfare of the endemic raiding variety continued to develop in the northern portion of the frontier. Indeed, the Spaniards felt forced to respond by expanding their presidio system; they founded Janos in 1685 and, farther west, Fronteras in the next decade. In the Casas Grandes district trouble began anew, almost as soon as the 1685 incident was over. Raiding was reported in 1686; one of the enemy groups was said to be Chinarras from Las Salinas and Los Médanos, but at least one person with them was a Suma from the Río de la Toma (near El Paso) and another was described as half Chinarra, half Concho. Sumas continued to be mentioned among the attackers, although they quickly lost their earlier position of importance in this western part of the Conchería. The resulting prominence of the Janos and Jocomes, however, did not endure for very many years, and by the early 1700s, Apaches from farther north began to be the dominant force among the raiding Indians. However, some Janos, Jocomes, and Sumas were in the area at least into the 1720s (DiPeso 1974: 866–75; Spicer 1962: 234; AHP 1685Dc; 1686Bb; see *Janos* entry, Chapter 3).

The fate of these raiding bands will be taken up later. In the meantime western Conchos became less involved with them than they were with their southern and western neighbors, the Tarahumara. During the 1690s, after about a decade of rather intensive missionization, the latter people rose up three times, and on each occasion some Conchos cooper-

ated with them. After the last rebellion in 1696-97, aside from a small amount of trouble with the Tarahumara during the next 10 years or so, Concho and Tarahumara alike remained peaceful during the 18th century, with the exception of a few bands of raiding Tarahumara that were occasionally reported. The Conchos and many of the Tarahumaras along the borderlands between the two peoples seem to have rather rapidly assimilated (or otherwise disappeared) into Spanish colonial society, probably in part because of Spanish slave raids against them. The Tarahumara farther away in the mountain hinterland either became relatively adjusted to the Jesuit mission system or managed to avoid it entirely, retiring even farther into the Sierra Madre, away from Spanish civilization (Spicer 1962: 33, 36).

It was during the decade of the 1690s that the western Conchos seem to have been most influenced by events that occurred in the Tarahumara country. When rebellion broke out among the Tarahumara, trouble also brewed among the Concho, and instigation for these disturbances may have come mainly from the Tarahumara. In 1690, when the first rebellion began, Tarahumaras, Conchos, and Jovas from the mountains west of the Conchos took part, and they also carried on some raiding into Sonora. Indeed, it was reported that there were still many gentiles (i.e., unconverted people) among these nations who had tried to mislead the good (Christian) people. However, by June of 1691, Captain Juan Fernández de la Fuente of the Janos presidio reported that two Concho governors, Alonso from Namiquipa and Felipe de Santiago, in the company of all the chiefs (*capitanes*) of their nation, had come to him to establish peaceful relations with Spanish authorities. These leaders told Fernández that they would try to bring in other Conchos who were still in the backcountry (Spicer 1962: 34; BL 1693a; CPP 16: 475–89, 511–20, 538-43).

Two years later these peoples again became restless. In 1692, Tarahumaras contacted neighboring Conchos and stated that they wanted to go on the warpath, as soon as the harvests were gathered, in order to avenge the past deaths that the Spaniards had inflicted upon them. The Western Concho governor, Don Felipe de Santiago, who lived at San Diego del Monte, was among several who informed the Spaniards of the plot. During Lent a number of Concho *principales* and others had gone off to confer with the Tarahumaras; many had remained up in Tarahumara country, mostly around the Sierra de Nácori. Further details of this movement are unknown, although the leaders were listed as Martín Pelón (the main instigator) and three other men who were definitely Conchos – Alonzo el Canote, El Tiguere, and El Pato; three other leaders were also mentioned – El Guajolote, El Mapre, and El Guacamayo – and these too were probably Conchos, although their tribal affiliation was left unmentioned. This particular movement apparently died out, and in December of 1693 it was reported that 30 gentile Concho families who had been hiding in the Guainopas mountains (west of the Santa Isabel area) – possibly part of a group of 50 families who in June of 1691 were said to have taken refuge in *la sierra* – had returned to the Spaniards and had settled in peace. Both nations, Tarahumaras and Conchos, remained quiet for a short while, only to rebel again within three years (AHP 1692A; BL 1695a; 1695b; CPP 16: 538–43).

For the next couple of years the province suffered epidemics of smallpox and measles. Among both the Tarahumara and the Concho, men who were probably often medicine men began to preach against the Europeans. By 1696, the Spaniards were well aware of the impending trouble; General Juan de Retana marched to Sirupa, west of Yepómera, to attempt to nip any rebellion in the bud. By making prisoners of many of the Tarahumara leaders, he succeeded only in precipitating a general revolt. About this same time, Lieutenant Antonio Solís from the Fronteras presidio went south and captured and executed three Concho leaders who had attacked the settlement of Nácori (Spicer 1962: 34–5, 235).

The rebelling Tarahumara held a meeting of war at Teseachic, near Papigochic, and both Conchos and Jovas attended. The Conchos had a stick with them that had many marks (*rayas*) on it, and they bragged that all of the marks represented Indians who had joined their side. Some Conchos (including Conchos from Aguaripa, Guainopa, and Chuhuichupa) also went to the Aros River, very near the Jovas, and gave a talk of war to both Jovas and gentile Pimas. Jovas from Natora also attended, and it was noted that at Guainopa Conchos and Jovas were intermarried, and that the latter spoke the Concho language. These Conchos, apparently claiming they were in league with Sumas, Janos, and Jocomes, were trying to obtain more allies to attack the Conchos at Namiquipa and Casas Grandes who had remained loyal to the Spaniards (AHP 1697Aa; 1697b; 1697Ac; 1697Ad; BL 1697–1703).

In Concho country, between San Diego del Monte and Casas Grandes, an attempted Concho action was led by the Concho governor at Casas Grandes, Juan Corma, a man who had on at least one occasion fought with Spanish forces against the nomadic Janos, Jocomes, and their allies. Some nine other leaders were also involved, but the movement was aborted by Spanish authorities, who learned of it from some Indian women, before it had actually gotten off the ground (AHP 1695; BL 1697–1703).

An investigation followed, and it appears that Corma was attempting to lead a nativistically oriented movement. According to Corma's own testimony, when he and his people were living at San Diego del Monte, he had had some contact with the devil, and afterward he had begun to preach against the Spaniards. People listened to him, especially after Commander Juan Fernández de la Fuente of the Janos presidio had picked up some medicine men at Las Cruces and taken them to Namiquipa, where they had been executed. Corma had then preached at settlements in the western valleys, including San Diego, Las Cruces, Namiquipa, and Casas Grandes, and a number of the people who listened were willing to take up arms against the Spaniards. It was

claimed that Janos, Jocomes, and Apaches were allies, and that some Opatas (Quilme from the Bavispe River?), Pimas, Sobaipuris, and even some Julimes were also going to join them (Spicer 1962: 235; BL 1697–1703).

In 1700 and in 1701, Conchos and Tarahumaras were speaking of rebellion again. Northern Tarahumara settlements, including the Santa Isabel mission and its towns, San Andrés, Bachíniva, and Yepómera, Tosoborachi, Papigochi, and Batopilas, as well as Tabalaopa, a hacienda where some Conchos lived, were all mentioned. Janos, Jocomes, Apaches, Chinarras, and Pimas were also said to be involved (AHP 1701; 1706).

A few years later, in 1709, trouble with Conchos and towns of the Upper Tarahumara mission district brewed anew. Satevó was very important in this movement, and a number of other pueblos were also mentioned. Apparently, Tarahumaras were the princpal movers, and they sent envoys both east to the Conchos and west to Lower Pima pueblos. On the Concho side, towns as far away as San Pedro, Julimes, Nombre de Dios, and Namiquipa were contacted. However, nothing serious came of this movement (AHP 1710a).

The wilder peoples had continued their attacks and raiding over the area. Along the two flanks of the Sierra Madre, Janos, Jocomes, and Sumas were the principal groups after the 1685 incident, and somewhat farther west, Pimas such as those under the gentile leader Canito were often involved. In 1686 Sumas and Janos raided settlements on the upper Moctezuma River in Sonora; two years later, Janos, Jocomes, and Sumas assaulted an Opata settlement of Santa Rosa, forcing the Opata to retire southward. For something like a decade, Mansos from around the El Paso area were also mentioned. In 1690 Chinarras, Sumas, Janos, Jocomes, and Apaches were accused of attacking Carretas, Casas Grandes, and San Buenaventura, and the same groups, plus the Pimas-Sobaipuris and Jovas, were making war on Sonora (Spicer 1962: 233–4; AHP 1686Bc; BL 1693a; CPP 16: 475–89, 511–20, 538–43).

In the following year, 1691, these same peoples continued to carry out hostilities all along the frontier border region of the northwest Conchería. The principal leaders of these activities were the Janos, closely seconded by the Jocomes. These two groups were accused of bringing Mansos Indians from El Paso to the Janos area, as well as Sumas from El Ojito, Guadalupe, and other pueblos of this area. Some of these Mansos were from the two or more bands of Mansos settled at their town and church of San Francisco de Los Mansos, some nine leagues from El Paso. These Mansos maintained communication with Apaches and Sumas, as well as with Janos and Jocomes. Indeed, at this time they were said to be intermarried with the two former groups, and this was probably also the case with the Janos and Jocomes, for in 1684 it was reported that Janos, Sumas, and Mansos were all interrelated. These bands were raiding as far east as El Paso itself (AGN 1691a; 1691b; 1691d; 1691e; 1691f; CPP 16: 538–43; 23: 10–4).

Farther west, these rebel bands maintained alliances

with Pimas and the Pima-speaking Sobaipuris, carrying out raids into Sonora. All of these groups – including Pimas of the west, and Mansos of the east (specifically the band of Captain Chiquito) – were said at one time or another to be roving into Apache territory as far as the *sierras* Florida and Gila. On occasion, Apaches would even come southward – once they showed up under peace at the Janos presidio to trade deerskins, but stole some hundred head of horses when they retired (AGN 1691b; 1691c; 1691e; 1691f).

Again in the early spring of 1692, Pima-speaking Sobaipuris, Janos, Jocomes, and "other nations" were raiding into Sonora, although the Sobaipuris were quieted down by March. Then in April, Captain Fernández de la Fuente and the forces of the Janos presidio fought with some 2,000 Apaches and others about eight or ten leagues from the presidio. The Indians at this time surrendered and promised to settle in peace, although it was soon evident that they had no intention of doing so. The rebels continued on the warpath, and around July Fernández met them again in another large battle at the Sierra de Enmedio. On this occasion, only 300 Indians were involved, but these included Janos, Jocomes, Mansos, Sumas, a few Apaches, and a couple of Pimas (AHP 1692A; 1695; BL 1693a; 1695b; CPP 17: 205–11).

By the middle of August, 20 Indians had come to the Janos presidio to see about arrangements for peace, and they wanted Fernández to visit them at their rancherias. The Janos were apparently the dominant group at this time, and their captain was said to govern all the rest, although the *tabobo* (also called "captain") of the Jocomes was cited as an important leader. The Indians agreed at this time to return to their own territories: the Mansos and Sumas were to go to the Rio Grande, which was their territory ("donde era su tierra" – apparently an indication that the Sumas of the Casas Grandes jurisdiction were fairly well out of the picture at this time); the Jocomes would go to their country (unstated), and the Janos would stay attached to the presidio and its environs because this was their area. The Indians were going to live during the winter by hunting and gathering until they could plant in the spring (BL 1693a; CPP 16: 586–92).

Whatever measures were actually carried out at this time, they had little effect. The following year Janos, Jocomes, Sumas, Apaches, and Pimas were again wreaking havoc in the northern area of the Conchería and in Sonora. At the same time these hostilities were continuing, Spanish power in the northwest part of the Conchería was weakening, giving the Indians an even stronger foothold in the region than they might otherwise have had. Spanish forces were diminished because of the many people who left to take part in the reconquest of New Mexico; this shortage was much felt, and was described in December of 1692 by Fernández de la Fuente, commander of the Janos presidio (BL 1693a).

In 1693, Janos, Jocomes, and Sumas, as well as Pimas and others, continued spreading death and destruction in the region. The next year, the Spaniards carried out four campaigns against these rebels, but with little success. Then in 1695, from May into September, the Europeans armed a large punitive expedition into what is now the southeast corner of Arizona against these warring nations of the north. They first went after an allied group of five nations – Janos, Jocomes, Sumas, Chinarras, and Mansos (Spicer 1962: 124–6, 234; AHP 1695).

When the Spanish forces first met this five-nation confederation in 1695, it was reported to them that the Janos were the principal leaders, as they had been in previous years. Indeed, their chief was said to "govern" all the rest, including the great chief (*el gran tabobo*) of the Jocomes. One report the Spaniards managed to obtain on the enemy forces stated that they consisted of 70 Janos, 60 Jocomes, and another 60 Sumas, plus 6 Mansos and 7 Chinarras. The Mansos and Chinarras numbered so few, it was said, because the Pimas and Sobaipuris had been fighting these five nations with such force that most of the Mansos and Chinarras had returned to their own territories; actually, according to this source, it was only the Janos and Jocomes who wanted to keep up the hostilities. During this first portion of the campaign, reports were in conflict with respect to the relations these people had with Apache groups. One source stated that the allied bands were at war with all Apaches but one band; other information indicated friendliness with more than one Apache group, including the people of Chief el Chilmo (now dead), Gila Apaches, Salinero Apaches, and others. Some Apaches (of unstated names) were said to war against each other (AHP 1695).

At this point the Spaniards were forced to interrupt their campaign and turn their attention farther westward, when Pimas in Sonora revolted in the area of Caborca and Tubutama. The Spanish troops left the Janos and their allies, after having begun to establish peace with them, in order to put down the new rebels. By September, the Spanish forces were back in the north, and this time they were also faced with the Apaches.

When the Spanish forces returned to consummate the peace that they had begun with the five-nation alliance, they received various reports that the Indians were with the Apaches in the general area of the Gila River. Specifically, Apaches, Sumas, and Chinarras were together on the Gila River; Janos were at a marsh (*ciénega*) on the north side of the Sierra de Santa Rosa; and the Jocomes and some Apaches were on the west side of the same mountain. The Indians were clearly avoiding the Spanish troops, and the Europeans figured that the Indians' previous overtures had been made simply to buy themselves time, particularly because the raiding in Sonora had not stopped. While the Spaniards finally gave up the chase and returned to their respective presidios, one lieutenant, Antonio de Solís, did manage to battle one Jocome ranchería, and he took some 43 prisoners (Spicer 1962: 124–6, 234; AHP 1695).

Hostilities continued in the area. The following year

Spanish troops pursued these raiders to the Gila River, but they were never found. By this time the Pimas-Sobaipuris were regularly fighting the rebel Indians. Sobaipuris met Jocomes in September of 1697, and this battle was considered to be a defeat (*golpe*) for the Jocomes; in March of the following year Spanish arms delivered a resounding defeat to the Janos, Jocomes, Sumas, Mansos, and Apaches. However, assaults from these peoples still went on: they raided Sobaipuris in the upper San Pedro River area, and these Pima-speakers eventually won what was deemed to be a large victory over the Jocomes and Apaches. Jocomes and Janos also raided into the Upper Pima country, attacking the mission of Cocóspera (Spicer 1962: 127, 235; DHM 1697; 1698a; 1698b).

In this same year of 1698, some Sumas tried to make peace, apparently having had their fill of warfare. The next year 32 Sumas and 28 Janos were sent from the Janos presidio to El Paso. The Sumas were relocated at Nuestra Señora de Socorro and the Janos at the El Paso presidio, where other Janos were already settled. All the Janos but one were captives taken by the troops of the Janos presidio (30 persons had actually been captured, but two had died and one very sick person had not been sent). The 32 Sumas included the captain of the de la Toma band (AHP 1699c).

The settlement of these Indians proved to be an extremely small victory for the Spaniards. Many rebels remained in the hinterland with Apaches and warred in the region well into the 1700s. By 1701, they had extended their raiding down the San Miguel River in Sonora to a place called Saracachi, 50 miles below Cocóspera. They also carried out an assault on the town of Janos this same year. In 1704, the Janos, Jocomes, and Apaches were reported to have continuously invaded a number of Sonoran towns, including Vaca, Teuricatzi, Bacanuchi, Cuaripe, Opodepe, Cocóspera, Senoquipe, Corodeguachi, Terrenate, and the mining town of Aygame. Also, in this very year, some Janos and Jocomes who had been settled at the Janos presidio fled to the back country. Between 1690 and 1710, these raiders had forced the abandonment of many Spanish holdings in the Casas Grandes district, through the areas of the Janos and Fronteras presidios and into Sonora (Spicer 1962: 236; AHP 1699c; 1704Ab; 1708; BL 1695b; DHM 1704).

Around 1707, the Sumas who had been settled in the jurisdiction of El Paso rose up and joined the Apaches. Their combined forces attempted to invade the El Paso area several times, but commander Valverde finally managed to reduce the Sumas to peace and to a pueblo (DHM 1707).

In 1711, the Janos, Mansos, and Sumas at both Janos and El Paso went on the warpath. These people had raided as far south as Chihuahua, and in December of this year they hit the town of Santa Clara. A detachment from the San Buenaventura presidio went after them – they could not locate the Indians, but they did pick up six bodies of the slain at Santa Clara and bury them. Among the Sumas, it was reported, there were four Conchos from Nombre de Dios. Following this, it was hoped for a while that the Sumas might surrender, but later these Indians sent word to the Spaniards that they would die before they would agree to peace with the Europeans (BL 1709-1715).

The history of the Janos, Jocomes, and Sumas becomes more and more obscure during these years. While there is no doubt that numbers of these people allied themselves with the Apaches to such an extent that they were eventually assimilated by the Athapaskans, it is not certain that all did; indeed, the history of these Indians and their relations with both Spaniards and incoming Apaches still very much needs to be worked out precisely.

In 1714, some "barbarous" (apparently meaning "wild") Sumas were still said to be in the area of Janos. Then, 10 years later in 1724, it was reported that the Suma of El Paso as well as some Suma of the Casas Grandes district were restless; at the same time it was noted that there were many Suma dwellings (*residencias*) only 30 leagues from the Casas Grandes jurisdiction! In the meantime, in 1717, a group of 155 Janos and Jocomes were settled at the Janos presidio, and apparently they remained at this place at least for a decade. Around 1725, Sumas were reported to be causing trouble in the Janos vicinity; a year later a band of 143 Sumas was relocated at this presidio, although it is not known if these were the same people referred to the previous year. While it is unknown how long these peoples remained at Janos – whether they were assimilated or whether they later rose up and joined the incoming Apaches – during the 1720s, both groups, following the dates of their settlement at Janos, were cited as auxiliary troops of this presidio. At about this same time, in 1728, a group of gentile Sumas were reported to have been brought into El Paso from the mountains; they were being maintained at the expense of the commander of that presidio. Finally, up to around mid-century, Sumas were sometimes reported to be associated with various Apache groups – Gilas, Chiricagues, Organos, Mimbres, and Mescaleros – raiding in the general desert region, especially from the San Buenaventura Valley and El Carmen to Chihuahua City (AHP 1722Bb; 1725Ab; 1727Ab; BL 1728; CPP 27: 195-224; 35: 329-34, 336-8, 364-76).

These few glimpses of the remaining original native populations of the region during the first 30 years or so of the 1700s show them near the end of their existence as distinctive cultural systems or societies. After this period, apparently from about the 1730s on, of the uncontrolled native groups only the Apaches survived, and they became the sole occupants of the non-Spanish-held territory. Concurrently, Spanish population and the Spanish way of life were spreading in the mission Indian area, while the indigenous mission population on both sides of the Sierra Madre was decreasing and in some cases disappearing (see Spicer 1962: 96-7).

It should be pointed out that this expansion of an hispanicized populace and Spanish cultural elements probably included an increase in the population of European domestic animals, one of the principal sources of subsistence of the

Apaches; the Apaches could never have occupied the position on the frontier in the manner that they did without this increment to their subsistence techniques. The Apache dominance led to the depopulation of many Spanish and Indian (e.g., Opata and Concho) settlements; ultimately, they caused the Sobaipuri to abandon the upper San Pedro River Valley, driving them west and south in the 18th century, as they also did the Spanish population. On the east side of the Sierra Madre much of the Casas Grandes district was depopulated by the 1760s – including the area around San Beunaventura, San Luis, El Torreón, and El Picacho (Spicer 1962: 127-8, 236; CPP 34: 103-8, 111-3; DHM 18thb).

The Conclusion of Conchería History

Finally, in the latter half of the 1700s, Apaches raided far into the old Conchería, both in the eastern and the western zones. In the 1770s and 1780s their war and raiding activities were exceptionally heavy, peaking in these years. In one report that covered the period between 1778 and 1787, most of the assaults in the area were said to have been made by Apaches (a few were by raiding Tarahumaras) (AHP 1787A). During this era the parish records of such towns as San Buenaventura, Julimes, and Santa Clara de Tapacolmes note deaths caused by the marauding Apache bands. While the intensity of Apache hostilities varied partly according to Spanish policy and actions in the region (Spicer 1962: 239-40; AGN 1793), the nature of the Indian population and, consequently, of Spanish–Indian contact, had changed radically between the time of the Spaniards first entry into the Conchería and the end of the colonial period.

3. TRIBAL GROUPS AND SETTLEMENT

INTRODUCTION

There seem to have been a number of basic, broad cultural similarities within the general geographical area of concern here, regardless of the specific language and ethnic identity of any particular group, band, or settlement. In the main, the peoples who dwelt in the desert regions were the more nomadic and relied more on hunting and gathering as subsistence activities, while those along the river valleys were more settled and put more reliance on horticulture than did their desert relatives; however, all may have done at least a little crop growing. The most settled people in the entire region were those inhabiting the La Junta district, at the confluence of the Rio Grande and Conchos rivers.

Despite the large number of names for specific groups of the region that occur in the documentary sources, most of the peoples referred to are not placeable, linguistically or geographically, except within rather broad limits. The early accounts, such as those of Gallegos and Luján in the 16th century, are often vague, and the expeditions that produced these *relaciones* actually visited only a small part of the country. The major portion of the Conchería was contacted at later times and was reported on only haphazardly; there are, in effect, only poor accounts, many quite indirect, for most areas of the Conchería during the colonial period.*

The geographical ranges or areas of occupation and exploitation of the various native groups shifted with the changing conditions under which the people lived, as Spanish settlement penetrated farther north and became more entrenched in the region. Unfortunately, for the general area there are no adequate inventories that geographically locate the various tribes or rancheria groups relative to each other at any

one time before these peoples became extinct. Such lists as Marin's in 1693 (Hackett 1926: 390-4) simply cite a large number of names, many of which occur in no other source. Therefore, most of the information about the various native groups has to be pieced together from references in several accounts that usually are not very clear with regard to ethnographic and linguistic data, or to general ethnic affiliation. Except for the La Junta towns, there is considerable doubt about the geographical and ethnographic placement of most of the aboriginal peoples dealt with here.

The general area of the Conchería and neighboring territory seems to have included two broad linguistic areas; one was that of the Conchos, the other that of the Sumas-Jumanos to the north.*

On the south, the peoples called Conchos bordered the Tepehuanes, the line between the two groups lying north of Parral and Santa Bárbara; south of the Conchos River, the border was said to be, variously, 15 leagues north of Santa Bárbara in 1575 (Miranda 1871) and 14 leagues away from San Bartolomé in 1622 (CPP 5: 102-5). The eastern boundary ran northeastward in the desert east of the Conchos River to just south of the present-day Coyame-Cuchillo Parado region. This last spot is agreed upon by both Gallegos and Luján, the chroniclers, respectively, of the Rodríguez-Chamuscado and Espejo expeditions. However, this was not the northeasternmost extension of Conchos from a linguistic standpoint. The Chisos, who from most evidence were Concho speaking, appear at the time of contact to have been inhabiting an area east of this point, and there is fair circumstantial evidence that they dwelt as far east as the Big Bend country of Texas, as well as in some of the mountains near La Junta proper. Indeed, it may well have been that Concho speakers were extending their territorial boundaries in this northeast direction at the time of the entry of the Europeans.

From the area of Cuchillo Parado, Concho-speaking groups were distributed as far westward as the Santa María valley, but it is quite uncertain where the actual northern boundary between Concho and Jumano speakers was. Both Sumas (Jumano speakers) and Chinarras (Concho speakers)

---

*For example, one report of about 1622 gives a census of 1,003 persons for the Indians of the Province of Santa Bárbara. Unfortunately, it is not known exactly what geographical extent this covered, or what ethnic groups. Missions as well as other settlements known to exist at this time, such as Atotonilco and San Francisco de Conchos, are not mentioned. Certainly, this figure included Tepehuanes and others, as well as Conchos who lived in the immediate area; the total is about the same as given eight years later for the Indian laboring force of the area and hence quite probably refers only to the hacienda Indians of San Bartolomé and Santa Bárbara, and environs (see *Labor* in Chapter 5). For purposes of comparison, in this same report of 1622 the total Indian population of Nueva Vizcaya — excluding Nayarit and the Tarahumara country, which was said to be unknown, but including the Sierra country farther south as well as the coastal areas of Sinaloa and Chiametla — was given as 101,563 souls. The Sierra of San Andrés and San Hipólito had 5,280 people, the district of Durango had 1,041, and the Parras and Laguna missions 1,569 (CPP 5: 278-84).

---

*This dual division, largely stemming from evidence supplied by the early 16th century expeditions into the area, has been fairly well substantiated by Sauer (1934). All information, much admittedly indirect or circumstantial, that I reviewed in the several archival sources supports Sauer's general conclusions. For a somewhat different view, see Forbes 1959b.

were reported to live in the sand-dune country of this desert area. The northwest extension of Conchos lay someplace between Las Cruces and Casas Grandes. My guess is that this border may have been as far south as upriver from San Buenaventura, but it is possible that the line was somewhere north of this settlement, for in 1684 it was reported that there were some Chinarras at the nearby mission of Santa Ana del Torreón (CPP 23: 13-4; see entry for these missions in Chapter 6). Certainly some Conchos were living at Casas Grandes during the colonial period (for instance, during the 1690s), but these Conchos, it was stated, had been moved into this place by the Spaniards themselves. One of the earliest statements of Concho distribution in this area, about 1650, simply reads "de la parte Concha . . . de mas alla de namiquipa," which probably indicates an area including Las Cruces but not necessarily any territory farther north (BL 1649-1700). A year later, in 1651, Fray Birvés and Juan de Munguía noted that the Río del Torreón (probably the Santa María River in the area of present-day Galeana, judging from the description) was the "land of the first Sumas" (CPP 8: 323-6, 329-30).

From the area of Namiquipa (and perhaps as far west as Babícora*), the southern Concho border ran southward, north of Bachíniva, which was Tarahumara (see Map 1). The boundary may have dipped as far south as the Cuauhtémoc Valley (in the area of Lago de Bustillos), since Conchos were reported living at San Diego del Monte in the latter part of the 17th century. From here the line moved eastward, passing around the Santa Isabel Valley (said to be on the border of the Conchos in 1648 [UTD 1648]), between Chuvíscar (which was Tarahumara) and Nombre de Dios. It then curved southward, between the mission of Babonoyaba (Concho) and that of Satevó (Tarahumara), three leagues west of Babonoyaba. Continuing southward, it took in a portion of the Conchos River, west of the town of San Francisco de Conchos, possibly some seven or more leagues, and included at least the old Concho town of San Luis (possibly under the present-day Toronto Lake). From here the southern border ran east again to the Florido district.

The Jumano-speaking country lay north of this Concho territory and will be dealt with in this paper only as it pertains to the general theme of Indian assimilation (see Chapter 8). However, the Spaniards, who for their purposes did not necessarily pay a great deal of attention to ethnic or linguistic boundaries of the aborigines, included a portion of Jumano territory, especially around the La Junta district, in what they called the Conchería – for them essentially an administrative division.

In the documentary sources, many different names occur for groups or "nations" of the Conchería. Since the Concho speakers occupied a rather broad geographical area and lived in separate settlements or rancherias, a reasonable assumption would seem to be that many of the names refer to Concho-speaking groups. However, in contrast to their references to La Junta and to some other regions, Spaniards when describing Concho country seldom gave much of a hint as to which groups might have been of the Concho language. Yet they do appear to have been fairly definite in indicating when they were dealing with Conchos proper, which implies that the Conchos (whoever they were and however they may have designated their specific rancherias) were for the most part quite homogeneous linguistically and culturally. Even the early expeditionary reports give no hint of what the separate designations of Conchos might have been.

The first real indication of Concho rancheria names comes during the 1644-45 revolt (see Chapter 2), some 70 years (and several generations) after the Spaniards had contacted these people. However, because the Conchos Indians occupied a region that was most attractive to the Europeans for economic (mine and hacienda) reasons, and because the Spanish settlements no doubt disturbed the Indians here more than in many other areas, the names that occur in the 1640s do not necessarily reflect the situation of the 1580s with much accuracy.

Neither the *relación* of Gallegos nor that of Luján is very precise with regard to Concho settlements. Putting both reports together, however, we can obtain a rough notion of the human settlements along the Conchos River. These settlements ran from a point somewhat upriver from the junction of the Florido and Conchos Rivers down to La Junta. According to these two accounts, in 1581 and 1582 Conchos were settled in the area of the Florido-Conchos confluence. Luján indicates that for about three leagues down the Conchos from this juncture Espejo's party was met by many people, and Espejo estimated that there were about 1,000 persons in this region when he passed through (Hammond and Rey 1927: 13; 1929: 49-50).

In regard to the area from this point to about Cuchillo Parado, Gallegos simply records that there were many people who belonged to the Conchos nation. Luján, however, states that about seven leagues from the location of the first groups (around the Conchos-Florido juncture), the Espejo party met some more Indians at a place the Spaniards named El Vado. No more natives are mentioned after this for another 13 leagues, at which point Espejo's people came to the San Pedro River, somewhat up from its confluence with the Conchos (at the later Santa Cruz or San Pablo?). On the San Pedro, the Europeans again encountered many Concho Indians, and later, after they had begun marching down the Conchos, some Indians came out to meet them at a spot the Spaniards called El Xacal, which Kelley interprets as possibly in the area of modern Julimes (Hammond and Rey 1927; 1929: 45-53; Kelley 1952b).

Espejo's group marched for several days from El Xacal, leaving the Conchos River for most of the journey. After 17

---

*A 1698 source reported Conchos at Chuhuichupachi (Chuhuichupa), west of Babícora (AHP 1697Aa).

leagues they crossed the Conchos River again, and three leagues farther on, at a place said to be two leagues from the river, they came to many Indian squash fields, a spot they named El Calavazal (place of squash fields). Here they were visited again by some Conchos Indians, and about a dozen of them accompanied the expedition farther down the river (Hammond and Rey 1929: 53).

From El Calavazal, after traveling another seven leagues, the Indians led the Spanish party to a broad marsh (*ciénega*). No people were mentioned at this site or any other along the way until the expedition had marched another four leagues back to the Conchos River. It was in this area that the Espejo expedition crossed from the territory of the Conchos Indians and entered that of the Passaguates (or Pazaguates), said to be more warlike than the Conchos (Hammond and Rey 1929: 53-4).

It was approximately at this point that Gallegos, the chronicler of the Rodríguez expedition a year earlier, resumed his description of the human population of the region. He noted that immediately before meeting a nation called the Cabris – quite clearly the same as the Passaguates of the Espejo party – the Spaniards had encountered a different nation from the Conchos, but one that spoke the same language. This group Gallegos called the Rayas, but the basis for distinguishing it from the other Concho speakers met thus far on this journey is not given, except that they lived on the boundary (*raya*, Spanish for "border") between the Conchos and Jumanos. It is possible that the Rayas were a band of the people later generally designated as Chisos (Hammond and Rey 1927: 13-4).

Strangely (and perhaps significantly), the accounts of the Espejo expedition are the only ones that detail to any extent the native settlements along the Conchos River from the area where the Florido joins it to about Julimes. In the 17th century, from the 1640s on, when more adequate documentary sources begin to appear, this region is simply taken for granted and little is mentioned with respect to aboriginal settlements – probably indicating that the Spanish had already occupied at least portions of this river valley, and that a fair amount of depopulation of the native settlements had already occurred.

It seems probable that Spanish penetration into this area had begun long before the 1630s. In 1619 Governor Albear described the richness of the Conchos River between the mission of San Francisco and another point, most certainly downriver, but unknown. In any event, the development of the region was given great impetus by the discovery of the mines at Parral in 1631. By the 1650s a number of places are mentioned where Spaniards seemingly had holdings: Xaguey, nine leagues from Parral on the Conchos River (AHP 1654Ab); El Nogalejo, on the Conchos River and apparently upriver from San Francisco; and Los Mimbres, near the Conchos River and the highway to New Mexico (AHP 1656A). Other places are cited in this district in the 17th century, but little or no information is available on their locations or history. Places like Bachimba and Tabalaopa, which became important Spanish haciendas in the last half of the 1600s because of such favorable attributes as water supply, almost certainly supported Concho Indian rancherias; indeed, Tabalaopa (adjacent to the later mines of Chihuahua, which were not opened up until the first decade of the 1700s) was a going hacienda by the time of the 1684 revolt, when it was mentioned together with Nombre de Dios and El Sacramento (the latter two to the north of Chihuahua City) (AHP 1684Aa; 1684Ab; 1685Db).

It is my guess, on the basis of circumstantial evidence, that at least by the 1650s Franciscan missionaries were also working in this river region, treating the settlements here as satellite parishes of the missions they had established at San Francisco, San Pedro, and probably Santa Isabel (see Chapter 6). San Antonio is referred to from the 1650s on (AHP 1658Aa), and in 1684, the Concho Indian governor, Obregón, mentioned such spots as San Pablo and San Gerónimo (near present-day Aldama?) (AHP 1684Aa). During the mid-1600s, then, the region around the Florido and Conchos Rivers had several Spanish settlements. One report confirms this, but then goes on to state that many had been abandoned by the 1670s, because of raids by Indians from the eastern desert country (AHP 1673a).

Because of this paucity of data from the early years, one can only guess which of the named groups may have been Conchos. In the 1645 hostilities, the following were mentioned as having joined the nations at La Junta: Conchos, Mamites, Julimes, Olozasmes (probably the same as the Olhasmas), Oposmes, Xiximbles, Tocones, Mosnales, Bachichilmes, Tapacolomes, Hovomes, Zabasopalmes, Bacabaplames, Ayozomes, Zolomes (Cholomes), Nababayoguames, Tatamastes, and Chisos. However, some of the groups cited were clearly La Junta peoples, and some seem to have been Chisos. The Oposmes and Tapacolmes were from the La Junta towns; the Zolomes were most certainly Cholomes from the Cuchillo Parado area. Xiximbles (Sisimbles) were not La Junta dwellers, nor were the Chisos, although some of these people may have lived close by. Also, there is no information concerning what bands the designation "Chiso" might have included, except that Sisimbles were generally considered to be Chisos by the Spaniards in later years. The Tatamastes may also have been Chisos, and the Bachichilmes seem to have been a Cholome group (Alegre 1959: III, 37; AHP 1645Aa; CD 1650a; DHM 1645).

On the Concho side, the Julimes and Mamites were Conchos by association, being mentioned quite consistently together with Conchos Indians from the 1640s on. To judge from this historical association, they appear to have been specific Concho peoples or settlements living in the area of San Antonio de Julimes and perhaps as far upriver as San Pedro; however, there is some evidence that the Julimes (and probably also, consequently, the Mamites) were early immigrants from the La Junta area (see *Julimes* entry below).

Olozasmes were the companions of the Mamites during the revolt, which may indicate a close ethnic connection between these two. The Tocones are first mentioned in 1606 as having been given in encomienda to an hacienda in the San Bartolomé Valley, and presumably, therefore, were one of the Concho rancherias who lived fairly close to Spanish settlement at this time, rather than one of the more distant-dwelling Jumano peoples. Because of the early dates and long association with the name Conchos, then, it does seem that these four groups – Julimes, Mamites, Tocones, and Olozasmes – may have been Concho groups. The remaining names cited may be designations of Concho rancherias that disappeared during the 17th century, since they cannot be correlated with later lists of names, or they may simply be alternates for groups or villages known elsewhere by other names (for some of the names, of course, both possibilities may apply).

The above-named bands or peoples from the 1640s are those who lived mainly along the Conchos River and its immediate tributaries, down to Cuchillo Parado or possibly even to La Junta. The same lack of specificity in information on bands or rancherias obtains, but to an even greater degree, for the Conchos who dwelt in the northwest portion of the Conchería. Many Concho groups probably existed, judging from the number of Concho towns, missions, and satellite parishes – such as San Diego del Monte, Namiquipa with five visitas, and possibly Bachíniva (basically Tarahumara), with a like number of satellite parishes, some of which may have been Concho. However, no names for specific Concho rancherias or groups seem to be known, with two possible exceptions. One is the name "Chinarra," which apparently referred to Concho-speaking desert dwellers, north and west of Nombre de Dios, but which probably included more than one group of people. The other is the name "Otaguas," applied to a Concho-speaking group from a place called Los Otaguas, north of Nombre de Dios, roughly in the area of Las Encinillas (AHP 1688A).

The records also offer little on the Concho peoples reduced to mission life at San Pedro and at San Francisco de Conchos. Possibly Julimes and Mamites lived at San Pedro; however, this information is from the 1650s and consequently too late to be very reliable (see *Julimes* entry below). At San Francisco, the first missionary in the early 1600s reportedly ministered to some 4,000 Indians, and such a large number of people no doubt belonged to many different rancherias. Possibly some of the peoples deduced as Conchos above, such as the Tocones, were among the early groups settled at San Francisco.

In summary, then, little can be said of the number and distribution of the Indian rancherias in the Concho-speaking area. Because there are practically no documents available on the early years of Spanish settlement in this region, the nature of the Conchería populations at the time of contact must remain unknown until new documentary sources are discovered.

The situation in the La Junta district is only slightly better. Some of the names of the groups belonging to the aforementioned Concho confederation in 1645 refer to La Junta peoples, but again, as with the Concho groups, it is impossible to determine precisely which ones. The same holds for the list of peoples given by the Indian governor, Obregón, in 1684 and that by General Juan de Retana in 1693. Many, or most, of these names cannot be connected with the names for the various La Junta peoples that occur in the 18th century, nor do they show up in local baptismal and other parish records. There is no attempt here to give a history of the use of these La Junta district ethnic names, beyond the entries given in the summary list below. However, a few more observations on the peoples and population of the region should be made.

Neither Gallegos nor Luján uses anything other than the generic term "Conchos" for the populations of the Concho area (with the exception of the Raya), although a number of different settlements are obviously involved. By contrast, however, both chroniclers note two to three different groups in the small area from Cuchillo Parado to La Junta. As noted above, they report, after leaving Concho country, a new nation at Cuchillo Parado. Luján called this group the Passaguates (Espejo's version was Pazaguates) and Gallegos named them the Cabris, but both terms clearly refer to people living in the area that was later Cholome country and, in effect, they probably were Cholomes (Hammond and Rey 1927: 13-4; 1929: 53-4). After the Cabris-Passaguates, both men agree that the next group their respective parties encountered was a different people; Gallegos called them the Amotomanco, Luján the Otomoaco. Luján distinguished them from the inhabitants of La Junta proper; he called the latter the Abriaches. Both writers also agree upon the essential linguistic unity of this area as against that of the Conchos (see *Language*, Chapter 4) (Hammond and Rey 1927: 13-4, 16; 1929: 53-5).

The over-all picture from these two reports is basically the following. The Cabris-Passaguates spoke a language that was intelligible to the Otomoacos-Amotomancos. While the latter were distinguished by Luján from the Abriaches at La Junta, these two groups also spoke mutually intelligible languages. According to Luján, moving up the Rio Grande, away from the La Junta towns, people who were Otomoacos were again encountered, including a group the Spaniards gave another name (or for whom they learned of another name) – the Caguates.

These accounts seem to indicate two things: first, Otomoacos had a wide distribution, and they were related to the other peoples in the area, including some called Jumanas (or Jamanas) living on the north side of the Rio Grande; second, the Spaniards distinguished the peoples of this general region on the basis of overt cultural differences, such as house types and settlement patterns, but these did not necessarily reflect linguistic differences. Some kind of unity may have been recognized or implied when the Europeans referred to this entire region as the province of the Patarabueyes. Farther up the Rio Grande, when the Spaniards ran into some Jumanos who were hunting, these Jumanos could be understood by the Patarabuey (Otomoaco) interpreter the Spaniards had with them. They noted that some Jumanos lived in tents and others lived in a settlement with houses. People of the same language, then, had somewhat varying ways of life (Hammond and Rey 1927: 16-8; 1929: 63-9).

While the documents are never very clear, this representation is borne out to some extent by later information. The Abriache-Otomoaco distinction in particular, but also that of the Passaguates, seems to have continued into the 18th century, until the La Junta region was finally depopulated of aborigines and inhabited by Apaches. By the 1700s, the La Juntans proper were sometimes lumped together as the Norteños, or "del Norte" (Abriaches), and distinguished from the Cholomes (Passaguates) and from the Jumanos and Cíbolos (probably in part the Otomoacos). Of course, on many occasions the individual La Junta settlements, as well as many neighboring rancherias, were called "nations" and designated with special names by the Spaniards; for example, in 1693, Commander Retana reported 13 separate nations at La Junta and environs (BL 1695a). The Cíbolos and the Jumanos dwelt in the area north and east of La Junta. In the 18th century, people living up the Rio Grande toward El Paso were often called Sumas. While Cholomes were frequently separated from the Suma, they sometimes seem to have been confused with them.

In the western part of the Conchería, Sumas extended into the Casas Grandes valley area and westward to border on the Opatas of Sonora. The exact distribution here is hazy, but it would seem that the Sumas probably extended as far south as the Santa María Valley around Galeana (as noted above) and also occupied areas to the north, adjacent to Janos – at least, the missions of Casas Grandes and Janos contained Sumas at the time of the trouble in 1685, for many of the Suma witnesses were said to live at either of these places. One Suma witness came from the mission of San Buenaventura; however, since Spaniards often moved Indians from outlying areas into their missions, this does not indicate that San Buenaventura was actually in Suma territory.

Although there is good evidence that Sumas resided at the Janos visita of the Casas Grandes mission and also at Carretas in the 1680s, in 1692 it was stated that the Janos were from the area of the Janos presidio (at a later date, in the early 1700s, Janos Indians claimed that this was their territory), that the Jocomes were from around Santa Rosa de Corodeguatzi, and that the Sumas and Mansos were from the Rio Grande. This, however, was after a good many Sumas

of the Casas Grandes area had been exterminated. About this time a number of different bands of Suma were recorded – those from Los Médanos, from El Ojito, and from La Toma (near El Paso), as well as others – in the Casas Grandes district. Somewhat earlier than this, Sumas who visited the Sonora Opata missions were divided into "Eastern Suma" and "Northern Suma" by Jesuit missionaries in the area. Later, in the 1700s, as the Suma were disappearing from the scene, they showed up mainly from around the El Paso area and southeastward to La Junta (BL 1693a). As late as 1748, a number of Suma were reported from this area; some of them were said to be allied with Cholomes and Apaches.

Practically no information on the Janos or the Jocomes has turned up. The Jocomes bordered the Janos on the north and northwest and were basically a northern band of the Janos; the two groups were reported to speak the same language. In the 1685 testimonies, some of the other band names cited possibly referred to Jano-Jocome groups, although they may have been Suma rancherias.*

Finally, the principal peoples who lived in the greater Casas Grandes district were occasionally reported to travel to some of the towns and settlements of Sonora. In 1678, the Jesuit mission of Baceraca was said to be on the border of many Conchos and Sumas, people who often went to Huachinera, Babispe, and Baceraca to trade. Also, Janos and Sumas would show up at Teuricatzi, Cuquiaratzi, Tebideguatzi, and Cuchuta (AGN 1678).

BAND AND GROUP NAMES

The following is a summary of the various bands, groups, or "tribes" of the greater Conchería. These summaries of necessity are short, but they should afford a rough notion of the ethnic complexity of the region as contained in documentary sources with respect to possible alternate designations of the several groups, their geographical locations, and

---

*The Ziquipinas were mentioned by several declarants, and seemingly this group was most closely associated with the Janos and Jocomes in recorded oral statements, although in one statement one could guess it was a western Suma band. Considering that some of the Suma who testified were from Janos and Carretas, this was possibly the case. In any event, the Ziquipinas appear to have dwelt west or northwest of Casas Grandes. The Amochimisquina were also mentioned several times by Indian witnesses (probably including the one occurrence of Amazimiisnaguaq), but are unplaceable geographically and ethnically from the contexts of the declarations. The Amjiqui (see entry below) were mentioned only once but were distinguished from the other groups. The Otames occurred several times in the testimonies, and were apparently from around the Janos area. It is possible, by comparing two of the declarations that refer to the same event, to infer that the Otame were a Jano band – "two Janos and a Ziquipina," and "a Janos, an Otame, and a Ziquipina."

The most revealing testimony regarding ethnic complexity came from the Suma ex-governor of the La Soledad mission (AHP 1685Db). He stated that there had been seven nations together at the time of the second attack (at El Peñol del Diablo?) during the previous uprising in 1684: Janos, Jocomes, Zhiquipinas, Otames, Amjiqui, Amazimiisnaguaq, and another group whose name he did not know. He distinguished these peoples from Mansos, Piros, and Apaches, but whether they were basically Sumas or Janos-Jocomes (assuming a distinct linguistic division between the two) cannot be determined from the documentary source. They are, however, Suma renditions re-rendered by a Spanish scribe!

approximately the period or years for which there are data on their existence. This list is not exhaustive of all names discovered during the course of this study. The major omissions are (1) names of the Tepehuanes, Tarahumaras, and Tobosos, all of whom are basically outside the scope of the present problem and who are otherwise well known, at least with regard to their geographical locations; (2) names for groups which, although little known, on circumstantial evidence seem to be outside the geographical province of concern here; and (3) a few stray names that occur in church records (see mission entries in Chapter 6) but are otherwise irrelevant to this study or are unplaceable geographically with respect to their place of origin.

Lists of band and tribal names that are found elsewhere – such as those of Marín in 1693 (Hackett 1926: 390-4) and of the Spanish military commander, Juan de Retana, taken from his 1693 campaign (Griffen 1969: 176-7; BL 1695a) – have not been utilized or have been used only slightly, because they afford little information and because they quickly spill into areas not relevant here. I have dealt with the above lists and other band and tribal names elsewhere (Griffen 1969).

NOTE: Names given in *italics* within the entries below refer to entries elsewhere in this summary list.

Abasopaeme. This is a group over which the Indian governor of the Eastern Conchería claimed jurisdiction in 1684, the only time this name occurs (AHP 1684Aa). They are probably the same as the Zabasopalmes cited some 40 years earlier.

Abriaches. This was Luján's term for the inhabitants of La Junta.

Amazimiisnaguaq. This is almost certainly a variant rendering of *Amochimisquina* (AHP 1695Dc).

Amjiqui. This name was given by a Suma from the mission of Nuestra Señora de la Soledad at Janos; it could refer either to a Suma band or to a band of Janos or Jocomes (AHP 1685Dc).

Amochimisquina. This name was cited by several Sumas in 1685; it could have been either a Jano-Jocome or a Suma band (AHP 1685Dc).

Amotomanco. The chronicler of the Rodríguez-Chamuscado expedition of 1581, Gallegos, gave this term to the people who dwelt immediately downriver from Cuchillo Parado. It clearly refers to the people whom Luján called the Otomoacos a year later (Hammond and Rey 1927: 16; 1929: 54-5). It is not quite clear, however, who the Amotomanco might have been in later years.

Apaches. This name begins to show up in the northwest corner of the greater Conchería, in the Casas Grandes district, around the 1680s, but not until the 1700s in the northeast portion of the region. It was not until after the 1740s that the Apaches began to have real prominence in the northeast of the Conchería, although they became important in the northwest three or four decades earlier. In 1693 and in 1715, Apaches were said to be north or east of La Junta and of the Jumanos and Cíbolos, and their territory was said to extend to the Pananas (Pawnee), toward the coast of the "northern sea" (Gulf of Mexico) (AHP 1715Ac; BL 1695a).

Asisimbres. See *Sisimbles*.

Auchanes (variants: Aochanes, Ochanes, Nauchanes; also Yauchanes, in the Julimes parish records). The Eastern Conchería governor claimed the Auchanes as part of his jurisdiction in 1684. By 1715, at least some of them lived at San Antonio de Julimes, although earlier they had inhabited the town of Santa Cruz de Ochanes, downriver from Julimes (at the modern site of Pueblito) (AHP 1715Ac). If these people were living at Santa Cruz at the time of contact, then they would most certainly be Conchos, since the Rodríguez and Espejo expeditions placed this town within Concho territory.

Aycalmes. These people were claimed as falling under the authority of the Eastern Conchería governor in 1684 (AHP 1684Aa). They are quite possibly the same as the Ayozomes cited some four decades earlier, since in manuscript orthography the cedilla is often left off the *c*.

Ayozomes. This group was said to be from the La Junta area, and was one of the members of the Concho confederation in 1645 (CD 1650a). See also *Aycalmes*.

Bacabaplames. These were one of the peoples in revolt with the Conchos in 1645, and were said to be from La Junta (CD 1650a). They are very possibly the same as the Bapacolani and/or the Baopapa cited in later years.

Bachichilmi (variants: Bachichimi, Bachichilme). This name first appears in 1645 as one of the groups from the La Junta area that formed part of the Concho confederation (CD 1650a; AHP 1688Ca). In 1684, the Eastern Conchería governor, Hernando de Obregón, claimed that the Bachichilmi were under his authority (AHP 1684Aa). The Bachichilmi were probably a Cholome group or, at least, closely associated with the Cholomes (if the latter name is interpreted narrowly). In one place an Indian was said to be "de nazion Bachichimi y Cholome," although later he was called a Cíbola (AHP 1688Ca).

Bachicyolic. This name occurs once in the documents, where an Indian is reported to be a "Bachicyolic Concho"; this man was variously said to be from Las Salinas, Nombre de Dios, and San Lorenzo (AHP 1684Aa). The name is possibly a variant of *Batayolicla*.

Bamichicoami. These people were living in the Rio Grande-La Junta area in 1693 and were said to be "gentile," that is, not yet missionized (although there had been a Franciscan entrada to La Junta around 1684) (BL 1695a). The name is probably a variant of *Guamachicuama*.

Baopapa. This group was cited by the Eastern Conchería governor in 1684 as under his jurisdiction (AHP 1684Aa). The name is likely an alternate of either *Bacabaplames* or *Bapacolani*.

Bapacolani. The Bapacolani were in the La Junta area in 1693 (BL 1695a); they were probably the same as the Baopapa and/or the Bacabaplames.

Batayolicla (variants: Batayoligla, Batayolila, Batayolicua, Batayulica, Vatayocua, Batlaboylas). This was a Chiso band involved in the disturbances of 1684 and said to be in the La Junta area in 1693 (AHP 1684Aa; BL 1695a). In this latter year, although it was at (or near) La Junta, it was considered separate from the other 11 nations who resided permanently there at this time. However, it apparently was closely associated with the Sunigugliglas (Seuliyoliclas), also at La Junta at this time, and the two groups together were reported to comprise 300 persons (Hackett 1926: 426; BL 1693b).

Batlaboylas. This group was reported to be in the vicinity of the La Junta district in 1715 (AHP 1715Ac); the name is probably a variant of *Batayolicla.*

Cabris. This was the name given by Gallegos, the chronicler of the Rodríguez-Chamuscado expedition, to the people who were almost certainly the Cholomes of later years (Hammond and Rey 1927: 14). The Espejo party called these people the Passaguates.

Cacalotes (from Nahuatl *cacalotl,* "crow"). These people were reported at La Junta in 1693, 1715, and 1724, and to about the middle of the 18th century (AHP 1715Ac; 1722Bb; BL 1695a). See also *Cacalotitos.*

Cacalotitos (from Nahuatl *cacalotl,* "crow," plus *-ito,* Spanish diminutive). The Eastern Conchería governor claimed the Cacalotitos as being under his jurisdiction in 1684. In 1715, some were reported working in the San Bartolomé Valley but were said to be from the Rio Grande (AHP 1684Aa; 1715Ac).

Cacuitataomes (variants: Cacuitathumet, Quaquithatome, Tacuitatomes, Cacuitatahumet, Tacuiyttattaomes, Oraquitatomes). According to testimonies in 1684, this was definitely a Chiso band that had its home on the Rio Grande; however, at this time it was living on the San Pedro River at the town of San Lucas, which belonged to the mission of San Pedro de Conchos, and the group was sometimes referred to as "la nación de San Lucas." Later, in 1723, they were reported to be living near the mission of San Francisco de Conchos (AHP 1684Aa; 1723A; BL 1695a).

Caguates. This was apparently an Otomoaco group reported by Luján to be living up the Rio Grande from La Junta in the 1580s; they were probably some of the Suma, or Cholomes, of later years (Kelley 1952a; Hammond and Rey 1929: 63-9).

Chacuiyacua. The Chacuiyacua were cited as a Chiso band in testimonies of 1684. They are possibly the same as the Yacchicava mentioned by the Eastern Conchería governor in this same year as falling under his jurisdiction (AHP 1684Aa).

Chalomes. See *Cholomes.*

Chichitames (variants: Chichitamen, Chuchitamen). This group (probably a Chiso band) was said to be involved in the disturbances of 1684 and after; it was cited again by the Spanish commander Retana in 1693 as living in the Rio Grande-La Junta region (AHP 1684Aa; BL 1695a).

Chinarras (these were apparently the same as the Chinarrasa mentioned by Mota Padilla [1870: 518]). The Chinarras comprised several groups that inhabited the desert country west of the Conchos River, roughly along the northern Concho border, some being reported as far west as the mission of Santa Ana del Torreón in 1684 (CPP 23: 13-4). In the 1680s, a Chinarra was said to be from a place called Los Pescados, and another was from Las Salinas (AHP 1686Bb). In 1715, the Chinarras were said to live between La Junta and El Paso. Shortly after this date they were reduced to mission life by the Jesuits at Santa Ana de Chinarras, near the present-day town of Aldama (AGN 1725); however, some of these Chinarras had previously lived at the missions of Nombre de Dios and San Pedro de Conchos (CPP 24: 120-240). They were possibly Concho-speaking, desert-dwelling peoples; in one place they were referred to as "Conchos Chinarras" (AHP 1684Db; see DiPeso 1974: 842, 992, fn. 38).

Chisos (variant: Chizos). In the later 1600s, this name clearly referred to a number of different named bands, including the Batayolicla, Cacuitataomes, Chacuiyacua, Chichitames, Cotoholomes, Guesecpayoliclas, Osatapas, Osatayoliclas, Seulilolicla, and probably the Sisimbles and the Tonmamar. There is also some evidence that on occasion "Chiso" was employed for a specific band (rather than used generically) (AHP 1684Aa). In 1645, the Chisos were reported to be members of the Concho confederation that was in rebellion at the time (CD 1650a); in 1653, in the title issued to the Eastern Conchería governor, the Chisos were explicitly stated to be under his jurisdiction (AHP 1652A). By 1684, several of the Chiso bands were settled on the San Pedro River, although their home was the Río del Norte; they worked on haciendas at San Bartolomé and elsewhere. From this time into the 18th century, Chisos of one kind or another were settled in the southern portion of the Conchería. Occasionally Chiso groups were reported to be north of the Rio Grande (AHP 1684Aa; AHP 1653Aa). Chisos were often said to be allied with Tobosos and other eastern Chihuahua desert raiders; the name "Chiso" occurs in the sources until about 1720 (see Griffen 1969).

Cholomes (variants: Chalomes, Zolomes, Chocolomos). In 1645, the Zolomes were reported to be one of the nations of the Concho confederation. Later, in 1715 and 1724, Cholomes were said to live at Nuestra Señora de la Redonda y San Andrés, the last of the towns downriver from Julimes just before La Junta proper (AHP 1715Ac; 1722Bb). In 1693, the Spanish commander, Juan de Retana, reported that the Cholomes were still gentiles but that they, together with the Cíbolos, were very *domésticos.* Retana added at this time that the Cholomes were a very widespread nation that bordered on the Sumas, who extended to El Paso (BL 1695a; DHM 1778). It would seem that specifically the Cholomes of the Cuchillo Parado area were the Passaguates and Cabris of the 16th-century expeditions into the area; however, the designation "Cholome" was apparently sometimes also employed in a less specific sense and was sometimes extended to or confused with some of the other groups and names in this region. For example, on one occasion an individual identified as a Cholome was also said to be a Cíbola; on another, an Indian accused of collaboration with the enemy was called both a Cholome and a Suma (AHP 1688Ca; 1688Cb). At this same time (1688), Cholomes and Sumas were said to be together at a place called Nuestra Señora de Guadalupe (no location given) (AHP 1685Dc). Since the accounts made in the 1580s indicate a general linguistic unity of the area, perhaps these examples do also. (See also *Coyamit.*)

Chuchitamen. See *Chichitames.*

Chulimes. See *Julimes.*

Cíbolos ("buffaloes" in later colonial Spanish; variants: Cibolitos, Civolitos, Sivolitos, etc.). This group originally dwelt north and east of the La Junta pueblos; eventually some lived at the rancherias located on the Rio Grande, downriver from La Junta, and some at La Junta proper. They were often associated with the Jumanos in recorded oral statements, and occasionally the Spanish called people in the area *Síbolos jumanas;* the bases for distinguishing Cíbolos from Jumanos are not clear. Some Cíbolos were town-dwelling and some, at least, acted as mediators between the La Junta peoples and others who lived farther out in Texas, such as the Tejas (Hackett 1926: 234-6, 240, 242-4, 248, 256, 260; Sauer 1934; BL 1693b; 1695a).

Conchos (Spanish, "shells," from the many shellfish found in the Conchos River, originally called El Río de las Conchas). This was a general name given to peoples who dwelt along the Conchos, San Pedro, and Florido Rivers and some of their tributaries, as well as along the Santa María and El Carmen rivers to the northwest. Apparently it referred originally to peoples speaking a single language, but this was not necessarily true in the later years. Names of specific Concho bands are unknown, although the Tocones seem to have been one of these. Possibly Mamites and Julimes were also Conchos, but there is some evidence that they may have been Jumano speakers (see *Language* in Chapter 4). Partly by historical association and partly by a process of elimination, a case could be made for considering some of the early names – such as Cupilames, Mosnales, Olozasmes, Tatamastes, and even Zabasopalmes – as having been names for specific Concho groups, but this is mostly a guess. Chisos were certainly Concho-speaking, apparently being an eastern desert extension of the basically river-dwelling Concho. Chinarras were likewise seemingly Concho-speaking, a northern extension of the Concho into the desert country west of the lower Conchos River; however, the evidence for the Chinarras being Concho speakers is much less substantial than for the Chisos. The La Junta area was not Concho country at the time of first European contact; one account in 1715 indicates that some Conchos were living at La Junta at this time, but since this is not supported in other sources, the evidence for a move of Concho speakers to La Junta during the colonial period is very weak.

While the Spaniards appear to have been fairly definite in indicating whether they were dealing with Conchos or with non-Conchos, sometimes they did employ this term in a generic sense, possibly using it at times for any Indians who lived along the Conchos River. In 1715 Don Andrés, general of the Cholomes, who apparently spoke a different language from the Conchos upriver from his group, said he was of the Concho nation, and his interpreter was a Concho Indian named Pedro Cosme. A 1684 report mentioned that Chisos, Julimes, and others who had taken part in the revolt of this year were all called "Conchos"; however, many of the "others" who had participated in this rebellion were Jumano speakers, and yet they were included in the designation "Concho" at this time. Such generic usage may have arisen from the fact that the Spaniards included both Conchos and non-Conchos in the administrative province of the Conchería (Hackett 1926: 221; Miranda 1871; Sauer 1934: 59ff; AHP 1715Ac; DHM 1715).

Conejos (Spanish, "cottontails"; variant: Conexo). This was a group that inhabited a couple of spots at La Junta. In the early 1650s, they were reported to live on the south side of the Rio Grande, and some continued to dwell in the La Junta area until the middle of the 18th century. In 1653 the Conejos were decreed explicitly to be under the Eastern Conchería governor; when the latter was brought to testify in 1684, the Conejos were again mentioned as being under his authority (AHP 1652A; 1684Aa; 1715Ac; 1722Bb).

Cototoholme, Cototoolome, Cototoolocme. See *Totoholme.*

Coyamit (possibly from Nahuatl *coyametl,* "pig" [Molina 1944: 24]). This name occurs only once, when cited by the Eastern Conchería governor, Hernando de Obregón, as a group that fell under his jurisdiction in 1684. The obvious association of this term is with "Coyame" – El Coyame was the "General" of the Cholomes in 1715, and *Coyamit* was probably Obregon's designation for *Cholome,* a name that was not mentioned in his testimony (AHP 1684Aa; 1715Ac).

Culebras (Spanish, "snakes"). This group was claimed by the Eastern Concho governor as under his authority in 1684 (AHP 1684Aa); otherwise the name is unplaceable.

Cupilames. This was very likely a Concho group. In 1653, these people, distinguished from both the Julimes (Chulimes) and Mamites, were reported to be at the town of San Antonio de Julimes (AHP 1653Bd).

Geulimes. See *Julimes.*

Guamachicuama. These people were cited as being under the jurisdiction of the Eastern Conchería governor in 1684 (AHP 1684Aa). The name is probably a variant of *Bamichicoami.*

Guelajipicmi. This group was said to be under the authority of the Eastern Conchería governor in 1684 (AHP 1684Aa). The term is possibly a variant of *Guesecpayolicla.*

Guesapame. This was a Chiso group, and the name is clearly a variant of *Guesecpayolicla.* In testimonies taken in 1684, both forms of the name were said to be the nation from "la tierra de las auras" (AHP 1684Aa).

Guesecpayolicla (variants: Guesecpayoliclao, Guasapa-yoligla, Guasapagoligla, Guasipayoles, Guesipayoles, Guesec-pamot, Guesapame). These people (probably a Chiso band) were also referred to, in testimonies from the year 1684, as the nation from "la tierra de las auras" (AHP 1684Aa). In 1693, General Juan de Retana reported that these Indians were in the Rio Grande area (BL 1695A).

Guiaquita. This name was cited once, in 1684, when the group was expressly claimed to be under the authority of the Eastern Conchería governor (AHP 1684Aa).

Guitates. In 1684 the Guitates were said to be under the jurisdiction of the Eastern Conchería governor, Hernando de Obregón (AHP 1684Aa); otherwise they are un-placeable.

Hobomes (variants: Obomes, Ovomes, Jobomes). The Hobomes first show up in 1645 as part of the Concho confederation then in revolt (CD 1650a). In this same year some Hobomes were reported working on an hacienda in the San Bartolomé Valley (AHP 1645Ab). In 1684, the Eastern Conchería governor, Hernando de Obregón, while citing the nations that were under his jurisdiction, mentioned the name *Hobome* twice – the second time stating that this Hobome nation was different from the first one. Possibly one of these was a Concho group. Again in 1684, Hobomes were laboring in the San Bartolomé Valley (AHP 1684Aa).

Hulimes. See *Julimes*.

Janos. These were a non-Concho and probably non-Jumano-speaking people who lived in the northwest part of the present state of Chihuahua. They were apparently from the area around the Janos presidio and settlement, and in the early 1700s they claimed that this site was within their territory; however, the Janos settlement may have been in Suma territory, or at least at the Suma-Janos border. These Janos were closely associated with the Jocomes and were reported to speak the same language (see DiPeso 1974: 839-40; AHP 1716A; DHM 18thc; CPP 16: 586-92; see also Chapter 6, entry for Janos settlement).

Jobomes. See *Hobomes*.

Jocomes (rare variant: Jacomes). This was clearly a group closely related to the Janos, said to speak the same language and to live to the north-northwest of them. In Sonora, they were associated with the town of Santa Rosa de Corodeguatzi (see DiPeso 1974: 839-40; DHM 18thc).

Julimeños. The Julimeños were a group of natives, re-portedly from the town of Julimes, who moved into the area of Coahuila. Included with them, at least part of the time, were a number of people from La Junta, specifically from the towns of San Cristóbal and Guadalupe. The latter people had left La Junta during the upset in 1749-50, when the Spaniards had attempted to establish a presidio there. It is unknown when the people from the town of Julimes went to Coahuila. About 1745, the combined group was settled at San Ildefonso in Coahuila (Kinnaird 1958: 188; Morfi 1935: 195; Oconor 1952: 106; Portillo 1886: 317-8).

In 1767, during Lafora's trip, many of the Julimeños were living in a small pueblo named El Carrizo, a visita about one and a half leagues to the south of the cabecera mission of San Francisco Vizarrón; some 160 Julimeño men and their families had moved there after having had difficulties with the Pauzanes Indians at San Francisco (Morfi 1935: 195). Lafora himself had at least some Julimeños with him, as he mentions that two were sent out from his party to scout (Kinnaird 1958: 151, 188).

Oconor, during the early 1770s, reported that the Juli-meños were constantly on friendly terms with the Apaches who were now in the area; it was assumed that these Juli-meños were involved in the many robberies and attacks in the region (Oconor 1952: 106). However, Morfi noted that these Julimeños had excellent records as auxiliary military personnel and were much sought after by the commanders of the Coahuila presidios (Morfi 1935: 196).

It was suggested during this period that these people be forced to move back to their town of Julimes; while it is unknown whether any actually did so, census reports of 1789 and 1816-1817 cite Julimeños as one of the groups at Julimes (AGN 1816; BL 1789a; 1789b).

Julimes (variants: Xulimes, Hulimes, Jeulimes, Geulimes, Chulimes). The Julimes may have been a specific Concho group, but there is some evidence that they were Jumano speakers, or at least not Concho speakers (see *Language* in Chapter 4). All 17th-century references except one indicate that the Julimes dwelt on the Conchos River in the area of the present-day town of Julimes. In 1684 Domínguez de Mendoza reported that Julimes occupied the settlements along the Rio Grande at La Junta, but this might have been an erroneous identification based on the fact that some of the people who lived at Julimes at this time were from the La Junta pueblos. Indeed, the fact that the governor of Julimes in 1715, Don Antonio de la Cruz, was from La Junta only points to the general migration of La Juntans south-ward, up the Conchos, during the last half of the 1600s and the 1700s, and does not necessarily indicate that the "orig-inal" Julimes people were Jumano speakers. However, if they were Jumanos, then they would have been one of the first groups from the La Junta area to migrate southward and settle in Concho country. In any event, they were closely associated with Conchos from the 1640s on; in 1677, they were explicitly included with the Conchos (CPP 39: 318-29).

The Julimes, often cited together with the Mamites, were part of the Concho confederation of 1645; in 1653 and 1684, they were noted as being under the Eastern Con-chería governor, Hernando de Obregón, who was said to be a Concho, and sometimes a Julime, but more frequently a Mamite. The Franciscan Urbaneja wrote in 1653 that the Julimes and Mamites had crop fields in the area of San Pedro. In a 1708 report, it was noted that one of the many nations in the Coahuila area was called "Julimes de dipos [*sic –* tipos?] Gavilanes"; this statement is uninterpretable unless it refers to some early precursors to the Julimeños (Bolton 1930: 325; Kelley 1952b; Sauer 1934: 59ff; AHP 1652A;

1653Bc; 1684Db; CD 1650a; DHM 1715b; UTD 1707).

Jumanos (variants: Jumanas, Xumanas, Sumanas, Chouman [the French form], and others – see Sauer 1934: 65ff). These people were located at La Junta proper and in the surrounding region; they were apparently related to the Sumas, the two names being alternates of each other.

Mamites (variants: Mamit [CD 1650a]; Mame [Julimes Parish Records]; Mamimetes [Mota Padilla 1870: 518]; each of these variants occurs only once, the regular transcription being *Mamites*). By early historical association (for instance, in the 1640s), these would seem to have been a specific Concho group, closely related to the Julimes. Possibly the homeland of the Mamites was near or adjacent to that of the Julimes, perhaps upriver from the Julimes around San Pablo, or even San Pedro. The Mamites were one of the confederated rebel groups during the 1645 uprising, reportedly closely associated with Julimes and Olozasmes. After this revolt many Mamites were settled in the area of the mission of San Francisco de Conchos – which does not necessarily indicate, of course, that this was their original homeland. Later, they were stated to be under the jurisdiction of the Eastern Conchería governor, Hernando de Obregón, often said to be a Mamite (AHP 1652A; 1653Bc; CD 1650a; DHM 1645).

Mesquites. These people were specifically claimed by the Eastern Conchería governor in 1684 as under his authority; in the years 1693, 1715, 1724, and into the 18th century, they were reported to dwell in the Mesquites pueblo at La Junta (AHP 1715Ac; 1722Bb; BL 1695a).

Mosnales. This was cited as one of the rebel groups allied with the Concho confederation in the 1645 revolt (CD 1650a); it was possibly a Concho band.

Nabobayoguames. These people were listed as one of the groups of the Concho confederation during the 1645 revolt (CD 1650a); they are probably the same as the Olobayapuame recorded in later years.

Nauchanes. See *Auchanes.*

Norteños (Spanish, "northerners"). This term became current as a generic reference to the La Junta peoples, as their specific pueblos and corresponding names became unimportant or lost to the Spaniards. It seems to have gained its major acceptance or use in the 1720s, and it apparently was employed for all peoples from the general La Junta area by mid-century; however, in 1730, José de Berroterán distinguished 30 *norteños,* 19 *cholomes,* and 13 *cíbolos* in a summary of the ethnic identity of some Indians who had gone to see him at the San Francisco de Conchos presidio (AHP 1730Cc).

Obomes. See *Hobomes.*

Ochanes. See *Auchanes.*

Olobayapuame. These people were reported to be under the jurisdiction of the Eastern Conchería governor in 1684 (AHP 1684Aa); most probably they can be identified with the Nabobayoguames.

Olozasmes (probable variant: Oljasmas). This was one of the rebel groups confederated with the Conchos in 1645. They appear to have been closely associated with the Mamites, since the chief of the latter made peace with the Spaniards for them in their name (CD 1650a).

Oposmes (variants: Opoxmes, and probably the Oppomes of Mota Padilla [1870: 518]). This was one of the more "stable" of the group names of the Conchería. The Oposmes were reported as part of the Concho confederation of 1645. In 1653 they were cited as being under the authority of the Eastern Conchería governor; later, in 1684, they were claimed by him to be within his jurisdiction. In 1693 General Juan de Retana recorded the Oposmes as living at La Junta, and they were reported to be there again in 1715 and 1724 (AHP 1715Aa; 1722Bb; BL 1695a; DHM 18tha).

Oraquitatomes. See *Cacuitataomes.*

Osapayoliglas (variant: Osatayoliclas). Probably a Chiso band (BL 1695a).

Osatabay. See *Osatapa.*

Osatame. This band was reported to be active during the 1684 disturbances (AHP 1684Aa); the name is almost certainly a variant of *Osatapa-Osatabay.*

Osatapa (variants: Osataba, Osatabay, Osatame, Osatapai, Osataopa). This was a Chiso group; in 1684, some were settled at San Francisco de Conchos, and some Osatabay were also reported downriver from the town itself (AHP 1684Aa).

Osatayoliclas. See *Osapayoliglas.*

Otaguas. Only one source refers to some people called Los Otaguas. They were most probably Concho speakers, from a place called Los Otaguas in the general area of Las Encinillas, north of Nombre de Dios (AHP 1688A).

Otames (possibly from Nahuatl *otlatl,* "cane, reed," pl. *otlameh*). This group was reported in 1685 testimonies to be allied with Janos, Jocomes, and various Suma groups, plus the Amochimisquina, Ziquipina, Amjiqui, and some Mansos, in the Casas Grandes district (AHP 1685Dc). In 1717 Otames were cited once from Santa Ana de Chinarras as if they were roughly in that area (CPP 24: 219-58).

Otomoacos. According to Luján, these were people who dwelt between the Passaguates of Cuchillo Parado and the Abriaches who lived at La Junta proper. Obregón claimed that these people called themselves the Jamana. The Otomoacos were closely connected to the Abriaches at La Junta – their languages were mutually intelligible dialects and the two groups were interrelated by ties of kinship. The Spanish soldiers called the people of the whole area Patarabueyes (Hammond and Rey 1929: 53-5, 58).

Ovomes. See *Hobomes.*

Palos Blancos (Spanish, "white trees" or "white poles"). This name for a group at La Junta was given in 1724 by the Julimes governor, who claimed he had never visited the area (AHP 1722Bb).

Passaguates (variant: Pazaguates). This was the name Espejo and party gave to the peoples that dwelt in the area of Cuchillo Parado; apparently they are the same as the Cholomes of later years. They are called Cabris in the Gallegos *relación* (Hammond and Rey 1929: 54).

Patarabueyes. According to Luján, this was a name the

Spanish soldiers made up (*patar a bueyes,* "ox kickers" – literally, "to kick oxen") for the peoples of the La Junta district (Hammond and Rey 1929: 54–5, 58).

Paxalames. See *Posalmes.*

Pescados (Spanish, "fish"). This was a nation from the general La Junta area, apparently named after their chief, El Pescado. They were first reported in 1693; in 1726, they were said to be located 10 leagues up the Rio Grande, toward El Paso (UTD 1710–1738a). In 1747, some Pescados living at the Puliques pueblo stated that they were from the downriver town of Tapacolmes (Kelley 1953), and they may have been the same as the Tapacolmes. They were cited again in 1749 (BL 1749–1750).

Polacmes (variants: Pualacmes; also, apparently, Polalmes, Poloaques, Polulamas, and Poltemes). The Polacmes were cited as being under the authority of the Eastern Conchería governor in 1684, and were reported to be living at La Junta in 1693, 1715, and into the middle of the 18th century (Kelley 1952; 1953; AHP 1684Aa; 1685Db; 1715Ac; BL 1695a; 1697–1703; DHM 18tha).

Poricas. See *Pulicas.*

Posalmes (variants: Poxsalmes, Pocsalmes, Paxalames, Pusalmes, Poxalmas). In 1684, the Eastern Conchería governor stated that the Posalmes were part of his jurisdiction; they were said to be living at La Junta in 1693, 1715, 1724, and apparently into the middle of the 1700s (Kelley 1952; 1953; Mota Padilla 1870: 518; AHP 1685Db; 1715Ac; 1722Bb; BL 1695a).

Pualacmes. See *Polacmes.*

Pulicas (variants: Puliques, Publicas, Poricas, Puliza). This group was reported to be living at La Junta in 1693, 1715, and into the mid-18th century (Kelley 1952; 1953; AHP 1715Ac; BL 1695a; UTD 1710–1738a).

Pusalmes. See *Posalmes.*

Quaquithatome. See *Cacuitataomes.*

Rayados (Spanish, "painted," "striped," "streaked," "marked"). Mentioned (DHM 18tha) as one of the peoples in or around La Junta, this was probably a Jumano group.

Rayas (Spanish, "stripe," "border," "boundary line"). According to Gallegos, the Rayas were the last group of Concho speakers before crossing to Cabris country. They may have been a Chiso band (Hammond and Rey 1927: 13–4).

Satapayogliglas (variant: Satayolila). This was a Chiso band reported to be raiding in the 1690s (BL 1693a). They were almost certainly the same as the Osapayoliglas.

Sensibles. See *Sisimbles.*

Seuliyolicla (this name has a great number of variants, some of which are: Senayoligla, Seulilolicla, Simplolila, Sinilolila, Siniplolila, Siui.Anouigla, Solinyolicua, Sonololila, Suniloligla, Sunilolila, Suninolila). This was a Chiso band, involved in the rebellion of 1684; in 1693 and 1694, the group was reported to be at La Junta, together with the Batayoliclas (Hackett 1926: 426; AHP 1684Aa; BL 1693b; 1695a).

Silaloya. In 1648, a Spanish Indian auxiliary was said

to belong to this group; the name is probably an early form of *Seuliyolicla* (UTD 1648).

Simplolila, Sinilolila. See *Seuliyolicla.*

Sisimbles (variants: Zizimbles, Xiximbles, Sensibles, Sinsimbles, Sisinbres, Asisimbres, Simbles, Sinibles). This was apparently a Chiso group, first reported in 1645 (as Xiximbles) as one of the nations in revolt, allied with the Concho confederation. In 1724, the Sisimbles were said to border the La Junta pueblos on the south (AHP 1645Aa; 1722Bb).

Sivolitos. See *Cíbolos.*

Solinyolicua, Sonololila. See *Seuliyolicla.*

Sopolmes. This is possibly a transposed form of *Oposmes,* since the group was distinguished from the Pualacmes and the Posalmes in the account in which it occurs; it was reported living at La Junta in 1724 (AHP 1722Bb).

Sucayi. The Sucayi were named by the Eastern Conchería governor in 1684 as falling under his jurisdiction (AHP 1684Aa).

Sumanas. See *Jumanos.*

Sumas. This was an alternate form of *Jumano* or *Jumana.* The term was most consistently applied to the people in the west, from El Paso to the Casas Grandes district, although in the late 1600s and in the 1700s it was used for groups living west of Cuchillo Parado and from La Junta to El Paso (Bolton 1930: 321ff); in 1693, Retana reported that the Suma extended from the Cholomes (around Cuchillo Parado) to El Paso, some having been reported at the El Paso mission in 1659 (BL 1695a). In their far western extension, the Sumas bordered on the Opatas of Sonora. These western Suma were probably first contacted by Ibarra in 1564–65; in the mid-1660s the Spanish governor, Gorraez Beaumont, reported that there were many Yuma (Suma) Indians at Casas Grandes, Torreón, and Carretas (Schroeder 1961: 65; DHM 1668). In the mid–17th century, a Jesuit made a distinction among the far western Suma (from the standpoint of Sonorans): the eastern Sumas (*Sumas del Oriente*) and the northern Sumas (*Sumas del Norte*). These eastern Sumas (called western Suma by Spanish writers to the east in Nueva Vizcaya) bordered on the Opata at Babispe, and for a short while in the middle of the 1600s, the Jesuits maintained a visita of Babispe, some six leagues away to the east, for this group, reportedly numbering 244 souls; the northern Sumas were reported at Teuricatzi; and both eastern and northern Sumas were said to be in contact with the *partido* (district) of Guasabas (AGN 1653; 1662). In the 1680s, in the general western area, separate bands of Sumas were reported to be from El Río de la Toma (the mission of San Francisco downriver from El Paso), Las Salinas y Ojo Caliente, Los Médanos, the mission of Santa Gertrudis (at the edge of Los Médanos), and Carretas (DiPeso 1974: 906, 908; AHP 1686Bb). Some of the groups mentioned in the 1685 testimonies taken at Casas Grandes, such as the Ziquipina, Amjiqui, Amazimiisnaguaq, and Otames, may also have been Suma bands (AHP 1685Dc). (See also *Cholomes.*)

Suniloligla, Sunilolila. See *Seuliyolicla.*

Tacuitatomes, Tacuiyttattaomes. See *Cacuitataomes.*

Tapacolmes (variants: Tapacolomes, Topacolmes). These people were cited as one of the rebel groups of the Concho confederation in 1645 (CD 1650a); in 1653 they were listed specifically as one of the nations that fell within the jurisdiction of the Eastern Cherchería governor (AHP 1652A). General Juan de Retana stated in 1693 that this group was residing at La Junta (BL 1695a), but about this time a rancheria of Tapacolmes was reported to be farther up the Conchos River; they soon moved to the mission of Santa Cruz, on the San Pedro River (AHP 1722Bb). Since the Pescado Indians were reported to come from the town of Tapacolmes on the Rio Grande, possibly they were the same group as the Tapacolmes (Kelley 1953).

Tatamastes. These people were cited only in 1645, as one of the rebel nations of the Concho confederation (AHP 1645Aa; CD 1650a); possibly they were a Conchos River group.

Tecolotes (from Nahuatl *tecolotl*, "owl"). This name first occurs in 1693 for a Jumano group named after its chief or headman. These people may or may not have been the same as the Tecolotes referred to in the 1700s (for instance, in 1726), who lived up the Rio Grande from La Junta and in some of the La Junta pueblos, and who were apparently closely related to the Mesquites and Cacalotes. The Tecolotes were probably some of the descendants of the Otomoacos or Abriaches reported by Luján in 1582 (Kelley 1952a; BL 1695a; DHM 1748; UTD 1710-1738a). (These groups must not be confused with the Toboso Cocoyome band of the late 1600s whose chief was El Tecolote.)

Tocones. In 1645 the Tocones were cited as one of the member nations of the Concho confederation (CD 1650a), and some were reported working in the San Bartolomé Valley district this same year (AHP 1645Ab). The name is almost certainly a shortened form of *Toconibabas.* In 1643, a petition stated that a group of the "Toconibabas nation" had been working on a hacienda in the Valle de San Bartolomé since the mid-1620s; their caciques were named Don Diego and Don Gáspar. According to the hacienda owner, Diego del Castillo, these Indians had been chosen for work by the Concho Indian governor and his lieutenant (a *principal* of the town of San Francisco de Conchos); at the time they were picked up in the hinterland, they were reported to be wild (*bosales*) and had never before been under encomienda (CD 1643). At this same time, in another source, Castillo and one Diego de Porras were said to be fighting over the use of Tocones Indians on their haciendas in the San Bartolomé Valley (CD 1648).

Toconibabas (variants: Toconibibas; Tocanibabas). See *Tocones.*

Tonmamal (variants: Tonmamar, Tuimamar, Tunmamar). This was apparently a Chiso band; in 1693 it was reported

by the Spanish commander, Retana, as being in the area of the Rio Grande (BL 1695a).

Topacolmes. See *Tapacolmes.*

Totoholme (variants: Totoholome, Cototoholme, Cototoolome, Cototoolocme). This was apparently a Chiso group. It was reported by General Retana to be in the area of the Rio Grande in 1693 (BL 1695a).

Tuimamar, Tunmamar. See *Tonmamal.*

Unanalguit. This name was given to a La Junta group in 1724 by the Julime governor of the town of San Antonio, who said he had never been to La Junta; this nation was mixed with the Cíbolos at that time (AHP 1722Bb).

Vatayocua. See *Batayolicla.*

Venados (Spanish, "deer"). In 1724, reference was made to the gentiles whose chief was El Venado and who dwelt on the Rio Grande; two years later, in 1726, they were reported to be living 12 leagues up the Rio Grande from La Junta. The Venados were cited again in 1749 (BL 1749-1750; UTD 1710-1738a).

Vívoras (Spanish, "snakes"). These people were reported to be in the Rio Grande-La Junta district in 1693 by General Retana, who stated that they were considered the same as the Cíbolos. In 1749, a rancheria of Vívoras was said to be three leagues from La Junta and to consist of 78 persons (BL 1695a; 1746b).

Xatomes. This group was reported in 1715 to be a gentile people living between La Junta and El Paso (AHP 1715Ac); it was most probably a Suma-Jumano band.

Xulimes. See *Julimes.*

Xumanas. See *Jumanos.*

Yacchicava. The Yacchicava were claimed by the Eastern Cherchería governor in 1684 as under his jurisdiction (AHP 1684Aa).

Yaculsari. These people were said to be under the authority of the Eastern Cherchería governor in 1684 (AHP 1684Aa).

Yauchanes. See *Auchanes.*

Yeguacat. This group was claimed by the Eastern Cherchería governor in 1684 as under his authority (AHP 1684Aa).

Zabasopalmes. The Zabasopalmes were cited as one of the rebel groups of the Concho confederation in 1645 (AHP 1645Aa; CD 1650a); they are probably the same as the Abasopaeme noted in 1684.

Ziquipina (variants: Zhiquipinas, Zhiquiphina, Ziquifina). The Ziquipina were mentioned by Indian declarants in 1685 as being from the general Casas Grandes district. They may have been either a Suma or a Jano-Jocome band. The testimonies vaguely indicate that these people lived west or northwest of Casas Grandes (AHP 1685Dc).

Zizimbles. See *Sisimbles.*

Zolomes. See *Cholomes.*

4. GENERAL ETHNOGRAPHY OF THE CONCHERIA

During the course of this study, little has come to light on the ethnography and cultural characteristics of the Concheria that has not already been published in some form.* However, what little additional information has been collected is presented here for future researchers and to afford as complete a picture as possible of the nature of the aboriginal cultures that the Spaniards had to confront.

Partly for convenience and partly because of environmental and cultural considerations, the region can be divided into at least three ethnographic provinces. The first is the area of the central river valleys – those of the Conchos River itself, the Chuviscar, the San Pedro, and the other tributaries of the Conchos upriver from where the Chuviscar joins the Conchos; this was the territory of the Conchos Indians proper. The second includes La Junta proper and the neighboring areas extending down to Cuchillo Parado and along the Rio Grande drainage in both directions; this area included several somewhat differing ways of life, although apparently most of the people here belonged to basically the same language group. The third ethnographic province is the northwest portion of the area of the Santa María and Casas Grandes river valleys; living here were some Conchos, as well as Sumas and Janos-Jocomes tribal groups.

This classification is partly a matter of convenience. A more significant division, perhaps, would be simply one of river-dwelling as against desert-dwelling people. However, the historical information collected falls roughly into the above three provinces and consequently will be presented in this fashion.

Early accounts of the Concheria, beginning in the 1580s, are certainly impressionistic, since they were written before the Spaniards had had sufficient time to become very well acquainted with the Conchos or to integrate the region into their economic system. These accounts are not very positive or optimistic, and they generally share the following views. (1) The population of the area was fairly high or dense (however, no actual counts or censuses have been discovered). (2) The natives were docile and peaceful. (3) These people were rude and barbarous culturally (the same was said of most of the aborigines of this general northern region; probably they were often being compared implicitly to the village-dwelling Nahuas and others of central Mexico). In particular, (a) they were naked (not a true statement in the literal sense, but apparently an indication that the Indians did not wear anything like Spanish and probably Mexican dress), and (b) they practiced little agriculture. (4) In subsistence activities there was great use of squash (presumably cultivated), and also mesquite, prickly pear, *mescal* (maguey), and fish. Finally, (5) the natural resources of the region had potential from the Spanish point of view. Curiously, the accounts include no descriptions of settlements or house types (except for those of La Junta, discussed below), which seems to indicate that they were not impressive. Not all of the early descriptions include all of these points, and some disagree with one or more of them; however, this seems to have been about the consensus of the early Spaniards concerning the Concheria. As we shall see, in later times the emphases of the descriptions change.

From the standpoint of the economic potential of the region, the feelings of the Spaniards can be seen in some of their statements. Luján noted that the Conchos River was very large, implying that this was of value for the Europeans. In 1619, Governor Albear described the area around the Conchos River and the mission of San Francisco as quite fertile, and the river itself as containing abundant water; the area between San Francisco de Conchos and San Pablo (the later mission site?) contained a great many shellfish (*conchas*), *nácares,* and *madres de perlas* (UTL 1619).

Descriptive statements of the Concheria during the mid-17th century represent the area somewhat differently, and they usually mention the large size and great importance of the province. In 1649, the Nueva Vizcayan governor, Diego Guajardo Fajardo, stated that the Concheria extended from Parral almost to New Mexico, a distance of over 200 leagues, and contained some 50,000 inhabitants. In 1667, another governor, Oca Sarmiento, indicated the same general order of high importance of the Concheria. The importance of the Concho area, he said, rested on the facts that (1) it bordered the Tarahumaras; (2) the Indians lived along the Royal Highway to Sonora and to New Mexico, hence the problem of protection of traffic on these roads; (3) the Conchos were the "nation" that carried out the harvest of the local farmers, and the people belonged to the farmers' encomiendas (see Chapter 5); and (4) the salt flats necessary for the mining industry lay within Concho territory (BL 1649-1700).

---

*Previously published material is merely summarized here. Works that deal with the ethnography of the Concheria, especially that of La Junta, are: Beals 1932; Forbes 1959b; Kelley 1952a; 1952b; 1953; 1955; Kroeber 1934; Schroeder 1961; Sauer 1934.

In the early 1680s, Lope de Sierra Osorio reported that "the land of the Conchos is flat, fertile and watered by many rivers and streams, following a line from San Francisco de Conchos up to the river called Del Norte [Rio Grande], which is the one that divides the jurisdiction of Nueva Vizcaya from that of New Mexico" (Hackett 1926: 218-22). Arlegui in 1736 described the Conchos River as being quite fertile and having many fish; also, he said, its people were not as barbarous as those of other nations (by this time, the Indians of this region appear to have been quite acculturated) (1851: 76-7).

THE CENTRAL RIVER VALLEYS

The Conchos

The first description of the Conchos Indians is Miranda's in 1575, immediately after the Conchos had been first contacted. He stated that there were a great number of people who were "rude (*bruta*), incapable (*inabil*), and ignorant (*desabida*), because they do not have fields of corn nor of other crops (*semillas*), and they nourish themselves with very vile and low foods" (1871). The lack of agriculture noted here certainly was not true (see below). About 15 years later, the Nueva Vizcayan governor, Rodrigo del Río y Loza, characterized the general region, including the Conchos, by stating that "all of the people [are] very barbarous and they sow almost no corn for their food; they maintain themselves with a fruit from a tree that is called *mezquite* and with *tuna* and *magey* [sic] and fish (*tapas de pescado*)." A year later, in 1592, he noted that the only products of the Concho province were the crops of corn and squash, and fish (UTD 1592-1643; CPP 2: 143-156).

The descriptions of the Conchos Indians that come from the Rodríguez-Chamuscado and Espejo expeditions in 1581 and 1582 confirm the practice of agriculture but emphasize the use of gathered items, including fish. Gallegos stated that the people were naked and that they subsisted on large amounts of ground mesquite, squash, prickly pears, mushrooms, and fish (Hammond and Rey 1927: 14). Luján also reported that the people were naked, but he said that they covered themselves with rabbit skins (probably woven rabbit-skin blankets); the genital region of the men was left uncovered, while the women covered theirs with rabbit and deer skins but left their breasts uncovered. The Conchos were docile and peaceful, although when they fought they employed the bow and arrow. For subsistence they utilized fish, mesquite, and mescal from *lechuguilla* (that is, the *maguey* of Miranda). Toward the northeast boundary of Concho country, on the way to La Junta, Luján made note of the many squash fields; before this, at El Xacal, he had recorded the large and small gourd containers (*tecomates* and *xícaras*) that were given to the Spaniards as presents by the Indians (Hammond and Rey 1929: 49-53).

In the Laet version of the Espejo expedition, Concho subsistence consisted of hunting wild and other animals ("other" left unexplained), mainly "rabbits, hares and deer." In addition, but apparently considered secondary in this report, Conchos utilized corn, squash, and melons, and one would guess that these were mostly cultivated. The province was noted to abound in these products as well as in fish (Hackett 1934: 311).

On the Espejo expedition (Laet version), it was stated that Concho dwellings were simply "hovels," arranged in "wards," and that the settlements were governed by caciques. Later, in 1621, the houses in which Conchos dwelled were simply referred to as *jacales*, as were those of some Chinarras in 1716. In 1619, Albear added that all the people of the Concho area had sweat houses (*estufas*) like those the Tarahumara had (Hackett 1934: 310; CPP 5: 89-101, 114, 117; 24: 142, 147; UTL 1619).

In the first decade of the 17th century, Torquemada, who probably obtained his information from the first missionary to the Conchos, Fray Alonzo de la Oliva, described the Conchos as a docile nation that covered an area of many leagues (Torquemada 1944: 345).

Later archival sources, which of course refer to Conchos after several generations of contact with the European way of life, confirm these early descriptions fairly well, but amplify them little. Many important matters such as social organization and ceremonial life – including such possible features as military and other societies – dwellings, and settlement patterns are simply not mentioned in the sources consulted.

As noted above, the Conchos used the bow and arrow. In 1684, Conchos, Julimes, Mamites, and others were described as having this weapon, as well as shields (*adargas*), pikes (*chusos*), clubs (*macanas*), swords (*espadas*), and daggers (*dagas*) (AHP 1685Db). Concho arrows were made of both *caña* and *lechuguilla* (AHP 1684Aa). In one place it was stated that the *lechuguilla* shaft of Concho arrows had a characteristic mark (*mueca*) on it (AHP 1645Ab). An arquebus was mentioned as being in the possession of one of the rebels of the Concho confederation of 1645 (CD 1650a).

Material culture involved with horses was mainly Spanish. In 1684, items cited as being associated with Conchos were described as "unos lomillos y dos sudadexos de cuero de Sibola y unos bastos de silla de baqueta." These same items were later described as "unos lomillos aforrados En quero de Cavallo y dos Sudaderos y uno de cuero de Carnero Y otro de sivola" (AHP 1684Aa).

In the 1680s, a number of Conchos were questioned regarding how they made their living. Ten men, simply called Conchos, said that they planted corn for their sustenance in their own territories, and that they also worked on haciendas; another man, who was reported to be from the salt flats (*de las salinas* – where?), also said he grew corn (AHP 1688A). In 1684, a man described as a Bachicyolic Concho from the town of San Lorenzo said he raised corn (AHP 1684Aa).

In 1653, Fray Hernando de Urbaneja wrote from Babonoyaba concerning the Julimes (who may not have been Concho speakers) and the area where they were located, saying that "all of the land in this direction [that is, toward Babonoyaba] and all of the Conchos river is very good, and the Jeulimes [Julimes] and Mamites have great milpas and bean fields; they came to see me and they brought me corn and beans; they are very populated" (AHP 1653Bc).

Another Concho stated that he lived by hunting cottontails and jackrabbits (AHP 1684Aa). Other items of Concho diet were pinole (AHP 1684Aa), mescal (BL 1697-1703), squash (*calabasas*), corn, watermelon (*sandias*), and meat (AHP 1684Aa). Conchos at Babonoyaba in 1619 were reported to be engaged in hunting and fishing (this was under wartime tensions) (UTL 1619). Fishing was also reported for the Conchos in 1645 (AHP 1645Aa). Conchos and Chinarras who had been living in the desert country north of Encinillas in 1716 said they gained their livelihood by sowing *semillas de la tierra,* hunting, and stealing cattle (CPP 24: 124-5).

Other subsistence items were mentioned: *contra yerba de Julimes,* reported to be found in the area of Julimes, was said to be good for all kinds of aches and for counteracting poison (apparently from arrows) – supposedly it was the only antidote known; *yerbas de camotillos* were apparently gathered around the Julimes mission (use not given) (Arlegui 1851: 133). Mota Padilla states that the *contra yerba* was a small *camotillo* (small root). It was found in several places, but that from Julimes was the most efficacious. It was useful for all kinds of illness; many people carried pieces of it with them hanging as amulets, and a small piece in one's mouth purified the blood and settled the stomach (1870: 357-8).

The Julimeños, when they were in the Coahuila area, were reported to have the following characteristics: they used peyote, *patolillo,* and an herb called *tabaco julimeño.* They indulged in wild dances (mitotes) and had on occasion joined with Apaches (Mescaleros) in dancing with scalps; they also practiced witchcraft (*brujerias*) (UTD 1768-1792). A final item of ethnographic note is that Chinarras in 1716 tallied on a stick the number of persons on their way to Santa Ana de Chinarras (CPP 24: 160).

The Chisos

For reasons of convenience, the Chisos are kept separate from the Conchos in this discussion. Their subsistence patterns during the colonial period seem to have been somewhat more oriented toward hunting and gathering than were those of the Conchos, although this impression may be partly due to a bias in the documentary sources. Members of Chiso groups questioned in the 1680s concerning their means of subsistence included the following: Chichitames – mescal, tunas, and *elotes* (corn); Osatabay (Osatayolicla) – mescal, deer, rabbit (*conejos*), tunas, and *elotes*; Batayolicla – deer, rabbit, mice (*ratones*), snakes (*culebras*), and nopal cactus, and two men mentioned corn. Presumably the corn was all grown by the groups mentioned, and one document specifically states that a Batayolicla claimed he grew corn ("se sustenta de mais que siembra En Su tierra"). One Taquitataome cited eating pinole (AHP 1684Aa).

In the 1690s, it was stated that Chisos would go to the far (north) side of the Rio Grande in the cold season to hunt buffalo, sometimes in the company of Cíbolos (BL 1695a). Chiso arrows were said to be made of *lechuguilla* with turkey feathers (AHP 1684Aa).

Some notion of ceremonial life is given for the Chisos. The women of a combined group of Chichitame and Sisimble, and possibly Guesecpayolicla, were reported to have killed and eaten a Spanish girl captive (Hackett 1926: 332, 396). On one occasion, Chisos threatened to cut off the head of a person and dance with it; once a group of Chisos cut the genitals off their victims (AHP 1684Aa; for additional information on Chisos, see Griffen 1969).

THE NORTHEAST CONCHERÍA

La Junta

As noted above, for ease of presentation, the La Junta pueblos are treated here separately from the rest of the northeastern area of the Conchería. From the beginning, the La Junta region was noted to be different from the surrounding area, especially from the Concho territory; it was also noted to have some internal diversity in size of pueblos, and so on. Luján and Gallegos noted this difference, which has been published elsewhere (Hammond and Rey 1927; 1929). In 1640, Governor Bravo de la Serna wrote an interesting description that may refer to the La Junta area. He noted that the Tarahumaras were bordered on the east by the Conchos and on the northeast by a nation called Los Caciques ("the chiefs"; this is the only time this name occurs). He stated that of these people it was reported that they were rich in wheat and corn fields and in minerals, and that they lived in high, well-built houses. The territory of Los Caciques was said to border New Mexico, on the far side of a large salt flat ("laguna de sal") (AGN ca. 1640).

The La Junta peoples were definitely agricultural, farming along the flood plains and moist low places along the Conchos and Rio Grande rivers and clearing the land by burning off the cover. Crops grown were corn, beans, squash, wheat, *endejotes,* melons (*melones*), watermelons (*sandias*), and lentils (*lentejas*); one report adds "and other seeds" (*y otras semillas*) or plants (*legumbres*) (AHP 1715Ac; BL 1746; DHM 18tha). In 1730, Norteños (La Juntans), together with Cíbolos and Cholomes, reported that they planted corn, beans, squash, and wheat (AHP 1730Cc).

La Juntans proper also did some hunting, as well as fishing from the local river. Gathered products included piñon nuts, mescal, and tunas; one report mentions *gabalides*(?). Turkeys (*guajolotes*) are also mentioned, but it is not stated whether these were domestic or wild. The diet included gruel (atole) made from various kinds of seeds (BL 1746b). When Taagua, the Concho nativistic leader, was at La Junta in 1685, he was reported by different witnesses to have eaten, variously, cooked mutton (*obeja cosida*), lamb shoulder (*espaldilla de borrego*), *panochas,* watermelon (*sandias*), squash (*calabazas*), and *mesquitamal* (AHP 1685Db).

At least by the 1690s, some of the La Juntans had do-mestic animals – Chiso bands were reported to have raided the Mesquite pueblo for animals in 1693 (BL 1695a). Eighteenth–century accounts also note some domestic ani-mals, such as horses, held by the La Juntans (Kelley 1952b; 1953).

Little is mentioned of material culture. La Juntans lived in pueblo–like structures, apparently often of adobe con-struction, with flat roofs; sometimes, however, dwellings were stated to be *xacales,* apparently in reference to brush, thatch, or some other kind of construction. Some of the towns had well-marked plazas, and some had fences (Kelley 1952b; 1953).

La Juntans used a digging stick in horticulture, as well as a gourd or pitched basket for transporting water (Kelley 1952b; 1953). On one occasion the people at La Junta were reported to have made a raft ("balsa echa de lo ancho de una estola de las que robaron") (UTD 1710-1738a).

Nothing is known or reported regarding the social organi-zation or ceremonial life of the La Juntans, except that they probably used peyote in their ceremonies and they danced with the heads of their enemies (Hackett 1937: 410; AHP 1722Bb).

La Juntans carried on trade, and La Junta itself was ap-parently a trading center operating between the peoples to the south and those farther out in Texas. Items reported ex-changed with the less settled peoples were tame horses, hal-ters (*frenos*), knives (*belduques*), deerskins (*gamuzas*) and buffalo hides, dried meat, and corn and beans. In later years, Apaches are mentioned as coming in from Texas, and it is noted that occasionally captive children were also traded (BL 1746). In 1730, Norteños (La Juntans) and Cholomes, together with Cíbolos, reported that they did some trading in horses with Tarahumaras (AHP 1730Cc).

The Northeast Outside La Junta

Other peoples who dwelt in the eastern Conchería, roughly east of El Paso, but not at La Junta proper, were Sumas, Cholomes, and Cíbolos. Chinarras and Apaches are also mentioned in the region in the 18th century. Very little ethnographic information has come to light on these people, and for purposes of convenience they are lumped together in this single, vague geographical region.

Cholomes of the Cuchillo Parado area were reported to raise corn, beans, and squash, using basically the same dry-farming techniques employed by the people at La Junta proper. They were also said to eat pinole, to hunt rabbits, and to collect tunas. In 1747, they were said to live in grass huts (*xacalitos de zacate*) (AHP 1688Ca; 1688Cb; BL 1746).

On one occasion the Sumas who dwelt along the Rio Grande southeast of El Paso were reported to live chiefly on mescal that they baked in palms (Bolton 1930: 321). It was reported that there was a recognizable difference (un-defined) between the arrows of Apaches and Sumas (BL 1751b). One reference notes the use of smoke signals (*hu-maredas*), apparently by Apaches, Cholomes, and Sumas (BL 1746).

Cíbolos (as well as others) were said to do some buffalo hunting each year in the area of Texas, some between the Rio Grande and the Nueces River (BL 1693-1702).

THE NORTHWEST CONCHERÍA

No data on the cutural traits or characteristics of the northwest Concho population have come to light, except that these people lived in small and scattered rancherias as did the rest of the population of the area (BL 1649-1700). A little information has turned up, however, on the peoples such as the Sumas, Janos, and Jocomes, who were only pe-ripherally part of the Conchería. Most of this information comes from the 1690s, after considerable contact with Span-iards (and most of it comes from a single document). In the sources, very often Janos, Jocomes, and Sumas and their allies are treated together and, consequently, it is impossible to distinguish ethnographically among these several groups (see DiPeso 1974).

For subsistence the Janos, Jocomes, Sumas, and others of the 1690s hunted and gathered. Game animals were not specified, but plant foods included mescal or maguey, mes-quite, tunas, roots, *dátiles,* and seeds of various kinds (un-specified). *Tatemas* (places where meat was roasted?) were discovered by Spaniards at one abandoned camp (AHP 1695; BL 1693a; CPP 16: 586-92; 17: 200-5).

In 1695, footwear was reported but undescribed: *cacles* for the men, and *zapatos de teguas* for the women and chil-dren. One Indian man belonging to the combined group of Janos, Jocomes, and others was reported to be wearing a *tilma.* One abandoned camp contained the ashes of some 40 small hearth fires, around which were discovered a number of beds of grass (*camas de zacate*) where the Indians had slept (AHP 1695). In 1692, mats (*petates*) were found in the Sierra de Enmedio (BL 1693a; CPP 17: 205-10). In a campaign out of Janos in 1693, against people judged to be Apaches, in the Casas Grandes area near some springs called Santo Domingo, the Spanish forces came upon many tent coverings (*Ropa de tiendas*) as well as many buffalo hides; in 1730, some round houses constructed of grass (*sacate*) were judged to belong to Apaches (AHP 1730Ca).

Weapons of the Janos, Jocomes, and Sumas included bows and arrows, clubs (*macanas*), lances (*lanzas*), swords (*espadas*), shields (*adargas*), and pikes (*chusos*); some of the latter were constructed from the blades of swords hafted onto a stick. These people also had a number of Spanish leather military jackets or *cueras* with them. On one occa-sion, Apache arrows were stated to be "distinctive," but it was not specified how their arrows were distinguished from those of other peoples, such as the Janos and Jocomes. In 1693, Apaches were said to have large shields (*adargas*), and to make war whoops and throw rocks in battle; they also used smoke signals, as did the Janos and their allies. These Apaches on this occasion were reported to have thrown up some kind of defensive breastwork at the highest point of a mountain (*peñol*) (AHP 1695; BL 1695a).

Several other items of material culture were reported in 1695, some obviously stolen from Spanish sources, such as *justacos* or *justacales* (lances?), saddles (*sillas*), and halters (*cabrestos*). Carrying crates (*guacales*) and deerskins (*gamuzas*) were also cited (AHP 1695).

At the time of the cited reports, these people were relying to some extent upon stolen animals, and the Spanish encountered a number of these: horses, which were both eaten and ridden, as were mules. These two animals were the most desired because they could travel faster than many other beasts. However, on one occasion, the Spanish troops came across a recently killed bull, and a cow and a burro were also mentioned (AHP 1695; BL 1695a).

In battle, these Indians would send the women and children away to some safe place; then the men would stand and wait for the Spaniards. A Chinarra declarant stated that when the Janos and others would go out to raid, they would always leave the women and children at water holes next to the mountains; those who participated in the raid would all go together, and not until they got quite near the settlement of their destination would they send out scouts (AHP 1695).

Motivations for warfare were cited as vengeance (against Spaniards and Pimas [Sobaipuris]), but obviously the stealing of livestock, clothing, and other Spanish material items was also important. Both captives and Spanish goods, including weapons, were traded to Spanish troops in 1695 (AHP 1695).

The taking of scalps was common practice; these, as well as other paraphernalia of war, then functioned in the people's ceremonial life, as recounted by several informants. It was reported that at camp the Indians (with special reference to Janos and Jocomes) would dance wearing Spanish military jackets (*cueras*) and with Spanish scalps and clothing. At this time (1695), the chiefs of the Janos and the Jocomes possessed arquebuses, and they would dance with these firearms in their hands. One account cited the dancing with war booty – including two saddles, one arquebus, and a sword – and a jacket (*cuera*), as well as a scalp (AHP 1695).

A much more detailed account was given by two Opatas who had been captives of the Janos. According to these declarants, the Janos had invited some Apaches to their rancheria where they were holding a Spanish soldier prisoner. Both men and women took part in the celebration. The Indians first ordered their captive to load their arquebuses, which he did. The Indians donned their *cueras*, and with lances, swords, shields, and bows and arrows in their hands, they sang their war song. They brought the Spanish soldier in to dance with them and then began to beat him with their clubs (*macanas*) and bows. The Indians chanted to him, telling him that if he and his comrades (three of his companions, whom the Indians had killed at Guasabas in Sonora) had been from the Janos presidio, they would have fought with their arquebuses and swords (i.e., they would have shown more bravery) and would not have let themselves be killed without a fight (AHP 1695).

The Indians kept up this chanting and dancing until their captive fell to the ground from exhaustion. When the Indians finally saw that he could no longer get up, they killed him with their arquebuses; then, with their lances and knives they cut him into pieces and passed these out to everyone – men, women, and children – saying that all who ate this meat would be very brave. Later, they gave the Spaniard's head, and some scalps and a few animals, to the visiting Apaches so that they could take these items back to their own camp and dance with them (AHP 1695).

Sumas were reported to have ceremonies involving drunkenness, but it was not stated what intoxicant was utilized (AHP 1686Be). One Suma medicine man from the Bavispe region carried out "superstitious dances," congregating people in large drunken get-togethers. In one dance, called the Dance of Fire, he would spew flames from his mouth, walk on hot coals, and perform other such feats (AGN 1662).

The Spaniards reported that the Janos and others had a mourning wail for the death of some of their members (AHP 1695).

Chiefs or leaders, cited by the Spaniards as *capitanes* or *gobernadores,* were mentioned a number of times. While little specific information on these leaders exists, one Spanish report possibly indicates something of the manner of their recruitment at this time. The Europeans, while attempting to get the Indians to settle in communities, requested that the latter select their "governors" for these future settlements. According to the Spanish report – which may be very biased, given the Spaniards' own cultural orientations – bloodlines played a considerable part in the selection of these governors (AHP 1695).

The Jocomes elected a young man (*moseton*) to be their governor because he was a brave man and because he was the son and nephew of past governors. The Janos chose their current chief to continue as their representative because all his ancestors had been governors; he deserved the governorship because of his bloodline ("lo merecia por su sangre") and because he had governed them well in the past. The Sumas selected a very old, one-eyed man ("muy viejo y tuerto") because he and all his ancestors had led them well for many years (AHP 1695).

Two ethnographic items indicate that Spanish contact had occurred over some years. In 1695, Spanish troops northwest of Janos came upon a cleared and well-swept area that contained one very high cross and three smaller ones, placed "in the style of a church" – apparently some kind of syncretic ceremonial area. On one occasion, the Janos, Jocomes, and their allies gave the Spaniards a piece of paper, painted and marked up ("pintado y escarabajeado") in an unintelligible fashion, as a sign of peace (AHP 1695).*

---

*Sauer (1934: 75–6) quotes a description of a painted deerskin sent to the Spaniards by the Janos, Jocomes, Sumas, Mansos, and Apaches; this item seems to have been much more understandable than the painted piece of paper.

LANGUAGE

Only a small amount of information exists on the distribution of the various languages spoken in the general region of the Concheri\a. Unfortunately, none of the data are of the quality that would be supplied by vocabularies and grammars, which could point to definite, broader linguistic relationships.

According to the early chroniclers, all the people on the Conchos River down to about Cuchillo Parado, including the Rayas, spoke the same Concho language. A linguistic boundary just south of Cuchillo Parado is supported to some extent by later evidence; however, at least by the time the Parral mines had been in operation for a few years, non-Concho speakers (probably Jumanos) were moving southward, and this greatly confuses the ethnic and linguistic identification of the Concheri\a Indians in the 17th century. At no time is there any *direct* evidence that all the people dubbed Conchos by the Spaniards spoke the same language; for many years some language – including that spoken as far west as San Diego del Monte and Namiquipa – seems to have been consistently identified by the Europeans as the Concho tongue, and one can only assume that western Concho was quite similar to the Concho language spoken in the east. It still is not certain, however, that at the time of early contact all people who lived in what is defined here as Concho country actually spoke the same language.

Judging from the reports of both Gallegos and Luján, and especially that of Gallegos, north of the Concho language area another broad linguistic area existed, but it was divided into several mutually intelligible dialects. Gallegos stated that the Cabris (Passaguates) and Amotomancos (Otomoacos) Indians could understand one another, although their speech sounded different. Furthermore, the Amotomanco Indians gave the Spaniards to believe that there were many people of their language in an area that the Europeans interpreted to be more than 100 leagues long. This language, now generally identified as Jumano, extended for some distance north into Texas, along the Rio Grande upriver from La Junta, and across the northern portion of the Concheri\a, including the Casas Grandes district; it bordered on the west with the Opata of Sonora (Hammond and Rey 1927: 14–7; 1929: 54, 58; Kroeber 1934; Sauer 1934).

All available evidence points to the fact that Chiso and Concho were the same language (AHP 1684Aa; BL 1709-1715). This, of course, means that the Concho language extended eastward some distance from La Junta, probably at least as far as the Big Bend country. Curiously enough, this eastern extension is supported by a single word collected in 1674 during the expedition of Fernando del Bosque. Del Bosque's party left Ciudad Guadalupe in Coahuila, went northward across the R\io de las Sabinas, by the *puesto de Vicente Ferrer,* and crossed the Rio Grande; the Spaniards were in the company of some Pinanacas, Xaeser, Tenimamas, and Cocoma Indians, some of whom were from the band of

Esteban Quequesal (Hueyhueyquetsal) and from Coahuila (BL 1674). A river was encountered 11 leagues north of the Rio Grande, and the Indians informed the Europeans that in their language it was called *ona,* which meant *salina* ("saline") in Castilian. This is clearly a Cahitan word.* Kroeber, on the basis of the only three words recorded, has identified Concho as probably essentially a Cahitan language, and Sauer has supplied some documentary evidence that Concho may have been most like the language spoken at San Miguel de Culiacán on the west coast. Whether or not the name *ona* was a local word used by the people living at this river north of the Rio Grande, it was a term employed by peoples who dwelt east of the Concheri\a, and its occurrence points to the possibility of a fairly far eastern extension of Cahitan or Concho speakers (Kroeber 1934: 13-4; Miranda 1871; Sauer 1934: 59-60; BL 1674).

In the desert country south of the Chisos and east of the river-dwelling Conchos, the Toboso language was spoken. Most evidence indicates that Concho and Toboso were mutually unintelligible, although they may have been related (AHP 1655A; BL 1748; UTD 1749a; Griffen 1969).

From their association with Conchos over many years and from their geographical location from the 1640s, it might reasonably be assumed that peoples like the Julimes and Mamites were Conchos who spoke the Concho language. However, it is possible that these two groups were some of the first Jumano speakers to move southward from La Junta into Concho country. Evidence for this is rather weak, but it is a possibility.

In one account it was reported that of a group of attackers, some spoke in Concho, some in Julime, and others in Tepehuan ("que unos Hablaban en concho otros en Julime y otros en tepeguan") (AHP 1656A). This is the only explicit statement that the Julimes and the Conchos spoke different languages. However, one other bit of information may support this.

In 1689, when Don Juan Xaviata, chief of the "Z\ivola and Jumana nations," was in Parral, it was reported that there was no one in the city who could interpret the "S\ibola and Xumana languages"; therefore, one Don Nicolás, governor of the Julime nation, and another person who could also understand these languages (C\ibola and Jumano – probably actually only dialects of each other) were chosen as interpreters (BL 1693-1702). In 1683-84, Domingo de Mendoza reported that at least some of the people at La Junta were Julimes (Bolton 1930: 325); however, this is the only source in which these people were associated with La Junta (even Retana's inventory of 1693 did not mention Julimes at La Junta), and in any event Spanish reports often were in error about Indians.

---

*Modern Mayo *oona* (Collard and Collard 1962: 170), and modern Tarahumar *coná* (Hilton and others 1959: 200).

Sauer (1934) identified Chinarras as desert-dwelling Conchos. The fact that in 1716 the Concho governor from San Pedro de Conchos acted as interpreter for the Chinarras who were eventually settled at Santa Ana de Chinarras tends to support this, but it is the only such evidence (CPP 24: 135).

Farther westward, Tarahumara was distinct from Concho. In 1619, during the Albear campaign, Conchos could not communicate with Tarahumaras without interpreters (UTL 1619). Again, two years later in 1621, an interpreter (a Concho named Ambrosio) was needed to translate from Tarahumara to the Concho language (CPP 5: 126-31).

One somewhat ambiguous statement indicates that Concho was different from Yaqui. According to a declarant who apparently was a Concho, he could not understand a conversation the Concho governor at Casas Grandes had with a Yaqui because they were speaking in the Yaqui tongue (BL 1697-1703) (one would like to know how the Concho governor had learned the Yaqui language).

Almost certainly the Suma and Concho languages of the Casas Grandes district were distinct languages, although there exists no good evidence for this (except the evidence presented above for the differences between eastern Concho and Jumano). The Janos and Jocomes were reported explicitly to speak the same language – a statement in the 1680s noted that a person "ynterpreto en lengua Jana lo que el Yndio de dicha nasion o jocome (q toda es una lengua) declara" (AHP 1686Bc).

Other evidence of the linguistic complexities of this area is more circumstantial, and is based upon the use of interpreters. During the 1695 campaign, one man, Cristóbal Granillo, often served as an interpreter because, it was stated, he was knowledgeable in the language that all of the allied nations spoke and understood ("q izo ofizio de interprete pr ser mui yntelijente en la lengua q ablan y entienden todas las naznes coligadas") (AHP 1695).

However, apparently not all the people of these "confederated nations" actually did know the language that Granillo spoke. On one occasion, he interpreted in the interrogation of a Suma Indian. Later he interpreted for a Jocome woman, but this time it was stated that the woman spoke Suma although she was a Jocome ("Xptoval granillo yntelige en la lengua suma q hizo oficio de ynterpete y la yndia ablava dha lengua mui bien aunq ella era jocome") (AHP 1695). Immediately afterward, another Jocome was interrogated and a new interpreter was chosen, which indicates that Suma and Jano-Jocome were not mutually intelligible. At the same time, when a Chinarra was questioned, it was not Granillo but rather the Concho governor, Juan Corma, who served as interpreter; this supports information on ethnic associations suggesting that the Chinarra were most probably Concho-speaking (AHP 1695).

The Opata language from Sonora was unintelligible to a Jano-Jocome speaker (AHP 1695). No statement or other information has turned up, except that presented by Kroeber (1934), regarding the similarities and differences of Opata and Concho.

Unfortunately, I have discovered nothing that would help place "Apache" with respect to any of the other languages spoken in this northwest corner of the Conchería.

5. SPANISH CONTACT

The principal institutions of Spanish contact in Nueva Vizcaya were, as elsewhere on the Spanish frontier, the mission, the mine, the hacienda, and the military. The mission contact situation, handled by the religious arm of Spanish administration, will be discussed more fully in Chapter 6. In order to give a more complete picture of the context in which the missions operated, this chapter sketches some of the non-mission aspects of 17th- and 18th-century north Mexican society – in particular, those features of the Spanish civil administration that extended down to the local level of Indian life, and the use of Indians as laborers and as auxiliary soldiers.

THE NATURE AND SPREAD OF SPANISH SETTLEMENT

Many of the details of early Spanish-Indian relations in the central Chihuahua valleys are unknown. However, the natives were probably pressed into service by Spaniards soon after the first dates of contact, given the great need the Europeans always had for laborers for the mine and the ranch, and for auxiliary military personnel. Indeed, it appears that Conchos Indians in particular soon became regarded as a steady and important source of hacienda labor for the general region of Parral, Santa Bárbara, and the San Bartolomé Valley (today, Valle de Allende).

Miranda, in his 1571 account of the Florido River and the Santa Bárbara mine country (which originally fell within the territory of the Tepehuan Indians), noted the economic potential of the region. Along the Florido, about where there had been a *villa* named Vitoria that had been destroyed by Indians, there were at the time of his writing seven haciendas *de labor* where much corn was raised. Eight leagues to the west were located the mines of Santa Bárbara (founded about a decade earlier). Santa Bárbara, which was then at the edge of the zone of Spanish settlement on this frontier, could boast of 30 Spanish citizens (*vecinos*), and there were already haciendas, *ingenios,* and a number of mines established in the surrounding area (Miranda 1871).

Despite Miranda's somewhat optimistic account of the region, the Santa Bárbara district during the early years did not show a great amount of expansion and development. To be sure, a number of small mines were opened up, including Roncesvalles and Valsequillas, and the larger mine of Todos Santos (today, the settlement of Cordero) was established by 1691. However, the ores of these mines were of low qual-

ity and many of the operations did not endure. Nevertheless, during this same period, the Europeans began to work a number of agricultural holdings. In the very early years immediately after the turn of the 17th century, the town of Santa Bárbara had only some 12 *vecinos* still living there, and Todos Santos possessed only 18. A 1604 report on the Santa Bárbara valley (apparently referring to the entire district) listed four mines (without machinery), eight cattle ranches, and eleven grain farms; 34 men (*vecinos?*), half of them married and half single, and one merchant were also noted. These holdings, although possibly not extensive, no doubt were making their effects felt upon the local Indian population (Hammond and others 1932: 62-3; Mota y Escobar 1940: 198; West 1949: 10-11).

It was not until the third decade of the 17th century that the Santa Bárbara province began to develop as a really important mining region. The first big silver strike occurred at Parral in 1631, and shortly afterward another was made at the place that soon became known as San Diego de Minas Nuevas, a few miles to the west. With the opening of mining activity at these two locations, a veritable silver rush took place, bringing an influx of population from as far south as Nueva Galicia and Mexico City. Some 20 years later, in the 1650s, rich ores of gold and silver were discovered at San Francisco del Oro, about five miles northwest of Santa Bárbara (Tello 1891: 855; West 1949: 12-4). These large strikes and the many smaller mines that were founded, together with the expanding agricultural holdings needed to support the increased population, put greater and greater demands upon Indian labor. The Indians who dwelt along the Conchos River and its tributaries were no doubt hit earliest and hardest; however, by the mid-17th century, Spaniards also were shipping many Indians into the area from such faraway places as Sonora and Sinaloa, as well as from New Mexico (West 1949: 49; AHP 1653 Ae; Parral Baptismal Records).

The expansion of the different types of Spanish holdings continued in the area so that by the mid-18th century European settlements of some kind existed across the entire Chihuahua region that is of concern here. Agricultural settlements in the form of haciendas and ranchos dotted much of the area. Mines of different degrees of importance were established at places like Cusihuiriachi and Chihuahua City (beginning in 1707), each operation bringing with it a concomitant increase in the hispanic population of the local area. Particularly after 1685, Spanish military activities expanded, and presidios were established at crucial points around Spanish settlements to help mediate between them and the less controllable native population. Finally, the mission system, intimately related to the other Spanish frontier social units, developed greatly during the last half of the 17th century. While it lost considerable ground during the following century, some eight of the Conchería missions lasted until the end of the colonial period, operating as one of the forces of acculturation and assimilation in this region of the Spanish frontier.

POLITICAL ORGANIZATION

While nothing precise is known of the general level of native social organization in the Conchería, some of the formal aspects of the structure of the contact situation can be discerned from the documentary sources. Aside from such obvious Spanish social units as mines and haciendas, to which the Indians had to adjust, the Spaniards imposed other formal structures upon the Indians.

In the Indian pueblos, especially in the mission towns, regardless of the type of existing native social organization, the Spanish attempted to set up their own kind of administration and then selected natives to fill the positions. The number of these posts varied with the size of population of the town and its general situation, but they included civil administrative slots as well as roles within the mission church organization. The titles of these positions were *gobernador* (village governor), *teniente de gobernador* (lieutenant or assistant governor), *capitán, sargento, alférez, alcalde, alguacil, fiscal, topil, sacristán,* and *cantor.* The last two, particularly, were associated with the church organization, but many of the others may also have been church-related. Unfortunately, while it is known that the Spanish did attempt to establish some kind of local organization, it is seldom known how many and what kind of positions were set up in any specific town (although many documentary sources refer at least to governors and lieutenant governors of Indian pueblos; see also mission entries in Chapter 6). Moreover, even when these posts are known for a particular town, there is rarely any direct evidence regarding the rights and duties involved (AHP 1728Aa).

In addition to the Spanish-imposed town organization, the Europeans also appointed general governors of the Conchería. It is unknown when this practice was begun; however, apparently as early as the 1620s there was a general Concho governor whose jurisdiction extended over the entire Concho area. This situation lasted until 1653, when the Conchería as a political-administrative area was split into two separate jurisdictions.

The early governors, before the administrative split, are for the most part unknown. It is difficult to know whether the 1620s references actually refer to a general governor or not, and it is always possible that the post was not created until after the opening of the Parral district, when there likely arose a greater need for better management of local Indians for labor and other purposes. In any event, in 1621 there is

mention of one Don Francisco, Concho Indian governor (CPP 5: 82-9). Again, in 1643, a Don Francisco Gutiérrez (the same?) was said to be the Concho governor, and he was sent at this time to the hinterland to obtain laborers for the Spanish haciendas (it is always possible that this man was merely a town governor, but this seems somewhat doubtful) (CD 1643).

In 1648, Juan de Barraza wrote the Spanish governor that the Concho governor, Don Antonio Juan, had borne himself very well during the Tarahumara campaign – as a governor and as a great soldier; unfortunately, the rebel Indians killed Antonio Juan this same year (CPP 7: 406-12; UTD 1648). Possibly it was Juan Díaz who was next appointed governor of the Conchería, for in 1653 he was mentioned as the deceased holder of this office. However, Fray Lorenzo Canto in 1650 referred to one "Don Juan de la Cruz, Governor General of all of the nations of Concho and Tarahumar Indians," in whose company, along with Fray Hernando de Urbaneja, he had visited the Santa Isabel-San Andrés region. While it is impossible from this statement to determine whether the jurisdiction of Juan de la Cruz included the lower Conchos River settlements, it is quite possible that it was restricted to the Babonoyaba-San Pedro-Santa Isabel area, perhaps a *de facto* recognition of the east-west division that was soon to be formalized (CPP 8: 13-7).

On April 8, 1653, the Spanish governor, Diego Guajardo Fajardo, was at La Peña del Cuervo while on campaign in the Tarahumara country. Noting that the Concho Indian governor, Don Juan Díaz, was now dead, Guajardo stated that it was necessary "to name someone to govern [the Indians], and considering that it [the Conchos] is a very large nation, and among it there are other nations, and all are quiet, and in consideration that Don Pedro, Indian Captain of Babonoyaba, at another [previous] time has been governor of the said nation, he will govern one part of it with all care and vigilance, which is from the said town of Babonoyaba and San Pedro and all of the border of the Conchos Indians which extends toward the Tarahumara, as they [the Conchos] are many and voluminous; and for the other part, Don Hernando Obregón, Indian Captain of the Julimes and Mamites, has been named who will be obeyed by all those [people] of the hinterland (*tierra adentro*) . . . from San Francisco de Conchos along all of the [Conchos] River and hinterland of the Julimes and Mamites and the rest of their allies" (AHP 1652B).

Later, on June 19, a formal "title" was issued to Obregón, a Mamite, in Parral (AHP 1652B; AHP 1684Aa). This document stated that the eastern portion of the Concho country was assigned to Obregón, "governor and captain general . . . of the entire Concho nation, of all of this side (*vanda*) of the Río del Norte up to the land of the Tobosos, and including the Mamites, Julimes, Chisos, Oposmes, Conejos, Tapacolmes and all of the rest of the nations which are of the said area" (AHP 1652A). Unfortunately, the title of the Western Conchería governor, Don Pedro, has not been located. While the 1653 statements do not include the northwestern region of the present state of Chihuahua, probably because Casas Grandes was not yet founded (despite Arlegui's date of 1640 [1851: 95-6]), this area was later considered also to be a part of the Western Conchería (DHM 1667a).

Obregón's "title" stipulated his duties, and it shows something of the position of this office of Conchería governor within the legal or formal framework that tied the native peoples of this region to the Spanish empire. The Spanish governor stated to Obregón in this document that as governor "you will visit, help, and defend in good order and military discipline [the above nations] and when it is necessary you will be able to take out and you will take out with my order and with that of my Lieutenant Governor and Captain General the men of war which may be necessary for the defense of this Kingdom, and for this, and in order that the Indians comply with the encomiendas you will be able to take them out from whatever areas of your jurisdiction [necessary] in order for them to go on time to work at the *labores,* and for the other things for which they have obligation, and you will not consent that they be mistreated, nor that the Indian men and women be sold nor that they be taken outside of the Kingdom without first reporting it to me, and you will see that the said Indians live with order (*policia*), raise chickens, make their fields, and attend the doctrine, and that the dwellings (*hacales*) that they make are sturdy (*confundamto*); for all of this, you will wear the insignia of such Governor and Captain General" (AHP 1652A).

A number of documents attest to the fact that these Indian governors were indeed called upon many times to carry out the obligations that these titles imposed upon them. In the April *auto,* cited above, the Spanish governor specifically ordered Don Pedro and Don Hernando, as soon as they received their titles and had left Parral, " to go to get all of the people that they can for the harvest, Conchos as well as Julimes and Mamites, and the other nations which exist in the hinterland." Obregón also had another task at this time. He was to journey to the land of the Chisos to induce them to go to war against the Tobosos who were in revolt (AHP 1652B). On a number of occasions, Governor Obregón made trips into the backcountry to obtain laborers (e.g., AHP 1658Aa; 1658Ab; BL 1649-1700) or to pacify rebels, especially Chisos (AHP 1653Bd; 1654Aa; 1718Ab).

After the 1650s, the history of the governorships of the Conchería is quite obscure, and, indeed, it is unknown when the offices actually became defunct; after the beginning of the 18th century there are no more references to the Indian governors of the Concho country. The dual administrative division, however, lasts as long as named incumbents of the governorships occur in the sources.

The eastern governorship was held by Hernando de Obregón from 1653 until at least 1684 (AHP 1684Aa), which may have been for more than half of the life of the post. The Western Conchería saw several holders of the office of governor during the 17th century. It is unknown how long Don Pedro from Babonoyaba exercised his duties. However, at least during the late 1660s (possibly to about 1670), a Don Juan Constantino was the Western Conchería governor (CD [1671]). In 1666, a source refers to the "nacion conchos de la Raya de Tarahumares del govierno de Don Constantino," and the latter was apparently a resident of San Pedro de Conchos at this time. The same document makes note of the dual division of the Conchería, the next passage going on to state, "Y en otra Vanda en la mesma forma a todos los Indios que tenia consigo Don hernando obregon Goveror de la parte del rrio abaxo de conchos hacia El norte" (BL 1649-1700).

In 1692, a Don Felipe de Santiago seems to have been the western governor. He was from San Diego del Monte, which would have been a more adequate place for the residence of the western governor than either Babonoyaba or San Pedro, given the Concho population reduction in the south and its more northern concentration at this time. He had been appointed to his office by the Spanish governor, Isidro de Pardiñas, and his jurisdiction included the area of Casas Grandes. While still in office, Santiago was taken by the Spanish captain, Ramírez de Salazar of Casas Grandes, to Mexico City to testify to the viceroy regarding the conditions on the northern provincial frontier (AHP 1692A; BL 1695B). A few years later, in 1697, Don Juan Corma apparently held the office of governor of the Western Conchería (BL 1697-1703), but this is not entirely clear in the sources.

INDIANS AS A LABOR FORCE

The Indians first affected by Spanish labor needs for mine workers and farm hands in the Santa Bárbara district were probably Tepehuanes, although there is little direct information on the matter. One would guess that Conchos were put into service soon after 1575, the year of first reported contact, and it is known that La Junta peoples were affected by slave raiding by 1580 or so. However, the most intensive use of Conchería Indians may not have occurred until after the big silver strikes that were made during the first half of the 17th century at Parral, Minas Nuevas, and other places. In any event, Spanish demands for labor were always fairly high, and by 1621 Tarahumara were also reported working at Santa Bárbara (West 1949: 47-52, 72-4; CPP 5: 278-84).

The exact nature of the relationships between the Spanish land and enterprise holders and the laboring native population is, for present purposes, rather unclear. West, who has given the best single historical description of the labor system of the Parral district, has noted that the repartimiento system, as practiced in many other areas of New Spain, was not so well developed in the mines located here. While forced labor was used in the earlier years, it tended to be rather quickly replaced by labor of the "free" type, which then often turned into a system of debt peonage. The slave labor of Indians taken during warfare (as well as of a lesser number of Negroes) was also utilized to some extent in the Parral district mines (West 1949: 49-53).

The labor situation in agriculture seems to have been somewhat different from that in the mines, partly because ranchers and farmers had seasonal labor needs that differed from those of miners. Some Indian workers became permanent residents of haciendas and were employed in the regular, day-to-day farming operations. Other natives were brought in once or twice a year during the peak seasons for sowing and harvesting, and they were recruited from Indian settlements through the local governors and other officials. Indians living in both of these situations apparently were held in encomienda (West 1949: 72–4).

Repartimiento-type labor drafts, or what was called encomienda in Nueva Vizcaya, lasted in some form into the 18th century. Despite the obscurities surrounding the entire labor system, which needs to be investigated further, it seems evident that there was considerable conflict between local practice and official policy. On the one hand, from the 1570s, immediately following the founding of San Bartolomé, something called encomienda was utilized for labor recruitment on farms and ranches, as well as for mines. On the other, a number of royal orders were issued prohibiting the use of encomienda, or repartimiento-type forced Indian labor.

For example, in the early 17th century, a cedula of 1609, sent to Governor Francisco de Urdiñola, explicitly prohibited putting newly reduced Indians under encomienda (Porras Muñoz 1966: 512ff, esp. 514). A few years later, at the time of the Tepehuan revolt in 1617, a number of Conchos Indians were reported specifically to be working in the Santa Bárbara Valley, many or all apparently under encomienda obligations (Hackett 1926: 38, 98, 110; AGN 1617; 1618). However, three years earlier, in 1606, Governor Urdiñola had granted two rancherias of Conchos Indians in encomienda to one Diego de Porras, the son of Luis de Salvatierra, *vecino* of Valle de San Bartolomé (CD 1643).

In 1646 it was again ordered that the encomiendas of Nueva Vizcaya be abolished, but a cedula two years later requested that information on Vizcayan encomiendas be sent to the Crown because the latter did not have knowledge of the encomiendas of this province. A few years afterward, Governor Gorráez Beaumont denied the existence of encomiendas in Nueva Vizcaya. However, in 1667 his successor, Oca Sarmiento, noted that the Indians of the Conchería belonged to the encomiendas of the farmers of the region, and the following year he granted an encomienda of Sumas Indians of Carretas to Capitan Bernardo Gómez (Porras Muñoz 1966: 515; BL 1649–1700). Three years later, in 1670, a report of the *fiscal* underscored the fact that the encomiendas in the Nueva Vizcayan province were maintained by some kind of subterfuge (*maña*) (CD [1671]), while this same year the repartimiento in Nueva Vizcaya (here, the same as encomienda?) was abrogated by the Audiencia of Nueva Galicia, an action that was based on earlier royal decrees (West 1949: 73). However, as late as 1725 petition was made by a Spanish woman, Doña Rosa Ortiz de Campos, for a repartimiento of 30 Indians from the towns of San Pedro and Santa Cruz. This practice, it was stated at this time, was an ancient custom in the province (AHP 1725C). Finally, to add to the confusion concerning the labor situation in northern Mexico, in 1744 a report from the Nueva Vizcayan governor to the viceroy stated that repartimiento was still being used, and that abuses stemming from it caused considerable disruption to the Indian settlements. Although by law four percent of a community could be employed in this fashion, in effect so many people were taken from the towns that they were often left "depopulated" during the work season (Bancroft 1884: 586).

In only one instance have the specific provisions for an encomienda been found. In the Porras grant of 1616, mentioned above, the provisions were (1) that the natives were to be taught the Catholic faith (for which reason Porras was obliged to see that they settled at the mission of San Francisco de Conchos); (2) that the Indians could not serve against their will; and (3) that they had to be paid a certain designated wage for their labors (CD 1643). Nothing was mentioned about the Indians' having to pay tribute, and the 1670 *fiscal*'s report stated explicitly that the encomienda as practiced at San Bartolomé did not demand tribute of the Indians (CD [1671]). Elsewhere in New Spain it was common to collect tribute from natives in encomienda (Porras Muñoz 1966: 516; see also Simpson 1950).

Despite the differences in the ways the repartimiento or encomienda system was practiced in this northern area and in other sectors of the Spanish empire, the Nueva Vizcayan Spaniards felt that they held privileges regarding allotments of native labor for their own use. In the above-mentioned 1725 repartimiento, something of the system as it operated at this time can be seen. Governor López de Carbajal ordered that 15 men be taken as laborers each month, and that they be replaced by a like number the succeeding month – thus, it was a rotation system. This arrangement would endure, the governor said, only during the term of his office (AHP 1725C).

Innumerable references in the Parral and other archives note the use of Indians of the Conchería as laborers in the San Bartolomé Valley (e.g., AHP 1637B; 1644A; 1652B; 1654Ab; 1658Aa; 1684Aa; 1699b; CD 1643; 1648; DHM 18tha). A number of sources also mention the fact that these and other Indian laborers were often brought in from the surrounding hinterland (e.g., AHP 1685Aa). In November of 1621, a certain Don Mateo, said to be a *principal* of the Concho nation, arrived in Durango with word that the Concho cacique Alonzo had been sent to the interior of Concho country to obtain Indians for work on the haciendas of the San Bartolomé Valley – a labor, it was reported, that "they are used to do each year" (Hackett 1926: 130–2; CPP 5: 137–42). In the early 1640s, the Concho Indian governor and his lieutenant, a *principal* of the town of San Francisco de Conchos, selected Indians from the hinterland to work at San Bartolomé (CD 1643); on June 23, 1645, it was reported from the San Bartolomé Valley that a Don Miguel, a Tocón Indian from the hacienda of Diego del Castillo, and one Don Baltazar, an Hobome from the hacienda of Santa Ana, were involved in bringing about 100 Indians to the valley for the harvest (AHP 1645Ab). On January 1, 1667, the Spanish governor, Oca Sarmiento, made reference to the Conchos nation, from whose province laborers for the mines and haciendas were employed (BL 1649-1700; CPP 9: 463-83, 529-30).*

More specifically, although the decades after the founding of the Santa Bárbara district remain a blank, some data that hint at the extensiveness of the use of Indian laborers in the province begin to show up in the early part of the 17th century. In 1621 a number of persons were reported to have Conchos Indians working for them. These included Capitan Pedro Sánchez de Chávez, Pedro Sanches de Fuensalida, Alonso del Castillo (who had other Indians of unstated tribal affiliation, in addition to Conchos), Bartolomé Delgado (who, it was explicitly said, held an encomienda), and Juan de Morales (who had both Tepehuanes and Conchos on his hacienda). Some Conchos were also employed at the Estancia de Nava. A Jesuit, Father Nicolás de Estrada at San Pablo, had at least two Concho servants at this time (CPP 5: 75-107, 110, 112). Personal service by Indians for ecclesiastics was necessary in Nueva Vizcaya owing to the fact that the Indians did not pay tribute and this was the only way for priests to maintain their parishes (Porras Muñoz 1966: 516-7).

Nine years later, in 1630 (just before the Parral mines were opened), an actual count was given of the Indian laborers in the immediate area who were ministered to by the San Bartolomé convent. There was a total of 875 people living on 20 haciendas, which extended for a distance of some nine leagues downriver (Atotonilco was said to be seven leagues away), plus another 50 Indians living at San Bartolomé itself. Most of these people apparently were Conchos and were distributed among landholders as follows: Juan de Cobos had 55; Manuel Moreno, 40; Hernando de Bustillos, 50; Marcos Cortez, 20; Juan de Salazar, 15; Juan Sánchez de Ulloa, also 15; Andrés Cordero, 76; Bartolomé Delgado, 70; Luis de Salvatierra, 65; Diego del Castillo, 10; Alonso del Castillo, 76; Juan de Solís, 60; Diego Ximénez de Funes, 76; Diego Montesdoca, 75; Francisco de Porras, 50; Cristóbal Zapata, 20; Pedro Sánchez de Fuenzalida, 50; Pedro Sánchez de Chavez, 30; Juan Bexarano, 10; and Jacobo de Lafranca, 12 (Porras Muñoz 1966: 277-8).

Porras Muñoz cites another 200 persons at Atotonilco as *vecinos* (a term usually understood to refer to Spaniards) administered by the Franciscans; however, because this was

a mission, and because of the high figure, it is almost certain that these people too were Indians. He also states that there were Conchos in the environs of Santa Bárbara but gives no number (Porras Muñoz 1966: 277-8).

West reports that usually only 10 to 12 Indians were permanent residents on an hacienda, hence it would follow that the persons cited in this list probably lived elsewhere, although no information on residence is given. In any event, these Indians did not reside at the San Bartolomé mission, for its population was cited specifically as comprising 50 Indians (Porras Muñoz 1966: 277-8; West 1949: 73).

Despite the heavy use of Conchos and their neighbors during the 1600s, hundreds of Indians were brought or induced into the Parral district from the west coast and from New Mexico. These people, however, apparently tended to be used in the mines. Conchos and, increasingly as time went on, natives from the La Junta area were used intensively on the haciendas, and they continued to be regarded as an important source of agricultural labor throughout the 17th and into the 18th century. However, the general picture slowly changed as Conchería Indians died off or otherwise disappeared and as the system of free labor, with people hired for wages, developed and became more prevalent (AHP 1715Ac; 1722Bb; Parral Baptismal Records; West 1949: 47ff, 72-4).

A few reports afford some notion of the relationship of Indians to the Spanish work units, and hence also of the influence of haciendas and mines in the general processes of Indian assimilation. After the 1684 revolt and the Franciscan entry into the La Junta region, Fray Agustín de Colina penned a description of the conditions under which the missionaries there had been forced to labor. The efforts of the Fathers were hindered, he said, because many of the Indians would leave the La Junta towns to work on Spanish haciendas and, consequently, had little contact with the religious personnel. Even the local Indian officials (that is, those appointed by the Spaniards) had no interest in missionization, but only in getting the required number of Indians out for the hacienda labor force. Some of the Indians would remain away from La Junta for long periods because of the money they could earn (Hackett 1926: 249). Here it might be noted that La Junta Indians were still being employed as migrant laborers at least as late as 1755 (CPP 36: 568-71).

Frequently entire settlements or rancherias, including some from the La Junta area in the later years, would move to and take up living at an hacienda, no doubt under some kind of encomienda arrangement. Often these Indians would be located officially at some mission, although they would in actual fact be residing on an hacienda, where their children would be born and reared (e.g., AHP 1699b; 1715Ac). This situation continued well into the 18th century, probably as long as La Junta remained settled by Indians (AHP 1715Ac; 1722Ac). No doubt the people of many of these settlements would never return to their original homes.

In 1715, when a new push for the missionization of the

---

*The *fiscal*'s report of 1670 noted that there were three kinds of Indians in Nueva Vizcaya: (1) wild ones who were always on the warpath; (2) pacific town-dwellers who paid their tribute to the mission and who attended the religious doctrine, and who also worked voluntarily on the haciendas; and (3) the natives who were only at half-peace, hiding away in the mountains and hills, and on whom the Spaniards could not exert much pressure for settlement because they would always flee back to their home territories. It was the duty of the Concho Indian governors to get the people at half-peace to work, and the *fiscal* opined that the Indians who served at San Bartolomé were of this latter type (CD [1671]).

La Junta area was begun, the hacienda owners feared the effect that this might have upon the Indian labor situation in the Parral district. The Spanish governor had issued an order for the captains of Indian towns to pick up the Indian laborers on the various haciendas and take them back to their pueblos so that they would be available at their homes to receive the teachings of the missionaries. At this same time, when Trasviña Retis made his entrada to La Junta, he reported that of the 1,405 Indians included in his census of the area, only 80 were away at the San Bartolomé Valley working on haciendas there (Kelley 1952; AHP 1715Ac; DHM 1715b).

In reaction to the Spanish governor's order, the San Bartolomé landowners made a petition requesting that it be rescinded. This petition and later testimonies given in person by these same hacienda owners provide some further glimpses into the relationship of the Indians of the Conchería and the La Junta region to the Spanish production units. Of course, the hacendados felt that the action taken so far would be injurious to the operation of the haciendas and other holdings. The attempt to substitute Tarahumaras for the usual Indian labor force, which the Spanish governor had commanded, would be unsuccessful for several reasons. One of these was that Tarahumara were less efficient than the regular Indian employees, who were quite skilled, many of them having been either born or virtually brought up on the haciendas, as noted above. From the testimonies it emerged that while many of these hacienda Indians were not yet Christians or instructed in the faith, many did speak the Castilian tongue and were otherwise rather well acculturated (AHP 1715Ac).

According to the testimony of Captain Joseph Migueleña, a partial count of the Indians employed at this time in San Bartolomé was 174, excluding the wives and children of the laborers (this figure conflicts with the 80 reported by the expedition to La Junta in this same year). Migueleña's count refers only to La Juntans, but it may give some idea of the labor force on the haciendas in the district: 10 Cacolotes worked on the Bartolomé de Porras hacienda; 9 Mesquites were on Ana Moreno's place; 10 Posalmes worked for Andrés Delgado; 9 Oposmes were on the hacienda of Simón Cordero; 3 Cíbolos were in the employ of Joseph del Yerro; 5 Polacmes were on Diego Moreno's place; 4 Julimes worked for Manuel de Ascue y Armendáriz; and 8 Tapacolmes were on the hacienda of Francisco de Navarrete. The remaining haciendas of the San Bartolomé area, he said, either had no Conchos River or northern Indians or had only a very few (AHP 1715Ac).

A Franciscan, Pedro de Ortega, also reported during the 1715 testimonies. The convent at San Bartolomé had ministered to Indians for some 140 years, but the church records had noted tribal affiliation only since 1657; therefore, Ortega stated, he could not cite specific Indian groups working in the area before that year. In 1657, however, only Conchos and Tapacolmes were listed in the records; subsequently, these two nations as well as Oposmes, Cacolotes, Pusalmes,

Batlaboylas, and other groups had been ministered to by the convent, presumably while they were working at San Bartolomé and in the surrounding district (AHP 1715Ac).

Other records point up the fact that in the general Parral-Santa Bárbara district, Indians from a number of different ethnic groups were brought together. For example, Cacuitataomes, Batayoliclas, Guesapames, and Conchos were reported at Valcequilla, while Mamites, Julimes, and Batayoliclas were employed at the hacienda of Antonio de Molino (AHP 1684Aa); on other occasions Tobosos, Gavilanes (a specific Toboso band), Tarahumaras, Sonoras, Sinaloas, and occasionally a Suma and even a Nahua or Otomi (from central Mexico) were said to be living in the area (AHP 1640C; 1653Ad; 1654Ac; 1656A; 1669B; 1685Da; 1686Ba; 1688Cb; 1723A).

INDIANS IN MILITARY SERVICE

Another important contact situation involved the Indians who were employed as auxiliary troops for the Spanish military forces. While the amount of warfare that took place on the Spanish frontier varied somewhat, after 1644 hostilities and fighting were fairly constant. There were the more or less major outbreaks in 1644-45, from 1648 through 1652, in 1666, 1684, 1690, and 1697; before, during and after these dates there were the continuing raids and retaliations involving Cabezas-Salineros, Tobosos on the east, and somewhat later, Cholomes, Sumas, Janos and Jocomes, and eventually Apaches on the north. In practically all, if not all, of these military operations, the Spaniards employed Indians as fighting troops and also as scouts and couriers.

While it would not be feasible here to list all the occasions and all the Indian groups who were employed as auxiliary soldiers, some examples of this constant practice will demonstrate its importance in the acculturation process. Employment as soldiers gave Indians of widely scattered ethnic groups experience with one another, with vast new geographical areas, and with new cultural items and techniques, all under the direction of the Spanish command that organized and maintained them.

During the colonial period in northern Mexico, there was a change in the use of Indian auxiliaries that should be noted. It was to some extent related to two other changes that took place in the contact situation during the same period. These were, first, the alteration in the nature of the Spanish military itself, with the elaboration of the frontier presidio system that began around the end of the 17th century and continued with the military reforms of the Bourbons in the 18th; and second, the noticeable decrease in the number of Indian pueblos that could readily supply military manpower.

The practice into the 18th century was for the Spanish authorities to send an order to Indian pueblos, as well as to Spanish holdings where Indians were living, for a certain number of troops to be remitted from these places (often belonging to a mission) to some point that the Spanish command had designated. As the number of Indian towns and settlements diminished, this type of recruitment became more and more impossible to carry out, and by the latter half of the 1700s it was necessary to station regular Indian auxiliary garrisons outside or near some of the permanent presidios. For example, between the years of 1779 and 1794, a garrison of 22 to 24 Tarahumara was housed at Atotonilco to assist the presidio at Guajuquilla. From 1779 to 1798, an Indian garrison of some 23 or 24 Yaquis from the west coast was maintained at Parral. The report of 1779 states that this Yaqui garrison had in previous years consisted of 31 men, but that in this year it was reduced to 24. Indian auxiliary garrisons also existed at or were associated with such places as San Carlos (today, Aldama), Chuvíscar, Bachíniva, San Buenaventura, and a number of other locations (AHP 1779Aa; 1779Ab; 1784A; 1788Aa; 1788Ab; 1788Ac; 1788B; 1794a; 1794b; 1794c; 1795; 1797a; 1798A).

Something of the nature of the use of Indians by Spaniards may be gleaned from the following examples. During the Tepehuan revolt and in the hostilities that followed in the early 1620s, Concho Indians were employed as auxiliaries (CPP 5: 82-9; UTL 1619). In 1644 and 1645, a number of Tepehuanes and Tarahumaras, as well as 73 Conchos, were employed by the Spaniards against the Concho confederation (CD 1650a), and Conchos were used against Tarahumaras in the uprisings of 1648 and after (CPP 7: 406-12). In 1653, a year of much active campaigning, on one occasion 324 Indian auxiliaries were employed against rebel Tarahumaras. The roster included 147 Tepehuanes, 85 Sinaloas, 34 Sonoras, 16 Conchos, 22 Julimes and Mamites, 17 Laguneros, and 3 Indians from Copala (AHP 1653Aa). There were also times when the Spaniards did not accompany the Indians. In this same year, on another occasion, 85 Julimes and Mamites, including a few Chisos, were sent out to fight Tobosos (AHP 1653Ab).

For the various hostilities of the 1690s, a number of different lists of Indian troops are available. In 1691, one expedition included 181 auxiliaries: 28 Tobosos and Conchos from the town of San Francisco de Conchos, 23 Conchos from the pueblo of San Pedro, 61 Conchos from Namiquipa, 21 Tepehuanes, 16 Cabezas, 18 Babozarigames, and 14 Vovoles (Boboles), the last three groups from the Coahuila area (BL 1695a). On another occasion during this year Chisos, Conchos, Tapacolmes, Norteños, Cíbolas, and Tepehuanes were listed (BL 1751a).

When Retana went on campaign to the Río del Norte in 1693, he gave a detailed list of the Indians among his troops (while noting that those who worked on haciendas had no knowledge of the enemies' territory). In the list were Tobosos from the town of San Francisco; Indians from San Lucas and San Pedro, including Chisos, Cacuitataomes, and Conchos; and other Chisos who had recently been reduced to peace, including 16 Guasapayoliglas, 14 Chichitames, 27 Osapayoliglas, and 12 Sisimbles. There were also 96 men from the nations of the north: 10 Tapacolmes, 8 Opoxmes, 11 Paxalmes, 6 Pulicas, 20 Polacmes, 13 Mesquites and Cacalotes, and 28 Cíbolos and Cholomes (BL 1695a).

In 1697, Conchos from Namiquipa, Cruces, San Lucas

and San Pedro, Tobosos from San Francisco de Conchos, Cíbolos and Norteños (this actually reads "Del Norte"), and Tarahumaras from Babonoyaba, Santa Isabel, Santa Cruz, Papigochi, Santo Tomás, and Mátachic fought together during one campaign (BL 1697-1703). On another occasion this same year, the native forces were composed of 130 Tarahumaras from a number of different towns, 43 Conchos from Namiquipa and Las Cruces, another 28 Conchos from Nombre de Dios, 22 Cholomes and Cíbolos, 12 Babozarigames from El Pasaje, 17 men listed simply as Indians (12 from the town of San Lucas and 5 from San Pedro), and another 12 Tobosos (probably from San Francisco) (AHP 1697Aa).

During this same decade of the 1690s, Conchos in particular were often employed against the warring nations of Sumas, Janos, and Jocomes in the Casas Grandes district (BL 1693a; AGN 1692). In 1691 and 1692, both Conchos and Opatas served in operations out of the Janos presidio against Sumas, Janos, and Jocomes (CPP 16: 538-43, 586-92; 17: 200-5). In 1695, in a large campaign made into what is now the southeast corner of Arizona and west into the Pimería Alta, 17 Conchos from the town of San Diego del Monte y La Sierra (under Juan Corma), 32 Conchos from the towns of Namiquipa and Las Cruces, and 21 Opatas from the towns of Baseraca, Huachinera, and Babispe took part with the forces from Janos and other presidios (AHP 1695).

In 1704, Tobosos and Tarahumaras from San Francisco de Conchos, Indians from San Antonio, San Pedro, and San Pablo, Del Norte Indians, and a number of Tarahumaras (including some from the towns of Babonoyaba, San Andrés, and Santa Isabel) were employed as auxiliaries (DHM 1704). In 1715, against the Cocoyomes, Acoclames, and Sisimbles of the Bolsón de Mapimí area, the force included some 95 Tobosos, Cacuitataomes, and Tarahumaras from San Francisco de Conchos, 20 Indians (Tarahumaras?) from Atotonilco, and some Del Norte Indians. Many of these same groups, as well as Conchos from Nombre de Dios and San Pedro, were involved in another expedition at this time (AHP 1715Aa). In a large campaign against warring Indians from the Bolsón region, listed on the auxiliary roster were Tarahumaras from the presidio of San Francisco de Conchos and from some 28 other towns, as well as 12 Indians from Atotonilco, 17 from San Pedro, 11 from Santa Cruz, 9 from Julimes, 12 from Nombre de Dios, 20 from Santa Ana de Chinarras, 28 from San Francisco de Conchos, and 14 from the town of Cinco Señores to the south on the Nazas River (AHP 1721A).

Five years later, in 1726, when Joseph de Aguirre made his entrada to La Junta, he took 148 Indian auxiliaries with him. These included 51 Chinarras from Santa Ana, plus Conchos, Tobosos, Julimes, and Tarahumaras, some of whom were from the towns of Nombre de Dios, San Gerónimo, and Chubisca (Chuvíscar) (UTD 1710-1738a). And finally, in 1740, when Yaquis and Mayos rose up in Sonora, 50 Indians from San Francisco de Conchos and 100 from the La Junta towns marched to the west coast area to do battle with the rebels (BL 1746b; DHM 1748).

6. MISSIONS AND ASSOCIATED SETTLEMENTS

INTRODUCTION

The missionization of the Conchería, except in the one case of the Jesuit mission of Santa Ana de Chinarras (near present-day Aldama), was carried out by men of the order of Saint Francis, who for the most part were of the Province of Zacatecas. Unfortunately, the Franciscans' records for this province have not been located, and consequently much of the history of missionization of the natives that fell under their jurisdiction must be pieced together from the various sporadic references that occur in other sources. The most important single source that does survive is Arlegui's general work (1851), which was written in the 1730s, and a good portion of which was based on the first-hand records of the Franciscans, now lost. In the summary that follows, reference to the 18th-century writer Mota Padilla is omitted for the most part, since he usually simply quotes Arlegui (see Mota Padilla 1870).

Despite the lack of many of the original Franciscan records, the overall development of the mission system of the area under consideration here is fairly clear. The most active period fell within the 17th century. The missionaries, apparently following to some extent the settlement of the Spanish civilian population, extended their chain of missions northward through the lower river valleys of central northern Nueva Vizcaya, while the Jesuits, who followed them slightly later, occupied the higher elevations in the Sierra Madre (see López-Velarde [1964: Chapter 4] for a general historical summary of the Zacatecas Province).

This penetration was, in effect, through the heart of Concho country, although by no means were the Franciscans dedicated solely to the Conchos Indians. In some places, such as San Andrés and Santa Isabel, there seem to have been few or no Conchos, most of the people being Tarahumaras. Having established themselves fairly well in Concho country, especially along the western border with the Tarahumara, and having begun missions among the Opata in Sonora, Franciscans after the 1650s started to plant churches in the northwest among Sumas and Janos at Santa Ana, Casas Grandes, Carretas, and La Soledad.

Some years passed before they moved northeastward down the Conchos River, although they had probably visited as far as San Antonio de Julimes at least by the 1650s. In 1684 they commenced in earnest to Christianize the towns of La Junta, at the confluence of the Conchos River and the Rio Grande. By the early years of the 18th century, how-

ever, these hard-working padres experienced more and more difficulty (except possibly in the La Junta area after 1715), and the missions of the region dwindled in numbers to some extent during the remainder of the century.

Certainly one of the major problems for missionaries working in this area was that many of the places where the Franciscans had their establishments were also within or adjacent to the heart of Spanish civilian settlement. In these locations, the amalgamation of native groups and their assimilation into the Spanish colonial system went on at a faster rate than in other regions of Nueva Vizcaya, owing to the intense contact that the different tribal peoples had with each other at the mine and the hacienda. It would seem that the Franciscans, somewhat in contrast to the Jesuits working in the higher mountainous country of the Tarahumara, could not carry out their labors without considerable hindrance and interference from other segments of Spanish society. While the history of such civil-religious conflict on the local level for this specific region is for the most part unknown, occasional statements from priests regarding the proximity of non-Indian settlements show that this was indeed something of a problem (see below, *Conditions at the Missions*). This situation, coupled with the fact that civilian-military people often settled outside or alien Indian groups at Franciscan missions (for example, Chisos and Tobosos at San Francisco de Conchos), could only have resulted in disturbance of the stable conditions necessary for the missionaries to be able to instruct their neophytes.

In the history of the activities of the Zacatecas Province in the Conchería, there seem to have been two major periods of reorganization and expansion of the mission system. The first of these occurred around 1650 (which may account for the founding date of 1649 for San Pedro de Conchos), and the second about 1694. At the time of this second reorganization (when even long-established places were called "Las Nuevas Conversiones"), several former satellite parishes (visitas) were elevated to the status of head mission (cabecera). Other more minor shifts and alterations in the system took place at other times.

CHRONOLOGICAL OVERVIEW

The Spanish towns of Santa Bárbara and Valle de San Bartolomé were established around the late 1560s, the official date for the founding of Santa Bárbara being given as 1567 and that for San Bartolomé as 1570 (Jiménez Moreno

1958: 37, 62). From the earliest years, the Franciscans managed a convent at San Bartolomé; it was founded around 1570 (see site entry below for alternative dates), and apparently operated as some kind of administrative headquarters (*casa de administración*) (Arlegui 1851: 34, 59; Jiménez Moreno 1958: 139-40).

This Santa Bárbara-San Bartolomé district was well within Tepehuan country, and no doubt the first Indians touched by the activities of the Franciscans were mainly Tepehuanes. By 1575, however, Conchos, whose border was located some 10 leagues to the north of Santa Bárbara, had been contacted (Miranda 1871), and presumably it was some time after this that the Spaniards began to bring Conchos Indians into the European-Catholic fold. Probably most of this contact occurred in work situations at mines and haciendas, but the actual date that Conchos were first employed as laborers in this district is unknown. Writing in the 1730s, Arlegui commented that the administration of the Indians in Valle de San Bartolomé had been extremely arduous because the natives had been distributed on haciendas and there had been no way to reduce them to a town. A similar complaint had been registered 15 years earlier (Arlegui 1851: 59; AHP 1715Ac).

The first mission specifically dedicated to the Conchos Indians was that of San Francisco de Conchos, founded in 1604 by Fray Alonso de la Oliva on the Conchos River, north of the Santa Bárbara district (Arlegui 1851: 76; Jiménez Moreno 1958: 146-7; Torquemada 1944: 345; West 1949: 11). Oliva's actual work among these people had been started sometime in the 1590s. During the time of the Tepehuan revolt, about 1619, it was stated that Father Oliva had been with the Conchos for 24 years (UTL 1619), and Jiménez Moreno states that this Father had been working in the area for 10 years before the founding of the mission (Jiménez Moreno 1958: 146-7). This would place Oliva's entry into the Conchos River area about 1594 or 1595. In 1609, Torquemada reported that Oliva had some 4,000 Conchos at his mission of San Francisco in these early years (Torquemada 1944: 345). San Francisco lasted 156 years, and although much or most of its history is quite obscure, in the 17th century in particular it seems to have had a major role in the Zacatecas-based mission system. It was removed from this system in 1769, the year in which it was secularized (AGN 1816).

The next mission of the Franciscans in this area, San Buenaventura de Atotonilco, was founded a few years later, apparently principally for Toboso Indians. However, it seems likely that some Tepehuanes were also involved since the mission was located on or close to the border between Tepehuan and Toboso country; in later years it was the nomadic Toboso groups that were so often brought here to settle. While the exact date of the establishment of this mission is not clear, some kind of mission unit was at this location as early as 1611. Arlegui reported that the actual mission was not set up until 1619; previous to this the place had had the status

of *guardianía,* which was apparently what had been established at the earlier date (Arlegui 1851: 82-3; West 1949: 11).

San Pedro de Conchos, on the San Pedro River, and Santiago de Babonoyaba, farther west in the mountains near the Jesuit mission of Satevó, seem to have been the third and fourth major (cabecera) missions of the Franciscan system. Arlegui cites the founding date for San Pedro as 1649 and that for Babonoyaba as 1665 (Arlegui 1851: 97-8). However, there are statements indicating that both of these places had resident priests and were *misiones* before these years – Babonoyaba in 1640 and 1648, and San Pedro in 1644 and 1645 (AGN 1640; CD 1650a; CPP 7: 406-12; DHM 1645; UTD 1648). If Arlegui's statements have some basis in fact and are not simply errors, they may refer to the formal establishment of these missions as administrative centers (cabeceras); in this case, prior to Arlegui's dates they were most likely satellite parishes of some other mission, most probably of San Francisco de Conchos.

Little is known of the Babonoyaba mission except that it was in existence for many years. It did have, at one time or another, at least one visita named Guadalupe, as well as another place it administered called La Joya. Babonoyaba was still on the mission rolls at the close of the colonial period (AGN 1816), its long life probably owing in part to the fact that it was located at some distance from the main areas of Spanish settlement. It was principally a Tarahumara mission for most of its life, at least for the last 150 years (see *Babonoyaba* entry below).

San Pedro de Conchos was a mission of major importance during the mid-1600s. Arlegui describes it as having consisted of some 11 towns; however, the names of only six of these visitas are known. These were, moving downriver: San Pedro, San Lucas, Santa Cruz, San Pablo, Nuestra Señora de Guadalupe, and San Antonio de Julimes. Sometime after 1694, with the reorganization that took place at this time, San Antonio de Julimes became the administrative head of the three last-named places. Later, San Lucas was dropped as a mission, and Santa Cruz (by this time called Santa Cruz de Tapacolmes) became the cabecera of San Pedro, itself now relegated to a minor position (Arlegui 1851: 97-8; Hackett 1926: 358-60; BL 1695a).

According to Arlegui, in the decade of the 1660s several new missions were opened up in the Franciscan expansion to the northwest, along the eastern flank of the Sierra Madre. These missions were Santa María de la Navidad de Bachíniva in 1660, San Pedro de Namiquipa in 1663, and Santa Isabel in 1668. Probably the missions at Casas Grandes, Carretas, and San Buenaventura were also established about this time (Arlegui 1851: 94-7).

However, according to other sources, the impetus for new missions had commenced a decade earlier, probably partly as an effort to keep this portion of the Tarahumara border quieted down, given the general unrest and rebellions among the Tarahumara beginning in 1648. Arlegui's date for the founding of Santa Isabel in particular appears to be late, and probably refers to the formalization of cabecera status for this mission. In 1649 the Spanish governor, Diego Guajardo Fajardo, made note of the lack of missionaries in the province, particularly for the Conchos and for the other nations to the north. He and the Franciscans then began a concerted effort toward the conversion of the Conchos. In 1650 Guajardo reported that already a successful beginning of missionization had been made, although in fact some missionary work in the general area of Santa Isabel had apparently been started before this time. A year later, in April of 1651, this same governor noted that the Franciscans had established the town of Santa Isabel in the Concho province (Hackett 1926: 166–70; AGN 1651; BL 1649–1700; CPP 8: 13).

More specifically, in the latter part of 1649, Guajardo made an expedition into this region, visiting San Felipe, Satebó, Babonoyaba, San Lorenzo, La Concepción, San Andrés, San Diego, Santa Isabel, "and many other rancherias of the said province" (CPP 7: 595–601; 8: 2–9). Almost immediately afterward, in May of 1650, the Franciscan Fray Lorenzo Canto carried out his entrada into the hinterland, accompanied by Fray Hernando de Urbaneja from Babonoyaba, who, the former recounted, had been working the area for so many years. These men visited settlements in both Concho and Tarahumara country. The group went to San Gregorio Yaguna by way of Santa Isabel, San Andrés, and San Bernavé (these last two later became visitas of the Santa Isabel mission). At San Gregorio the Spanish expedition was visited by the natives from a place called San Diego (del Monte?). In San Bernavé, Fray Canto, with the local caciques and those from San Andrés, marked out a site for the church and convent of the new mission. It was here, Canto later reported, that the Indians from the settlements of San Gregorio Yaguna, San Diego, San Antonio, San Mathías y Santo Thomás, and Santa Cruz would attend. Some of these places were as far as 20 to 24 leagues away from San Bernavé (Hackett 1926: 166–70; CPP 8: 13–7).

Three years later, around the month of September 1653, another Franciscan, Fray Francisco de Cervantes, made an expedition down the Conchos River. His party traveled to a place called San Antonio (de Julimes?), where he conferred with the Cupilames, Chulimes (Julimes), and Mamites Indians regarding possible sites for Indian settlements. He spent two weeks at San Antonio, where he had a modest church of branches (*ramos*) built; he reported that neighboring rancherias had agreed to go to this spot later to assist in making a larger church. He also baptized some 48 children and sent word as far away as to the Rio Grande (probably to La Junta) for the people there to come to San Antonio (AHP 1653Bd).

Unfortunately, there seems to be no other information regarding the founding of the new missions in the 1650s and 1660s. The three most important of the missions cited above, in terms of their duration over time, were Santa Isabel, Bachíniva, and Namiquipa. Santa Isabel had as many as nine visitas at one period; after 1694 two of these satellites, San Andrés and Nombre de Dios, were raised to the status of administrative centers. San Andrés later was reported by Arlegui to administer seven towns (unspecified by name and place). Nombre de Dios eventually possessed three visitas, Chuvíscar (formerly belonging to the Santa Isabel mission), San Gerónimo (apparently a new establishment), and Los Alamillos (Arlegui 1851: 90–1, 97, 100–1; Hackett 1926: 360–2; UTD 1742–1754).

Less is known of the administrative arrangements of Bachíniva and Namiquipa. Arlegui claimed that Bachíniva had at one time possessed five visitas, although he did not give their names. By 1728, however, only one visita, San Luis Obispo, was listed in the yearly census. Namiquipa was also said to have five visitas; the name of only one, Santa Clara, is known, but Las Cruces was almost certainly a second. At least one other of the towns in the area in the 17th century, San Diego del Monte (still in existence), while not specifically cited as a visita, was probably attached to one or another of the missions of the area – possibly Santa Isabel, since it was an Indian settlement of some standing. Santa Isabel and Bachíniva survived until the end of the colonial period; Namiquipa, however, was secularized in 1753, and the site was abandoned sometime after this, to be resettled at a later time (Arlegui 1851: 96–7; AHP 1728Aa; AGN 1816).

The histories of some of the other missions of this area, such as Casas Grandes, Carretas, and El Torreón, are for the most part even more obscure. The geographical region of these establishments was sometimes referred to as the Casas Grandes district, since Casas Grandes was the predominant settlement of the area – or was assumed to be such, because of rumors of mines there as well as because of the ruins nearby that were said to date from the era of Montezuma, according to Governor Gorráez (DHM 1666; 1667a).

The Casas Grandes mission itself was established in 1640, according to Arlegui, although other information indicates that it was founded during the 1660s. Apparently the first missionary at Casas Grandes was Fray Andrés Páez, who worked during the second or third year of the term of office of Governor Gorráez Beaumont (1662–65). Páez spent two years here and was aided by Captain Andrés López de Gracia in the reduction of the Indians to mission life. After Páez left, he was replaced by two fathers, Pedro de Aparicio and Nicolás Hidalgo. Aparicio died at Casas Grandes, but not until he had brought a great number of natives under mission control, so it was reported. However, by August 16, 1667, López de Gracia noted that since the death of Father Aparicio, some of the Indians had abandoned the Casas Grandes mission, and work on the convent had stopped. Nevertheless, with some ups and downs, this mission continued well into the 18th century, until it was secularized in 1758. During its history it possessed as many as three satellite parishes, one of which was Janos; the other two visitas remain unknown (Bancroft 1884: 337; AGN 1816; DHM 1666; 1667a; 1667b; 1667c; 1667d; 1668).

Arlegui and other sources, including the Nueva Vizcayan governor Gorráez Beaumont, cite two other little-known missions, Santa María de las Carretas and Santa Ana or San Buenaventura del Torreón. These were probably established during the 1660s, about the time of the founding of Casas Grandes, and El Torreón was apparently the southernmost of the missions that were dedicated mainly to the Suma Indians. Arlegui, who gives no founding dates for these places, states that they were destroyed by Indians (he says "Apaches") between 1685 and 1700. The names of both of these missions occur in documentary sources that deal with the Indian troubles of the 1680s, and at least one of the Sumas executed in 1685 was from San Buenaventura. Soon after this, however, both missions drop from historical sight (see entries below) (Arlegui 1851: 43, 95-6; AHP 1684Da; DHM 1667a).

Despite the paucity of data on this area, it appears that for a period during the last half of the 17th century this northwestern region saw quite vigorous missionary activity. A Parral document, undated but falling either at the end of 1684 or the beginning of 1685, lists the missions of the region: Las Carretas, Janos, Casas Grandes, Santa Ana del Torreón, San Pedro de Anamiquipa, San Miguel, and Santa María Nativitas [Bachíniva]. Most of these were cabeceras; Janos, however, was a visita of Casas Grandes. San Miguel is an unknown place and possibly was also a satellite. Since the list as given clearly runs from north to south, apparently San Miguel lay somewhere between Namiquipa and Bachíniva (AHP 1684Da).

In the meantime, in the northeast portion of the Conchería along the lower Conchos River, several men of the order of Saint Francis began missions among the peoples of La Junta. The first indication of missionary activity here comes from a statement in 1744 by Fray Miguel de Menchero, who recounted that two Franciscans began religious establishments at La Junta in 1670. According to Menchero, these men remained two years before the Indians expelled them. A decade later, from the fall of 1683 until late in the following spring, missionization of La Junta was again undertaken, but was ended by the 1684 rebellion; it was resumed again around 1687, lasting this time for about a year and seven months (letter from Fray Agustín de Colina, November 18, 1688 [BL 1695a]). Somewhat less than 30 years later, in 1715, missionization was started again in the La Junta district and continued, with some vicissitudes, into the middle of the 18th century (Hackett 1926: 249; 1937: 407-8; BL 1695a).

After 1694 and the reorganization of the Franciscan mission system, several new missions were established, as noted above. However, as the 18th century progressed, missionary activity in the Nueva Vizcayan area slowed while the Franciscans put their labors into more fruitful fields. Few, if any, new religious establishments were begun, and in the second half of the century several of the existing missions were removed from the system by secularization. To be certain, Spanish power in the region in general was weakening during this period, but other factors were also at work, specifically affecting the mission system and its population. One of these was the continuing development of an hispanicized Indian and mestizo population, concomitant with a loss of Indian ethnic identity. Although the mission Indian population between 1765 and the end of the colonial period did not decrease greatly in some places in the central river valley area, this was apparently because of considerable Indian immigration, much of which was from La Junta (see Chapter 7).

In any event, the history of Nueva Vizcaya is one in which the Franciscans played a key role, promoting the acculturation of native peoples and their assimilation into Spanish colonial society. A rough count of the missions and their satellite parishes that existed in the latter part of the 17th century reveals that during this period the men of Saint Francis were actively engaged at some 50 locations in bringing the European way of life to the Indians.

In the first decades of the 1700s, the Franciscan system consisted of some 12 or 13 cabeceras, or administrative centers. These were the Convent of San Bartolomé, San Buenaventura de Atotonilco, San Francisco de Conchos, San Pedro de Conchos (which was soon to become a satellite of its own visita, Santa Cruz), San Antonio de Julimes, Santiago de Babonoyaba, Santa Isabel, San Andrés, Nombre de Dios (these last two having previously been satellites of Santa Isabel), Santa María de Bachíniva, San Pedro de Namiquipa, and Casas Grandes. The Jesuit mission of Santa Ana de Chinarras and the Franciscan San Gerónimo were founded in these years, the former becoming a satellite of San Gerónimo upon the expulsion of the Jesuits in 1767.

The La Junta establishments were abandoned sometime in the late 1760s or after. According to Berroterán, writing in 1748, from around the year 1720, when it was rumored that there were disturbances at La Junta, the missionaries began visiting their holdings there only during a portion of each year. This practice was followed, he said, because of a continuing fear of trouble among the Indians. Nevertheless, Berroterán pointed out that the natives had always received the missionaries *sin novedad*. In any event, when not at La Junta the missionaries would spend the remainder of their time in Chihuahua City (DHM 1748).

Dropped from the roster of Nueva Vizcayan Franciscan missions were Namiquipa and the San Bartolomé convent in 1755, Casas Grandes in 1758, San Francisco (the longstanding and original Concho mission) in 1769, and San Gerónimo in 1791. By the end of the colonial period, only eight missions were left: San Andrés, Santa Isabel, Babonoyaba, and Bachíniva, all Tarahumara establishments; and Julimes, Atotonilco, Nombre de Dios, and Santa Cruz. The latter four consisted of a varied assortment of peoples, including some Tarahumaras, for almost all of the original Concho population had now become extinct. Indeed, in the censuses of 1816-1818 only Tarahumaras are listed for Atotonilco. The fate of many of the previously listed visitas or satellite towns and parishes of these missions seems to have been lost to history (AGN 1816).

CONDITIONS AT THE MISSIONS

The quality and effectiveness of the missions is often difficult to determine, unfortunately, but fragments of information occasionally come to light that permit some judgment of the conditions under which the missionaries were obliged to work.

In 1715, the Bishop of Durango made an inspection tour (*visita*) of the northern missions of the province of Nueva Vizcaya, visiting Jesuit as well as Franciscan holdings. In his concluding summary of the journey, he drew an interesting and enlightening comparison between the mission systems of the two orders as he saw them at this time (UTD 1715a).

He reported that he was extremely pleased with what he had observed at the Jesuit missions. There had been little or nothing to remedy at these places of the Black Robes, "owing to the especial zeal with which the missionaries dedicate themselves in carrying out their obligation and ministry." However, at the missions entrusted to the Franciscans, he had observed quite the opposite situation. For the most part, the churches were in bad condition, without adornments or ornaments; in many there had not been even a repository for the Holy Sacrament, and the Indians were badly instructed and educated (UTD 1715a).

The bishop pointed out what he felt were some of the reasons for these defects in the Franciscan system. The missionaries never stayed at their missions for more than two or three years, and they were constantly transferred to new assignments by their superiors. Consequently, the good Fathers could only consider themselves as transients and could not look upon either their churches or their flocks with great affection; likewise, the neophytes did not have an opportunity to develop warm feelings toward their ministers. Because of this situation the Indians learned no skill or trade, nor how to read or write, and they did not know (church) music, for which they had a great aptitude. The natives, he said, also lived in great poverty and were poorly dressed (UTD 1715a). The bishop added an important note concerning the language employed at the missions. He said that the Fathers did not apply themselves to learning the native tongues, and that therefore they could confess only those Indians who might know the Castilian language (UTD 1715a). Two years later, in 1717, many of the bishop's observations were echoed in a report by Fray Joseph Sanz (CPP 24: 97).

Some of these matters were policy or practice of long standing. In 1592 the governor of Nueva Vizcaya, Rodrigo del Río y Losa, noted that the Franciscans had not learned the language(s) of the natives of this province; a year earlier he had written that the religious men of this order were little dedicated to their missions (UTD 1592-1643). Royal cedulas of 1594 and 1597, partly in response to these reports of del Río y Losa, note the lack of knowledge of the native tongues (except the Mexican, or Nahuatl, language) and compare the work of the Franciscans unfavorably with that of the Jesuits, who were said to apply themselves to learning the native speech (and who had been in the mission field a much shorter period of time) (Porras Muñoz 1966: 335ff; CPP 2: 194-5, 198-9).

Moreover, the Indians themselves sometimes registered dissatisfaction with their missionaries. These complaints for the most part can be reduced to the following four points: (1) the neophytes had to pay the missionary money when they could not contribute corn to the mission; (2) they were forced to work on the missionary's fields (the fields of the mission?), which did not leave them sufficient time to farm their own; (3) the Fathers would employ the Indians as messengers, sending them to distant places and causing them to be absent from their villages; and (4) the priest would not permit the Indian town governor to select and allocate men from the pueblos as laborers. While complaints of this nature were made occasionally, they were usually quite difficult or impossible for the authorities to substantiate, since the practices alluded to clearly fell within the rights granted to the missionaries and were necessary to keep a mission going. The documentary sources consulted do not afford sufficient information to make possible an evaluation of the alleged wrongs (AHP 1723A; 1725C; 1730A; 1731A).

There is, nevertheless, an impression that one gains from the documents from the general region. Apparently, the missionaries usually made little effort to keep the members of distinct Indian ethnic groups separate at the missions – for example, Franciscans readily put Tarahumaras and Conchos together in missions located near the Concho-Tarahumara border; however, it should be noted that some of these settlements may already have been mixed before the arrival of the Europeans. Sumas, Conchos, Janos, and Jocomes appear to have been placed together in the Casas Grandes district. Whether this practice was part of Franciscan policy or not (it may have been due mainly to outside political pressure), it does exemplify the great mixing of peoples in this central river-valley area during the colonial period – an amalgamation that took place at all Spanish contact institutions. It is probable that in many cases two or more languages were spoken at a single mission, and this would have made it impossible for a minister to learn the tongues of his flock even if he wanted to, unless these languages were very closely related. Furthermore, the demand for laborers, which kept the Indians moving between native town and hacienda, must have seriously impeded the ability of the Franciscans to carry out their mission program.

Indeed, the remarks cited above may render a much too severe indictment of the Franciscans. These missionaries elsewhere were reported to be quite dedicated men who lived in poverty and who were much maligned by the rest of the Spaniards (see Motolinía's *History of the Indians of New Spain,* quoted in Washburn 1964: 162-6). Unlike the Jesuits in the area they served, the Franciscans in the central river valleys of Nueva Vizcaya were certainly very close to, and much of the time in the middle of, the most heavily settled Spanish zones, where the economic life of the northern frontier was the most active.

Examples of this proximity and the difficulties that it could occasion the missionaries are found in various sources. As early as 1645, the Jesuit Nicolás Zepeda wrote that there were a vast number of gentiles who lived along the Parral River and in the Parral district itself. These persons were not yet Christianized, and the only interest the Europeans had in them was in their value as laborers; the civilians simply did not cooperate with the religious in the saving of souls and carrying out the laws of the church (DHM 1645; Rosales Parish Records).

A quarter of a century later, in 1669, Bishop Gorospe summarized conditions in the area as he saw them after a recent visit, noting particularly the unrest in the province. Because of subjection and ill treatment, many Indians, a large proportion of whom were *mansos baptisados,* found it necessary to take refuge in the backcountry, fleeing their towns and the Christian doctrine. Those congregated in pueblos were oppressed by the "governors" of the kingdom with a repartimiento that they made under the designation of encomienda in His Majesty's name to the mine and ranch owners, even though, Gorospe said, this was prohibited by a number of royal cedulas. The Indians were kept the greatest part of the year to work on Spanish holdings, absent from their wives and children, who were left without support in places far away from where the men labored. Furthermore, the workers were paid, not in money, but only in locally made clothing (*ropa de la tierra*) calculated at inflated prices. All this was substantiated by the Western Conchería governor, Juan Constantino, who had reported that when he went out to bring in the Indians who were under encomienda obligations to work for Spaniards, he did so with certain danger to his own person and life because the people would resist with force and violence (CPP 10: 315-32). In 1688, Governor Pardiñas, possibly unwittingly, supported Bishop Gorospe's assertions to some extent while explaining why tribute was not exacted from Nueva Vizcayan Indians. This was because they were extremely poor; only a few worked at the mines (other kinds of holdings were not mentioned), and if any impost were levied on them, they would run away (CPP 16: 91-2).

In 1715, the missionary of Nombre de Dios, who was supposed to care for the Indians of Tabalaopa, was forced to complain that his neophytes did not attend mass or care for the fields of the mission. Whatever the attraction was, the natives preferred to remain at the hacienda. Once, when they had been brought back to the mission, within three days they had returned to Tabalaopa (AHP 1716B).

Apparently by 1744 not a great deal had changed. Bancroft summarizes a report of this year from the governor. Not only were the Indian settlements practically empty of people at certain times of the year (as Bishop Gorospe had noted 75 years earlier), but "the Indians were cheated in the matter of time, left free from all control in respect of religion and morals, and forced to go long distances for their wages, which were paid in such articles as the agents happened to have rather than in such as the laborers needed. Thus they were forced into the mountains in quest of food not existing at their homes; and from being fugitives they readily became rebels" (Bancroft 1884: 586).

One missionary, Fray Juan de la Portilla, stationed at the mission of Santa Cruz de Tapacolmes, on two occasions penned some notes of his problems in the very entries of his parish records. One such entry was concerned with the Spaniards' use of Indians as labor and their attitude toward the natives. In 1759, Portilla buried an Indian woman, a servant at the Ballero hacienda. He noted in the burial record that he had not been notified in time to render the last rites to this woman, simply because of the carelessness of her masters, who were only interested in extracting all the service possible from their native help. Portilla added that the Europeans had no charity (*caridad*) toward the poor Indian servants, a situation that only increased the burden of the missionaries; this was the third time he had been brought someone so near death that the person was unable to make confession before dying.

Portilla noted that since the first time this had occurred he had tried to rectify the situation with the persons responsible, but that so far he had been unable to obtain any satisfactory results. Portilla's comments are quite consistent with the statement made by Zepeda more than 100 years earlier.

Indian customs, however, as well as the local contact social structure, inhibited Father Portilla at Santa Cruz. In a later entry, he reported that the Indians from the town of San Pedro had buried a person without his knowledge and without his having been able to give the holy sacraments. This had been due to the laxity of the Indian governor. When Portilla went to see this governor, this official informed him that there had been no one to send to advise the missionary of the impending death. Portilla reprimanded the governor, who in turn threatened the good Father with the Spanish Corregidor. Portilla wrote in the burial entry that in order not to be accused falsely to his superiors – a common experience for the missionaries – he had decided to say no more. However, some time after this he learned that the Indians had interred the person in question alive; this was the second time he had discovered such a burial of a person who had not yet expired (Rosales Parish Records).

MISSION SITES

In the material that follows, I have attempted to include data from all possible sources on the missions and associated settlements that played an integral part in the history of the Conchos and neighboring Indians. Most of the locally obtained documents are parish records that reach back to the mission or colonial period; however, for many ex-missions and churches of that era no local records could be discovered. Of those located, all are incomplete and some are only fragments. Nevertheless, from the material collected, a general, if synoptic, picture of the mission or other establishment can be gleaned, along with some notion of its role in the total process of Indian assimilation and population movement during the colonial period.

Unfortunately, the major portion of the parish records refer only to the 18th century and, consequently, pick up only the later stages of ethnic assimilation. A few, however, do go back into the 17th century, notably those of the Franciscan convent of Valle de San Bartolomé; these begin about 1663, and they afford an idea of the ethnic composition of the labor force in this part of the Parral district at that time.

One feature of the Franciscans' record-keeping which, fortunately, is not too crucial for this study, given the founding dates for most of the missions, is that apparently these missionaries did not record the tribal affiliation of their Indian neophytes during their first 90 years or so in Nueva Vizcaya. In 1715, Fray Pedro de Ortega of the San Bartolomé convent stated that, although by this time the convent had ministered to Indians for more than 140 years, it had not been the custom to list the ethnic group of natives who underwent holy rites until the year 1657 (AHP 1715Ac).

While general trends in the loss of ethnic identity and in population movement during the latter part of the colonial period are noticeable, one point should be underscored concerning the use of parish records. Priests were often inconsistent and were sometimes ignorant of Indian ethnic affiliation as well as of the *casta* or class-ranked group of those who were culturally non-Indian (e.g., Spaniards, mestizos, mulattoes, etc.). In the latter case, apparently it was often difficult for the priest to decide to what "caste" a person belonged, and different priests classified the same people differently. However, despite these difficulties in the accuracy of the sources, an overall pattern is discernible.

The entries for missions and other sites given below are arranged on a geographical basis, essentially from south to north. Sites located in the western portion of the Conchería are dealt with before those of the La Junta district in the northeast. This geographical order is also roughly the chronological order of the foundation or occupation of these sites by the Spaniards.

The Central Valleys and the Northwest

Convent of Valle de San Bartolomé

Valle de San Bartolomé (today, Valle de Allende, Chihuahua) is one of the oldest Spanish settlements in the northern Nueva Vizcayan area. It was established in the 1560s, approximately at the same time that the mines of Santa Bárbara were opened up. While it soon became the center of agricultural activity that supported the mining industry of the Santa Bárbara and general Parral district, Almada notes that it was possibly originally claimed as a mining town (*real*). The *convento* and mission established here served as an administrative center for many or most of the northern missions (Almada 1968: 28; Jiménez Moreno 1958: 38, 62,

99, 140-1, 145; López-Velarde 1964: 63-5; AHP 1641A; BL 1789a; 1789b).

Franciscan holdings were set up here soon after the founding of the town, which Almada dates slightly prior to 1565 (López-Velarde gives 1564 as the most probable founding date for the *convento* and mission). Arlegui calls the first establishment an *hospicio,* and notes that by 1570 a *casa de administración* had been erected (Almada 1968: 28; Arlegui 1851: 34, 58-9; López-Velarde 1964: 63-5).

From the beginning all, or almost all, of the natives brought in from elsewhere by the Spaniards to work on the farms and ranches were located as inhabitants of haciendas, which numbered some 15 or 20 (e.g., 20 in 1630 but 16 in 1674, though the geographical areas included in these counts may not be comparable). Reportedly there was never a way to reduce them to a town or pueblo at San Bartolomé proper. In 1622, the jurisdiction of the San Bartolomé convent was described simply as the Provincia de Santa Bárbara, comprising 1,003 Indians; in 1630, one figure for the area was 1,125 aborigines administered by the convent, 1,075 of whom lived outside of the town itself (Arlegui 1851: 34, 58-9; Porras Muñoz 1966: 277-8; AHP 1715Ac; CPP 5: 278-83; 39: 203-16).

Apparently, during most of the 17th and at least early part of the 18th century, the San Bartolomé establishment had two or three religious. In 1622, there were two, and in 1630, a *guardián* and two friars instead of one. In 1723, somewhat previous to Arlegui's writing, it had two priests, a *guardián* and a *cura doctrinero* (Porras Muñoz 1966: 277-8; AHP 1723A; CPP 5: 278-83).

In any event, whatever Indian population existed at the San Bartolomé convent formed only a small settlement that was unattached to any of the haciendas. In 1630, the resident Indian population was said to consist of 50 persons; around 1700 only eight or 10 natives were living here; and in 1723 it was noted that there was still a pueblo of Indians, but it had only a very few people (Porras Muñoz 1966: 277-8; AHP 1723). Again, in 1751, the Bishop of Durango, Pedro de Anselmo, reported that San Bartolomé still possessed what he called a *doctrina* of Indians but that this consisted of very few persons (UTD 1742-1754). A later source states that the *convento* at San Bartolomé was secularized in 1755, implying that it was not worthwhile by this time to maintain a missionary establishment here (AGN 1816). However, there is possibly a slight contradiction to this secularization date; 10 years later, in 1765, the Nueva Vizcayan bishop, Pedro Tamarón y Romeral, stated that San Bartolomé still had a Franciscan convent with a single guardian, though he did not give the Indian population (Tamarón 1937: 121).

The extant parish records of the old San Bartolomé convent reveal something of the make-up of the Indian population (and, consequently, of the labor force) of this region in the latter half of the 17th and the first quarter of the 18th century (see Tables 1 and 2). Conchos constitute a good portion of the native peoples in the early years (as

TABLE 1

Valle de San Bartolomé: Ethnic Groups Cited in Baptismal Records, 1663-1686

	1663-1664	1665	1666	1667	1668	1669	1670	1671	1672	1673	1674	1675	1676	1677	1678	1679	1680	1681	1682	1683	1684	1685	1686
Apaches	3	4	2	1					1	1	1	2	4	3	4	2	2		2	1	1		
Chisos														1		1							
Chivira (Quivira)																1							
Conchos	54	27	23	39	22	31	11	15	10	9	7	11	19	20	15	10	7	15	9	18	3	3	1
Julimes	2		1	3		1		1		1	1		1	1						1		3	1
Mamites								1		2					1					1			2
Mexicanos	1		2			3	1	1			1	1			1					1			
Obomes		1	3						1				1										
Ocolmes (Ocomes)									1	2													
Oposmes						1																	
Salineros											2	1											
Sinaloas									5														
Sonoras	2	4	7	3	3	3	3	5	8	5	9	3	12	9	10	11	3	5	4	4	7	3	2
Tapacolmes	18	2	6	1					1	1													
Tarahumaras	1	1		1																			
Tobosos	3								1							1							
Unspecified Indians			1			3	4		1													14	5

Source: Parish Church, Valle de Allende, Chihuahua.

they do in the 1630 count mentioned above), and one would guess that Tepehuan Indians also did so at an even earlier period. However, the numbers of these nearby Indians slowly dwindle in the records as the more local native population was being dispersed and acculturated. Concurrently, as the La Junta pueblos were being gradually opened up to increasing intercourse with the Nueva Vizcayan Spaniards during the latter portion of the 1600s, the names of the various peoples from this part of the Conchos River and the Rio Grande begin to occur more and more in the church books at San Bartolomé.

There is also a rather steady stream of Indians from the western side of the Sierra Madre, who are usually designated as Sonoras and Sinaloas. At the same time, there are only a very few of the wilder, more warlike Indians from the general desert east of the Valle, such as Tobosos and Chisos. Indeed, these peoples on occasion were brought into the region to settle and work, but often their stay was only brief; the first time there is record of Tobosos being brought into the Valley is in 1612. The term "Apache" as it occurs in the San Bartolomé records apparently was employed when the priest could not identify the Indians by ethnic group, judging from the high frequency of its use in baptisms of children of unknown parents; this inference is supported by the administrative reports of this same period, which do not use the term "Apache" and do not mention any Apaches in the area (UTD 1648; Valle de Allende Parish Records). While the

Bishop of Durango in 1765 did not note Indians separately, he reported that the Valley of San Bartolomé at that time had a total population of 1,833 persons, comprising 202 families (Tamarón 1937: 121).

San Buenaventura de Atotonilco

Arlegui gives 1619 as the founding date for the mission of San Buenaventura de Atotonilco (today, Villa López, Chihuahua). However, a place named Atotonilco was founded in this area for wild Toboso bands from the east as early as 1611, and Tobosos were settled here either at this date or the following year (West 1949: 11; UTD 1648). Father Arlegui reported that Atotonilco was first a *guardianía* before it gained mission status, which may explain the discrepancy in dates (Arlegui 1851: 82-3, 85).

Later, on at least one (undated) occasion the church was destroyed by the desert-dwelling Tobosos, but it was rebuilt afterwards. Almada reports that sometime following this a civilian, one Capitán Andrés del Hierro, settled the area and called his place Atotonilco; he was forced to abandon it in 1671 because of Indian hostilities. While this history is sketchy, the mission of Atotonilco retained this religious status until the end of the colonial period (Almada 1968: 311-2; Arlegui 1851: 82-3, 85; Porras Muñoz 1966: 278).

Atotonilco was located in Tepehuan country, near the eastern border with the Tobosos, the boundary of Concho territory lying a number of leagues to the north of it. The

TABLE 2

Valle de San Bartolomé: Ethnic Groups Cited in Marriage Records, 1686-1724

	1686-1690	1691-1696	1697-1699 M	1697-1699 B	1700-1701	1702-1704	1705-1706	1707-1709	1710-1713	1714-1715	1716-1717	1718-1724
Apaches				2		2	x	x	x	x	x	x
Batlaboylas			1	2								
Cacalotes		1	1	1					x			
Cacuitataomes		1							x			
Chisos	1	3	3	1	1	2	x		x			
Cholomes												
Conchos										x		
Conejos					1							
del Norte						10		x	x		x	x
Gozomas		1		2								
Julimes	3	1	1	6	1				x			
Mamites			5	2	2	1						
Mesquites										x		
Oposme				1		1			x			
Panana										x		
Piraymes (Piros?)					x							
Piro							x					
Polacmes		2	6	4		1						
Posalmes		2		2						x		
Puliques		5	1	1	1	2						
Sonoras	3	11	9	25	4	11	x	x	x	x	x	x
Suma						1				x		
Tanos				2								
Tapacolmes					3	1						x
Tarahumaras											x	x
Tepehuan								x				
Tigua						x						

x = Group name appears, but records inadequate for count.
M = Marriage
B = Baptism
Source: Book of marriages, parish church, Valle de Allende.

history of ethnic groups associated with it is spotty. A number of Toboso bands were settled here for short periods, and for many years during the 17th century Atotonilco was called the Toboso mission; however, apparently few of these groups ever stayed on. For example, after many attempts to settle Tobosos here in the 1640s, by 1654 there were only 17 residing at the mission — seven adults and 10 children (AHP 1644A; 1654Aa; CPP 5:230-3). More settled peoples, such as Conchos (for instance, in 1644) and later Tarahumaras, were often reported living here. In 1717 the Jesuit Antonio Arias, perhaps overstating the case, considered Atotonilco a Tarahumara mission (Arlegui 1851: 82-3, 85; AHP 1644A; 1704Bb; 1715Aa; 1723A; CPP 11: 515-41; 14: 181-4).

In 1630 Atotonilco was reported to have 200 *vecinos*, but this usage of the term almost certainly means Indian residents (Porras Muñoz 1966: 278). In May of 1700, the total population of the mission was said to be 260 persons, many of whom were Acoclames (a Toboso band) from the desert country to the east, settled since 1698; however, by 1701 a number of these people had fled from Atotonilco back to their desert haunts (AHP 1700a; 1704Aa; BL 1649-1700). By 1726, this mission possessed only 30 men who were judged able-bodied for work. This number excluded the town officials (*justicias*), those who were in the service of the mission, and those who were too old. It was also reported that during "the plague," apparently a recent one, some 30 other people (probably men) had passed away (AHP 1728Aa). Unfortunately, it is unknown what the total population of the mission was at this time. In 1751, the Bishop of Durango merely recorded that the mission of Atotonilco had a few Indians (UTD 1742-1754); 14 years later, Bishop Tamarón stated that there were 83 families of Indians, totaling 280 persons, living here (Tamarón 1937: 122). Two years afterward, Lafora noted 300 Tarahumara in residence at the mission (Kinnaird 1958: 66).

A report of 1789 stated that San Buenaventura de Atotonilco was a cabecera mission, under the jurisdiction of Valle de San Bartolomé, and was administered by a Father from the Santo Evangelio Franciscans. The total Indian population at this time was 227 people and consisted of both Tarahumaras and Conchos (BL 1789a; 1789b). However, the Concho population was seemingly very small. Garrison lists of Indian auxiliaries of the nearby presidio of Guajuquilla (present-day Jiménez, Chihuahua) for the years 1779, 1784, 1788, 1794, and 1795 contain only Tarahumaras, and their numbers run between 22 and 24 for these years (AHP 1779Ab; 1784A; 1788Ab; 1794b; 1794c; 1795). In 1793, the population was reported to have increased to 331 persons (Bancroft 1884: 657, fn. 39). Tarahumara Indians only are recorded for the censuses of 1816 and 1817, and they total 187 and 188 persons, respectively, for these years. Interestingly, at this time the nations said to live in the surrounding country were Tarahumaras, Mimbreños, and Gileños (AGN 1816).

Convent of Parral

Joseph de Arlegui, writing in the early 1730s, called this Franciscan establishment a *convento;* at this time it ministered to three nations: Tarahumaras, Conchos, and Tobosos (Arlegui 1851: 89). Whether it was the same place or not, by 1642 there existed a Franciscan *doctrina,* apparently a satellite parish of Valle de San Bartolomé, in Parral; certainly by 1656 the Parral convent had been established (López-Velarde 1964: 97-8; AHP 1641A). Bishop Tamarón's 1765 report noted that there were two Franciscan Fathers stationed at this convent, but stated nothing concerning the administration of the Indians (Tamarón 1937: 124). Whatever importance this Franciscan holding may have had for the native population, it was apparently on a very local basis. However, administratively, the convent of San Antonio del Parral was elevated to a *custodia* in 1717. (There was also a Jesuit *colegio* in Parral, presumably for Tarahumaras and Tepehuanes [López-Velarde 1964: 97-8; Mota Padilla 1870: 357].)

San Francisco de Conchos

The mission of San Francisco de Conchos was the first establishment dedicated exclusively to the Conchos Indians. It was founded in 1604 by Fray Alonso de la Oliva after 10 years of missionary activity in the area, and by 1609 Oliva had more than 4,000 Conchos under his ministry (Arlegui 1851: 76; Jiménez Moreno 1958: 146-7; Torquemada 1944: 345).

This cabecera mission had a life of some 165 years, with seemingly one interruption about 1650 when the Bishop of Durango converted it into a secular parish for a short period (AGN 1651). Both Almada (1968: 483) and Bancroft (1884: 303) indicate that the mission was destroyed after the 1644-45 hostilities and that it was not reoccupied again until some time later – 1677 (Almada) or 1667 (Bancroft). While it was definitely inhabited again after these mid-1640 troubles (see below), and is referred to various times during this apparent interim (e.g., in 1657 [AHP 1657B] and 1658 [AHP 1658Aa]), its history for the next decade or so after secularization is quite obscure. Whatever actually took place around 1650, it seems that San Francisco was soon returned to mission status, which it maintained until it was finally secularized in 1769 (AGN 1816). Some time before its demise, however, it lost its status as cabecera – in 1763, it was said to be a visita of Valle de San Bartolomé (Bancroft 1884: 598, fn. 24; CPP 41: 471-504). Some 80 years after its founding, between 1685 and 1690, a presidio carrying the same name was erected about a league away, and for a number of years afterwards it was to be a major center of Spanish military power on the northern frontier of New Spain.

Unfortunately, despite the great importance of San Francisco for the native population of the region, there is little direct information on the history of the site. During the 1645 uprisings the Conchos, together with nations from the Rio Grande area, attacked the mission, committing a great amount of destruction. Two cells of the convent were burned, many of the sacred objects were stolen or profaned, and the two missionaries there, Fray N. Ligarán and Fray Francisco Lavado, were killed (AHP 1645Aa; CD 1650a; DHM 1645).

It is not known specifically whether San Francisco had any satellite parishes (visitas) connected with it; however, considering the early reported population of the area, it is reasonable to think that it did. There are several places that at one time or another may have been under the administration of this mission – both Santiago de Babonoyaba and San Pedro de Conchos, for instance, in their early years. The founding dates given by Arlegui for both of these missions fall after the 1644-1645 revolt. Since he seemingly gives dates that refer to the actual founding of cabeceras and not to the time a town or place was first settled or established as a visita, or with some other status, his dates for Babonoyaba and San Pedro, if correct, probably refer to a formal founding of these two missions as administrative centers. Both were in existence by the 1644 hostilities, and if they were not missions in their own right at this time, they may have been under the administration of San Francisco (Arlegui 1851: 76; CD 1640a; DHM 1645; UTD 1648).

Two or three other places were possibly or probably also under the authority of the mission of San Francisco: San Luis Mascomalhua, Babiscuamalba, and San Marcos

Church at cemetery west of the town of San Francisco de Conchos, Chihuahua

Lintel with inscribed date of 1627 *(AÑO DE 1627)*
in cemetery church, San Francisco de Conchos

(see entries below). All of these places had a short existence, although they were Concho settlements, and San Luis was said definitely to have been under the administration of Franciscans. Still another location (if it was not actually San Marcos) may have been a visita site. In 1653, Fray Francisco de Cervantes reported that he was trying to get some Indians to settle at a place he called La Junta de los Ríos, five leagues from the Conchos mission of San Francisco. This distance could put the spot about where the Florido and Conchos Rivers join, a place where the Rodríguez and Espejo expeditions in the 1580s had found a settlement of Conchos Indians (see Chapter 3: *Introduction*). This place had probably been abandoned by the 1650s, and Cervantes was trying to get a new group from the hinterland to take up pueblo life here, following the customary Spanish practice (AHP 1653Ab). It is unknown whether this settlement was successful.

There is little doubt that San Francisco was founded well within Concho territory and that the original population of the mission was Concho. The 1575 Concho border was about 15 leagues from Santa Bárbara and probably about the same distance from Parral (see Map 1); since the mission was said to be 22 leagues from Parral, this would place the mission some seven leagues inside the southern line of Concho territory (Miranda 1871). However, as the local population dwindled because of disease, overwork, or flight, or for other reasons, new groups were brought in from farther away. Indeed, much of the history of the mission consisted of the settlement of new populations, in later years often non-Concho, at the mission town.

Descriptions of Oliva's early work (Torquemada 1944: 345) would seem to indicate that some neighboring rancherias were probably induced to settle at San Francisco at this time. Four thousand souls are no doubt too many people for this location to have supported aboriginally; however, gathering together persons from outlying settlements was in keeping with the Spanish policy of *reducción*. In 1606 it was ordered that two Concho rancherias, which had come from the hinterland and were already in encomienda, be settled at San Francisco de Conchos. One of these bands was under chief Baoyacat and the other under Natramolao (CD 1643).

Later, after the 1644–1645 revolt, a number of the members of the Concho confederation were resettled here. These consisted of 230 Indians "of all nations," including 57 Mamites. It was also reported at this time that a rancheria of Julimes was on its way to take up residence at San Francisco (CD 1650a). Sometime around or after 1673, a group of Tobosos, under their governor Don Francisco, went to live at the mission (BL 1649–1700). The relocations seem to have been carried out even more frequently after the founding of the San Francisco presidio (ca. 1685), apparently so that the bands could be kept under the watchful eye of the military In 1684 Guesecpayolicla and Osatabay were reported at the mission. In 1693 some 401 Chisos, comprising

148 families and belonging to four different bands (Chichitames, Osatayoliglas, Guasapayoliglas, and Sisimbles), were settled at San Francisco; however, by August 1 of 1693 these same Chisos had fled back to their desert territory in the northeast (AHP 1684Aa; BL 1695a). On a number of other occasions both Chisos and Tobosos were cited as inhabitants of San Francisco in the 17th century (AHP 1686Ba; 1687Aa; 1687Ab; 1697Ab). After the 1697 uprising among the Tarahumara, some of these people were also brought here to live, and during this same decade some Suninoliclas and possibly Cíbolos were also in residence (BL 1697–1703). By the end of the 1600s, and for many years to come, San Francisco was a multi-ethnic community.

In the 1700s Tobosos and Chisos continue to show up in references to the population of San Francisco (e.g., in 1710 and 1713) (AHP 1704Aa; 1715Aa; 1715Ab; 1723A; BL 1709–1715; DHM 1704); however, in 1717 it was reported by the Jesuit Antonio Arias that Tarahumaras predominated (CPP 24:181–4). In 1723, one report specified Chisos (mostly Cacuitataomes), Tobosos, Conchos, and a few Tarahumaras. Indeed, a minor incident at this time involving some of these people affords a glimpse of the structure of the town government. For reasons that are not totally clear, a group of Indians, mainly Chisos but including some Tobosos, picked up and retired to the hinterland. This movement was led by a chief (*capitán*) named Juan, who was tied by kinship to some 18 or 20 men and their families who lived in town. The total number of people who took part in this flight from the settlement was about 75. In the reporting of this incident, it was noted that there was one governor for two of the nations of the town – the Cacuitataomes (Chisos) and the Conchos – and another governor for the Tarahumaras. The Tarahumara incumbent and his wife were both stated to be natives (*naturales*) of the town; this apparently means they were born there, and thus indicates rather longtime occupation of the place by Tarahumaras. No governor of the Tobosos was mentioned, but Tobosos were probably with the Chisos and Conchos (AHP 1723A).

Military occupation of the presidio was ended in 1751, after which time it appears that no new peoples were brought in to settle. Probably a number of persons living there eventually left for other places once San Francisco was no longer a center for military activities (AGN 1816).

In 1765 Bishop Tamarón reported that the mission possessed 89 families of Indians, comprising 289 persons. He also noted that there were 139 families, comprising 1,330 persons, at the town of the old presidio (Tamarón 1937:121). Two years later Lafora stated that the Indian mission consisted of 200 Chisos and Tarahumaras, but that the old presidio town, which he called Nuestra Señora de Guadalupe, had (only?) 25 white families, who supported themselves by cloth weaving. He mentioned no other population for this place. However, about four leagues away, he said, was the hacienda of Nuestra Señora de Aranzazu; this may have accounted for some of the population cited by Tamarón

Town church at San Francisco de Conchos, Chihuahua

(Kinnaird 1958: 67–8). In 1723, there had been at least two haciendas close to San Francisco, one of which belonged to the captain of the presidio and the other to a certain Arauz (AHP 1723A). As noted above, the mission was secularized officially in 1769. By 1779, it was noted that there were only a very few old and useless (*Viexos y Ynutiles*) Indians at the Conchos town and, consequently, no auxiliary military unit had been formed here (AHP 1779Aa).

Locally there are almost no records that refer to the San Francisco de Conchos of the colonial period. The earliest extant church records are found in a book of baptisms, 1815 to 1842, located in the parish church of Camargo. From March of 1815 through the year 1822, Indians, mestizos, and Spaniards are noted separately. On the average, Indians make up about 18 percent of the entries, Spaniards constitute about 50 percent, and mestizos make up the remaining 32 percent. There is no discernible trend of population change during these few years, and after 1823 the various *castas* are not mentioned in the records.

In the present town of San Francisco de Conchos, I located a few fragments of a document of 1758 concerning a land dispute, apparently between the inhabitants of the town and a local landowner; accompanying the document was a map, also dated 1758, which is reproduced here as Map 2. Another fragment of a page dated 1813 refers to the

protector of the Indians; however, it does not seem that this title could have amounted to much at this late date.

San Luis Mascomalhua

San Luis Mascomalhua was a little-known and apparently short-lived Concho town, upriver from San Francisco de Conchos. There is no record stating when it was established or whether it was originally a Concho settlement, as is most probable. The name of San Luis first appears in the documentary record in 1644 and drops from sight after 1666; little is known of its history. The place was attacked during the hostilities in 1645, and some of the rebels of the Concho confederation were later relocated here (Alegre 1956: III, 39; CD 1650a). The town was reported to be under the administration of Franciscans (DHM 1645), probably as part of the mission of San Francisco de Conchos.

It seems highly probable that in the early 1650s the inhabitants of this settlement were merged with those of another spot named Babiscuamalba (see following entry), and that the people of the latter came to San Luis. While *Mascomalhua* may be a shortened form of *Babiscuamalba,* at least in the early years these two places should not be confused. A statement dated 1644 noted that upriver from San Francisco de Conchos were the towns of "Babiscuamalba y San luis Passo q llaman del Rio que dista siete leguas de San Fran^{co}

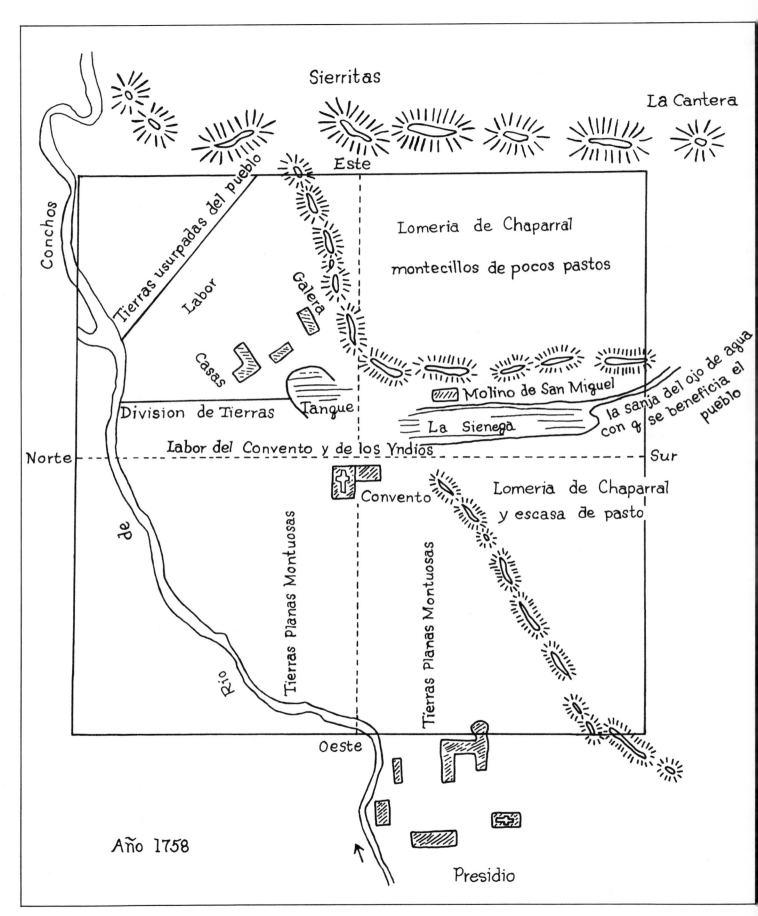

Map 2. Tracing of a 1758 map of the mission and presidio of San Francisco de Conchos, found in the *presidencia* of the town in 1964.

← NOTE TO MAP 2

In the area of the present-day settlement of San Francisco de Conchos, there are two churches that seem to date from the colonial period (see accompanying photographs). One of these is located in the town; the other is two to three miles west of the town, upriver, and today is identified as the presidio church. At first impression, the 1758 map seems to fit the present layout of the town. However, my investigations at the site raised some question regarding what areas the map actually covers. Assuming that the orientation of the churches on the map followed the orientation of the actual structures at that date, then the map does not refer to both of the present-day church buildings. The church corresponding to the presidio church of the map is oriented in the proper direction. However, the present-day town church is oriented exactly opposite to that of the map, the altar being at the west end rather than the east end of the church.

All documentary descriptions of the town dating around the middle of the 1700s agree that the presidio was to the west of the Indian town and church, as it is on the map. The Bishop of Durango reported in 1751 that San Francisco still had some Indians and that their pueblo was about half a league downriver (that is, east) from the presidio (UTD 1742-1754). Fourteen years later, in 1765, Bishop Tamarón also noted that the Indian town was about half a league to the east of the presidio (Tamarón 1937: 121); the same relative positions were also confirmed by Lafora (Kinnaird 1958: 87-8).

While all of these accounts conform to the 1758 map, except for the orientation of the town church, what does not coincide with other information is the dates inscribed on both of these colonial structures. What should be the presidio church carries a date of 1627 carved on a beam over a side entrance. This date is clearly too early for the church of the presidio, although it is always possible that it was inscribed at a later time. The roof of this building, which is for the most part intact, is of the type found on many colonial structures, with very large, slightly worked log beams running the width of the building, and smaller ones running lengthwise, with earth tamped on top. The entire building is in a very bad state of repair, and part of the cupola on the northwest front portion has already fallen in. The walls are of very thick adobe and clearly have been remodeled, or the surface has been reconditioned, several times. The floor is of earth, and the windows are small and located high in the walls, just under the roof, in the style of the old fortress-type frontier churches of northern Mexico.

At this particular site, there are no other buildings standing, although a number of mounds, covering many square yards, can be seen in front of the church — that is, roughly to the north toward the river. It is impossible without excavation to determine whether these buried foundations correspond to any of the structures represented on the map; none of the mounds that I inspected seem to be as close to the river as the structures noted on the map.

There is still a wall (renovated by the local inhabitants in the spring of 1967) enclosing the holy ground *(camposanto)* around the presidio church. The local people still bury their dead here, and many and sundry crosses and grave markers fill the area. According to the present inhabitants, this churchyard long ago filled up with burials; for some time now the newer graves have been dug on top of the older ones.

The church of the present-day town (lying some two miles to the east of the above-described church) also seems to be of colonial construction, although better made. It is still in use for services and is a visita of the parish of Camargo. This church has, in recent years, been renovated on the inside. It clearly corresponds to the pueblo church on the map (except, as noted, for its opposite orientation). However, this structure also carries a date, carved on one of the ceiling beams toward the back. This is an inscription to the effect that the church was finished at the behest of the executors of the will of General Juan Fernández de Retana (deceased in February of 1709 [Almada and others 1959: 3]), long-time commander of the San Francisco presidio. This inscription carries the date of May 30, 1710. (The entire inscription, clearly in the style of colonial orthography, reads: *Por los Albazeas del Genl D^n Ju^o Fern^z de Retana se acabo esta Yglesia Siendo Gua^n de este Com^{to} El R^o P^e p^{o}r$_y$ Ex Dilli. Fr. Diego de Orosco: En 30 de Maio de 1710 Anos.)*

This, in conjunction with the date on the previously mentioned church, plus the generally later construction style of the building, on top of a hill with heavily buttressed walls, would seem to make it more probable that this was the church that was part of the presidio. In the company of two local citizens, I was able to locate only tentatively some of the other features represented on the map, such as the marsh and the mill *(molino)*, at some distance to the east of the present town. Without more intensive investigation, including excavation, it will be impossible to determine to what extent the map corresponds to the present structures in the area. It is possible that the mission church represented in this 18th-century map is actually to the east of the present-day settlement.

---

de conchos y cinco de Babiscuamalba" (AHP 1654Ab). Later, in 1654, the two names are treated as belonging to a single place called the "pueblo de San Luis y Babiscomalba," said to be a Concho settlement upriver from Agua Escondida, which was two leagues from Todos Santos (AHP 1654Aa). In 1666, a Toboso group asked to be settled at San Luis, *puesto* of MaVisComalba, on the Conchos River, seven leagues from San Francisco. It is unknown whether or not this settlement was ever realized, but this Toboso group was apparently the same one living at San Francisco a few years later (BL 1649-1700).

Babiscuamalba

The settlement of Babiscuamalba was said to be some five leagues from San Luis, apparently upriver, to the west (AHP 1654Ac). Judging from the documentary sources, this place had an extremely short existence, although actually it may have been a Concho rancheria aboriginally. The data seem to indicate that the place was moved or abandoned by the early 1650s, the population probably moving eastward to San Luis or to San Francisco, or both (see *San Luis Mascomalhua,* above) (AHP 1654Aa; BL 1649-1700).

San Marcos

San Marcos is mentioned as being a Concho town during the 1644-1645 revolt, at which time it was abandoned. Later, some of the rebels of the Concho confederation were resettled here, and the place was cited again in the 1684 revolt (AHP 1685Db; CD 1650a). The location of San Marcos is unknown, but one source indicates that it may have been in the direction of Chancaplé, near where the Florido and Parral Rivers join (AHP 1654Aa). Because of the probable proximity of this place to the mission of San Francisco de Conchos, a guess would be that it was included within the administration of this mission.

San Pedro de Conchos

San Pedro de Conchos was an important Concho mission during the 1600s, possessing at least five visitas. During the next century, however, it rapidly lost ground, becoming a visita of one of its own satellite parishes, Santa Cruz (Tamarón 1937: 155; UTD 1742-1754). Arlegui states that the mission was founded in 1649; however, some kind of establishment, if not the mission itself, clearly existed before this date. In 1621 there is a reference to raids by warring Indians in the area of *la villa y rio de san Pedro,* possibly indicating that at this time there was already a town (satellite of San Francisco de Conchos?) at the later mission site (CPP 5: 89-101). Again, reports of the 1644-45 revolt definitely state that a mission named San Pedro de Conchos was raided by the rebels, who burned the church and profaned many of the sacred objects. Following the revolt, in 1645, some 170 Conchos Indians were relocated in San Pedro (Arlegui 1851: 98; CD 1650a; 1646c; DHM 1645). In 1648, General Juan de Barraza wrote that Fray Hernando de Urbaneja was *guardián* of the *convento* of San Pedro as well as of that of "Papasalagua" (Babonoyaba) (CPP 7: 406-12).

Until 1694, this mission was listed as comprising six towns. These, proceeding downriver, were: San Pedro, the cabecera; San Lucas, Santa Cruz, San Pablo, Nuestra Señora de Guadalupe, and San Antonio de Julimes. In 1694, or shortly after, the San Pedro mission was split up; the last three of the pueblos named above were converted into a separate mission, with Julimes as the administrative center (Arlegui 1851: 97-8; Hackett 1926: 358-60; AHP 1723A; BL 1695a).

In general, the history of this mission is quite obscure, and I could find no local documents or parish records to illuminate events impinging on this parish during the 17th century. Clearly the mission itself was located near the heart of Concho country. Nevertheless, as time passed and the original inhabitants of the Conchería disappeared, San Pedro was left as a small island of Concho Indians, surrounded by several other kinds of people. San Lucas, by the last decade of the 1600s (apparently as early as 1684 – see following entry), was settled by a group of Chisos called the Cacuitataomes, occasionally referred to as the "nation from San Lucas." Also about this time, Santa Cruz became the home of a group of Tapacolmes from the La Junta region, and thereafter it was often called Santa Cruz de Tapacolmes. Moreover, by 1715, some Auchanes Indians had located at Julimes (Arlegui 1851: 97-8; AHP 1684Aa; 1710a; 1715Ac; 1723A; BL 1695a).

Little is known specifically of the population of San Pedro. In 1722 it was reported that an Indian language, apparently Concho, was spoken at the town (AHP 1722D). In 1765, as a visita or satellite of Santa Cruz, San Pedro was reported by Bishop Tamarón to have a population of 74 Indians, constituting nine families (Tamarón 1937: 155). Two years later, the military engineer Nicolás Lafora noted that this parish was inhabited by Conchos Indians who, he said, were "not of the best reputation" (Kinnaird 1958: 68).

About the only hints of the earlier history of San Pedro de Conchos are Arlegui's brief comments. Interestingly, he states that in early times San Pedro consisted of 11 widely separated pueblos, the most distant lying some 60 leagues away. Some of these 11 towns were destroyed and some were assigned to other missions. Father Arlegui does not state which were reassigned and which were destroyed but, clearly, the later-created Julimes mission appropriated three of the known satellite parishes, leaving only two pueblos at the time of his writing (San Lucas having been abandoned by this time). Given any accuracy to Arlegui's account, one can only guess that the remaining five unmentioned towns lay roughly to the north, possibly in the direction of Santa Isabel (Arlegui 1851: 97-8).

San Lucas

San Lucas was a satellite parish of the mission of San Pedro de Conchos. It was said to be a Concho town in 1685 and again in 1710. However, by 1693 a group of Chisos called the Cacuitataome or Tacuitatome had located here, while some had come to its cabecera, San Pedro; these people apparently were here as early as 1684, for the Cacuitataomes were reported in this year to be living on the San Pedro River, which probably included San Lucas (Hackett 1926: 360; AHP 1684Aa; 1685Da; 1710a; BL 1695a). In 1723 "Chisos alias Tacuitatomes," said also to be called the "nation from San Lucas," were reported to be dwelling at San Francisco de Conchos (AHP 1723A). The ethnic identity of other inhabitants of San Lucas is unrecorded, except that one statement in 1697 lists, among the Indian auxiliaries employed by General Juan de Retana, a Batayolicla (Chiso) and a Coyame from the town of San Lucas (BL 1697-1703).

Sometime in the early 18th century, San Lucas was dropped from the Franciscan mission lists, although an hacienda by the same name, apparently at roughly the same site, gained prominence in the region. This hacienda was, according to Lafora, located about one league downriver from San Pedro (Kinnaird 1958: 68).

Santa Cruz de Tapacolmes

The mission of Santa Cruz de Tapacolmes (today, Rosales, Chihuahua) was originally a visita of the mission of San Pedro de Conchos; later, around the year 1694, it was converted into a cabecera, with San Pedro becoming subordinate to it (Hackett 1926: 360; Tamarón 1937: 155; AGN 1816; BL 1695a; 1789a; 1789b; Rosales Parish Records).

Church at San Pedro de Conchos, Chihuahua

Carved door on church at San Pedro de Conchos

TABLE 3

Santa Cruz de Tapacolmes: Tribal Groups Cited in Parish Records, 1757–1796

	Burials									Baptisms		Marriages
	1757–1759	1760–1763	Dec. 1766–1768	1769	1775–1778	1785–1786	1787–1788	1789–?	1794–1796	1763–1788	1789	1785–1790
Apache	2	3			2					1		1
Cholome	2	2								3		1
Concho							1				1	1
del Norte											1	
Pima							1					
Sonora	1								1	1		1
Suma	4	1								2		
Tapacolme	2										3	1
Tarahumara	1	9	4	2		1	1		6	15	12	4
Yaqui	5											
Yndio Xunchi (!)								1				

Source: Parish records (several books and scraps of books).

While few data exist on Santa Cruz in the early years, particularly in the 17th century, the parish records of the later 18th century provide some of the most revealing information on Indian assimilation in the central Chihuahua river valleys during the colonial period.

This mission was located several leagues down the San Pedro River from its original administrative center, San Pedro de Conchos. The population at the time of first Spanish contact was Concho; later Tapacolme Indians from the Rio Grande River were located here, some settling in town by 1693 or soon after, although in 1710 the town was said to be "Concho." In 1724, the Indian governor of the town, himself a Tapacolme, testified that the principal nation at Santa Cruz was the Tapacolme, but that there were persons from *all* of the nations around the confluence of the Rio Grande and Conchos rivers residing there at this time. Cited specifically were the Cacalotes, Mesquites, Posalmes, Sopolmes (Oposmes?), Conejos, Pualacmes (Polacmes), and Cíbolos, as well as Conchos (AHP 1684Aa; 1710a; 1722Bb).

Information from later years indicates that the ethnic heterogeneity of the town continued. In 1789, one document stated that the mission consisted of Cholomes (BL 1789a), but another listed Conchos, Tapacolmes, and Tarahumaras (BL 1789b). In the censuses of 1816 to 1818, the mission was reported again to have three nations: Conchos, Tapacolmes, and Tarahumaras (AGN 1816).

The extant parish records, however, indicate more tribal diversity than do these general reports, and the results of a simple count of the ethnic names are given in Table 3. Unfortunately, these records only cover the last half of the 18th century, but the earliest entries list Apaches, Cholomes, Sonoras, Sumas, Tapacolmes, Tarahumaras, and Yaquis. Although the name Concho appears in the 1780s, by this time Conchos had been pretty well assimilated, or at least had lost their identity as a separate group of Indians.

There are only five population totals for this mission, all coming late in the colonial period. The first, in 1765, from Bishop Tamarón, noted 23 families comprising 69 Indians (Tamarón 1937: 154–5). In 1789, there were 76 Indians listed at the mission; a report in 1793 gives 100 souls, and in 1816 and 1817 the population totals were 138 and 146, respectively. These figures, although they do indicate a population increase at the mission during the 18th century, do not seem particularly high when considering the number of people who received either burial or baptismal rites during this same period (see Table 4). The majority of the latter, from what can be gleaned from the parish records, were non-Indians, either Spaniards or persons belonging to other *castas,* especially mestizos. Santa Cruz obviously functioned as something more than a simple Indian parish, servicing as it did many places in outlying areas (Bancroft 1884: 657, fn. 39; López-Velarde 1964: 101; AGN 1816; BL 1789a; 1789b).

Among the settlements served by this mission were the haciendas of San Bartolomé and San Lucas (possibly the ex-mission of the old San Pedro de Conchos system). Other places mentioned were Los Sauces, de la Boquilla, and de los Saria; the ranchos de los Nietos and del Coronel, near Satevó; and the *labores* of Arenibal and of Blanco. Moreover, the names of many towns over a rather wide area are listed as the places of origin of a number of people cited in the records. These include San Pedro (de Conchos), San Pablo, Bachimba, Santa Rosalía, and Julimes. More revealing, however, is the list of towns known to be Tarahumara: Satevó, Temaichi, Caríchiqui, Papigochi, Nonoava, Coyachi, Mátachic, San Borja, San Andrés, Las Cuevas, San Xavier, Santo Tomás, San Mateo, Las Bocas, San José, San Gerónimo, and

TABLE 4

Santa Cruz de Tapacolmes: "Casta" Groups Cited in Parish Records, 1757–1811

	Coyotes	Indians	Lobos	Mestizos	Moriscos	Mulattoes	Negroes	Spanish	Unclassified
Burials									
Feb. 6, 1757–1759		23							1
1760–1763	1	42							5
Dec. 9, 1766–1770		23	1	26		30	1	42	13
1771–1774	1			24		24		24	3
1775–1778	1	14		44		7		27	2
June 14, 1785–June 23, 1789	7	11	2	16		19	1	26	12
April 1790–1795	1	7		39		13		19	11
1796–1799	1	15		45		1		35	2
1800–1803	1	15		54		2		25	15
1804–1807				6				1	74
1808–1811		12		64				21	19
Baptisms									
May 15, 1763–1764	3	46				6		2	2
Dec. 13, 1766–1768	1	8		13	2	20		31	
1769–1770	2	17	1	18		10		25	3
1771–1772		7		23		12		30	
1773–1774	1	2		21		19		18	
1775–1776	18	14		34		18		38	
1777–Feb. 1778	1	5		23		6		14	
June 21, 1789–1790	7	9		22		29		14	3
1791–1792	4	15	1	46		28		28	
1793	3	10		33		8		12	1
1794–1795	7	13		56		27		24	2
1796–June 24, 1797	5	9		20		19		20	2
March 31, 1798–1799		7		60				21	
1800–1801	1	18		81		5		45	7
1802–1803		5		82		1		33	12
1804		4		52				18	15
1805–1806									156
1807–1808		5		60				28	69
1809–1810		4		90				48	2

Source: Parish records (several books and scraps of books).

Santa Cruz (visita of Santa Isabel). While the actual name "Tarahumara" shows up infrequently in the records, these town names with the appended statement, "Indian from the town of . . .," occur quite often. This not only substantiates the general censuses that identify the Tarahumara as one of the ethnic groups of the mission, but it also indicates that these Indians were migrating into the town from a number of different locations (Rosales Parish Records).

In the burial records between the years 1767 and 1769, 48 persons are listed as having been killed by the "enemy" Indians, occasionally said to be Apaches. In the 1789 report of the Bishop of Durango, the nations that were reported in the area of Santa Cruz de Tapacolmes were the Apaches,

the Utes, and the Mescaleros. This same list, with the addition of one more group, the Comanches, was given in the 1816–1818 records (AGN 1816; BL 1789b).

San Antonio de Julimes

Arlegui gives 1691 as the official founding date of San Antonio de Julimes. However, the Spanish had clearly been active here before this year, and the mission may have been located in the general area of an Indian rancheria from the time of the first Spanish penetration into the region. Kelley (1952b) opines that San Antonio was possibly the spot called El Xacal at the time of the Espejo expedition down the Conchos River in 1582.

It is not certain what, if anything, existed at the place of San Antonio before the mid–17th century. Kelley (1952b) suggests that Julimes was founded around this time by a group of La Junta peoples, possibly from the town of San Francisco de la Junta, because a later Julimes governor came from that town; there is some support for this view (see Chapter 4: *Language*), but this evidence is shaky because Spaniards during this century often called the Julimes "Conchos." In any case, by 1658 some kind of Indian settlement was apparently in existence at San Antonio de Julimes, for in October of this year Fray Cristóbal de Arfián wrote that he had just visited the place of San Antonio (de Julimes) and had spent considerable time there with the Conchería governor, Hernando de Obregón (AHP 1658Aa).

Thirty years later, in October of 1688, a petition was received in Parral requesting missionaries for San Antonio de Julimes. According to the Franciscan Fray Miguel Díaz de Silva, the Indians living here had asked for a priest to minister to them two times before this occasion, once in 1684 and again in 1686. The third and last request of the natives had been made during Díaz's recent visit to the settlement (AHP 1686A). Nevertheless, though Díaz's statements imply that no priest had been sent, some kind of religious or missionary activity had apparently taken place at San Antonio by the time of his writing. In 1684 Mendoza had encountered Christian Indians living here and had noted that there was an adobe church in the plaza (Kelley 1952b). Whatever religious attentions this place had received up to this time had no doubt been sporadic; probably it was serviced mainly from San Pedro de Conchos, some 12 leagues away up the Conchos River. Possibly it had been visited by missionaries from San Pedro from the time the latter was founded in the 1640s (BL 1695a).

Arlegui reports that some time after 1691 the Julimes establishment was destroyed by "wild" Indians; Captain Retana then reestablished it (probably around 1693) on "this" side of the river (presumably the west side). By the time of Lafora's visitation in 1767, the presidio that had been at La Junta had been removed southward to Julimes El Viejo, which is shown on Lafora's map at the same spot where the present–day town is located. On this same map the Julimes mission is on the opposite (west) bank of the river, about where the present hamlet of La Regina is. Apparently, the original Julimes was on the east side of the river; in the 1690s it was moved (or refounded) on the west bank; finally, 70 years later, a settlement was begun again on the east side, this time as a presidio (Arlegui 1851: 97; Kelley 1952; Kinnaird 1958: 73, and map; BL 1695a).

Immediately after its founding, San Antonio de Julimes was administered by the cabecera mission of San Pedro de Conchos; this was stated in the information gathered around 1693 that was used to support the establishment of the "New Conversions" the next year, with a concomitant reorganization of the Franciscan mission system (Hackett 1926: 360; BL 1695a). At this time, San Antonio proper was re-

ported to have some 60 Indian families. The satellite parishes associated with it were Guadalupe (located some two leagues upriver), with 34 families, and San Pablo, with 30 families (BL 1695a).

It is not clear what the makeup of the population was at this time, beyond the fact that these Indians were some kind of "Conchos." The people at Julimes were Julimes, and apparently the Mamites lived rather close by and were no doubt included in the population figures for the above settlements. In 1710 the people of San Antonio were said to be "Conchos" (AHP 1710a); they possessed a town government of Indian officials, which included a *gobernador,* a *teniente,* an *alcalde,* and "others." San Pablo was at this time the only settlement belonging to Julimes, Guadalupe having been abandoned some time earlier (AHP 1710b).

By 1712, the Indian population of San Antonio was considerably reduced from what it had been in 1693. At this later time, it was reported that the towns of San Antonio and San Pablo contained only 30 men who were able to bear arms – all the rest were too old. The writer of this report, Fray Manuel Colomo, requested that another town be established with some 300 Tarahumaras, at a nearby place named San Diego, four leagues from Julimes; this was apparently a suggestion to create a buffer town for the defense of the area from the more warlike tribes to the north and east (BL 1709-1715). About this time Julimes seemingly did receive some new immigrants, for in 1715 it was reported that Indians who had abandoned the town of Santa Cruz de Ochanes had now settled at San Antonio (AHP 1715Ac). Fifty years later, in 1765, Bishop Tamarón reported that the town of Julimes was still a cabecera with one visita, San Pablo. The population at Julimes, he stated, consisted of 52 Indians, making up seven families (Tamarón 1937: 155).

The parish records (located today both at Julimes and at Aquiles Serdán, Chihuahua), which begin earlier and are somewhat more complete than those extant for many other missions, indicate that the native population of this town was quite heterogeneous during the 18th century. A summary of the various tribal groups that appear in the church books between the years 1719 and 1751 is given in Table 5. In the early years Julimes and Yauchanes (Ochanes or Nauchanes) occur with the highest frequency; the number of Indians from the La Junta district is fairly high. As time draws on, the Tarahumara immigrants into the area increase.

After about 1760, the numbers of Spaniards and of the various caste groups jump considerably; concomitantly, the Indians begin to disappear rapidly, and when the term *indio* does occur, the ethnic group is not usually cited. A count of the baptisms for the years 1761 through 1767 reveals this fact strikingly. During this seven–year period, only ten children of Indian parents were given the rite; eight had no ethnic or other affiliation, and the other two were a Tarahumara and an Indian from Cusihuiriachi, almost certainly also a Tarahumara. By contrast, baptisms of mixed bloods, mostly designated as *mestizos* (but including 17 *coyotes,* two *lobos,*

TABLE 5

**San Antonio de Julimes:
Indians Cited in Parish Records by Group
or Place of Origin, 1719-1751**

	1719–1723	1724–1728	1729–1733	1734–1739	1740–1750	1751–
Apaches			10	3	5	6
Babonoyaba					1	
Chiso		1				
Cholomes		2	3		2	4
Chuvíscar					1	
Cíbolos	2	1				
Concho		1				1
Conejos		2				
Coyame				2	1	
Cuchillo Parado				2	5	1
del Norte	1		1	2		8
El Paso			1			
Gentilidad					3	
Jobome		2				
Julimes	5	6				2
La Joya					1	
Las Cruces					1	
Las Cuevas					1	
Mame (Mamite)		1				
Mayo River					1	
Mazas River		1				
New Mexico		1			1	
Palmar		1				
Palo Blanco	1					
Papigochi					1	
San Andrés				2		
San Francisco de Conchos				1	3	
San Lorenzo				1	1	
San Pablo				2	12	
Santa Cruz (?)						1
Satevó				1	1	
Sonora		1		2	1	1
Tarahumaras					6	9
Yauchanes	4					

Source: Parish Records, Julimes and Aquiles Serdán, Chihuahua.

and 16 *mulatos*), numbered 60, and baptisms of people classified as Spaniards were by far the most frequent, totaling 94. In only five entries was the ethnic or caste affiliation unstated. The marriage records for this period reflect approximately the same proportions. It would seem, despite other reports of this century, that the aboriginal population of this region was essentially a minority at this time (Aquiles Serdán Parish Records).

In one portion of the 1789 report of the Bishop of Durango, it was noted that the population and language of the Julimes mission was Cholome, but elsewhere it was stated that the Indians of the town were Tarahumaras and Julimeños (BL 1789a; 1789b). Apparently, by this time the term "Julimeños" meant the conglomeration of Indians that called the town of Julimes their home; unfortunately, there is no further information that can assist in interpreting the discrepancy in the two sections of the 1789 report – Julimeños might have been largely Cholomes at this time (possibly they always had been). At any rate, many persons from La Junta had now migrated into the town.

The Indian population of the mission at the time of this bishop's visit was given as 76 souls (BL 1789b); 40 of these, according to the military *padrón* or census of two years earlier, were on the list of Indian auxiliaries for this town (BL 1787). A report for 1793 showed an increase in population over the immediately previous censuses, with a total of 112 people (Bancroft 1884: 657, fn. 39). In 1816 and 1817, the native residents of the town were said to be Julimeños and Tarahumaras, totaling 58 persons in 1816 and 64 in 1817 (AGN 1816). It is probably an indication of the general heterogeneity of the region at the time of the 1789 report that the surrounding or nearby nations were said, strangely enough, to be Yaquis, Pimas (!), and Chinarras (BL 1789b); in the 1816–1818 reports adjacent groups were Yaquis, Chicharras (probably Chinarras), Papes (?), and Apaches (AGN 1816). Apparently the latter report was largely repeating the report made a quarter–century earlier.*

Nuestra Señora de Guadalupe

The place or parish of Nuestra Señora de Guadalupe was (and still is) located on the San Pedro River about midway between the missions of San Antonio de Julimes and San Pablo. There are only a few references to it in the documents of the period. This may have been the location of a Franciscan hacienda, and also of a Cholomes-Sumas settlement (AHP 1688Cb). There is no further information on the ethnic affiliation of the inhabitants of this site.

In 1693, Guadalupe was reported to be one of the pueblos administered by the Franciscan mission of San Pedro de Conchos. At this time the visita of Guadalupe had an Indian population of 34 families (Hackett 1926: 360; BL 1695a). By 1710, it was reported that the town had been abandoned, at least for three years or so, but that it formerly was the place where the Nauchanes (Yauchanes, Aochanes) Indians had been settled (AHP 1710b).

San Pablo

The founding date of the visita of San Pablo (today, Meoqui, Chihuahua) is unknown. However, at least in the later years of the 17th century San Pablo was one of the satellites of San Pedro de Conchos. Later, when Julimes

---

*In the latter part of the colonial period, San Antonio was sometimes called San Andrés de Julimes (AGN 1790a; 1790b; 1790c; 1816).

became a principal or cabecera mission, San Pablo was transferred to it, together with the parish of Nuestra Señora de Guadalupe.

San Pablo seems clearly to have been a Concho Indian settlement. In 1693 it consisted of 30 families. A 1710 report refers to the Indian officials of San Pablo; testimonies in the early 1720s noted that in the formal political structure of the town the highest official was a *teniente* (one person said *alcalde*) under the governor of Julimes. By 1765, San Pablo, the only remaining visita of the Julimes mission, was reported to have a total Indian population of 36 persons, making up eight families (Hackett 1926: 360; Tamarón 1937: 155; AHP 1710b; 1723A; BL 1695a).

Bachimba

The site of Bachimba, located west of Julimes and northwest of San Pablo, was apparently the location of a ranchería of Conchos Indians in the early years of Spanish entry into the area. In later years it became a Spanish hacienda and in 1710 this hacienda belonged to one Fernando Colomo. By 1716 Bachimba was said to be abandoned (UTD 1715a; CPP 23: 528-32), but in 1730 it was reported to be an hacienda that employed many Cholome Indians on its labor force (AHP 1730Cb). The name was once rendered as Ibachimba (AHP 1684Da).

Santiago de Babonoyaba

Santiago de Babonoyaba (variants: Bamonoyaba [AHP 1653Bc; UTL 1619], Banonoyaba [AGN 1640], Bobonoyaba [Kinnaird 1958: 133], Babonoyagua [AHP 1723A; UTD 1715a]) was one of the early Franciscan missions for Conchos Indians, although it was heavily Tarahumara in later years. It was located on the Santa Isabel River, only some three leagues away from the Jesuit mission of Satevó. During the 18th century, the mission was described as having a visita named Guadalupe, some five leagues distant (Tamarón 1937: 139; AHP 1700b). Arlegui, noting that the mission possessed two pueblos, Babonoyaba and Guadalupe, added another place called La Joya; the parish, at the time of his writing in the 1730s, included many persons dispersed along the edge of the river. There were also several Spanish haciendas in the area (Arlegui 1851: 97; Sauer 1934: 61).

Arlegui cites 1665 as the founding year for this mission, while Urrízar cites 1649 (Arlegui 1851: 97; López-Velarde 1964: 99). However, there was some kind of Franciscan holding here even before 1649, and the site was known at least by 1619 (UTL 1619). As early as 1640, Fray Hernando de Urbaneja was reported to be the missionary at Babonoyaba (AGN 1640). Later, in some papers of Governor Diego Guajardo Fajardo dating from the Tarahumara uprising of 1648, it was recorded that Hernando de Urbaneja of the Order of Saint Francis was the *guardián* of the convent of Santiago de Babonoyaba de los Conchos (UTD 1648). In this same year, General Juan de Barraza noted that Urbaneja was guardian of this convent (which he called variously

Papasalagua, Pagalagua, Bamonayama, and Banonayama, apparently referring to the same place) as well as of the convent of San Pedro (CPP 7: 406-12). Urbaneja stayed on as resident priest of this mission until at least the mid-1650s (AHP 1655A).

Babonoyaba is often considered to be a Tarahumara mission, and these were the people who occupied it in later years. During the earlier period, however, it seems to have been entirely or predominantly Concho – as the abovementioned name, Santiago de Babonoyaba de los Conchos, indicates. In 1619, when Governor Albear stopped here during his campaign against the Tepehuan, the *puesto de Bamonoyava* was described as Concho (UTL 1619); later, in 1653, the Indian governor of the Western Conchería, said to be a Concho, was a resident of Babonoyaba (AHP 1652B). However, in this same year Babonoyaba was reported as one of the pueblos that had taken part in the recent Tarahumara rebellion (AHP 1653Ba; 1687Ac). Other information indicates that the mission at this time was mainly Concho but also included some Tarahumaras (AHP 1656A). Reference was made to a Tarahumara who lived at Babonoyaba in 1655 (AHP 1655A), and Tarahumaras were reported from here in 1697, 1700, and 1704. In 1700 the Indian governor of Babonoyaba was a Tarahumara named Don Nicolás, and in 1717 the Jesuit Arias considered the mission to be essentially Tarahumara (AHP 1700b; BL 1697-1703; CPP 24: 181-4; DHM 1704).

It appears likely that some Conchos were moved into this town by the Spaniards themselves. The Jesuits, in the 1660s and 1670s, claimed that Conchos had been transferred by the Franciscans to their Tarahumara missions. The men of Saint Francis had done this, it was alleged, in order to be able to claim that their missions consisted of Conchos Indians, in keeping with the original agreement that the Jesuits would have the Tarahumaras, and the Franciscans the Conchos (AGN 1677a; 1677b; 1677c). With the scanty historical documentation available, it is impossible to assess the truth of this assertion that Franciscans had settled Conchos in Tarahumara communities. One possible source of such Concho settlers may have been a group numbering some 170 who, according to administrative reports, moved to Babonoyaba from the San Pedro mission after the 1645 revolt because of a famine that occurred at the downriver site (CD 1650a).

The Jesuit allegations do appear to be supported by one earlier document, dating from January 4, 1640. It states that several Tarahumara with their chief Hernando appeared before the Nueva Vizcayan governor with a complaint. They claimed that Fray Hernando de Urbaneja had brought into and settled at the mission many Conchos from a number of different places and that these Conchos were causing a great deal of trouble with the Tarahumara population already settled there – taking away from them their womenfolk, lands, and corn. Hernando and the other Tarahumaras requested that these Conchos be ordered out of Babonoyaba and back

Church at Bachimba, Chihuahua

to their own pueblos, because Conchos and Tarahumaras were so antagonistic to each other (AGN 1640).

Taking this information at face value, by 1640 the area of Tarahumara settlement came very close to, or even included, Babonoyaba. However, this situation may have been well established even earlier than 1640, considering that Spanish penetration in the southern Chihuahua area had begun some 70 years earlier, and Spanish settlement always brought some shifts in the aboriginal population owing to the Spaniards' great demand for labor, the introduction of alien diseases, and the like. Because the earlier references to Babonoyaba, including the first one in 1619, cite Conchos Indians, and because the general trend under colonial conditions was for many of the Tarahumara to migrate somewhat eastward and northward (see Chapter 8), it would appear that in the earliest years of Spanish occupation of the region Babonoyaba was principally a Concho settlement located adjacent to the Tarahumara-Concho border. In the later years of the colonial period, as noted above, Babonoyaba was certainly a Tarahumara town. This is recorded a number of times not only in the documentary sources on Babonoyaba itself (see below), but also in church records of other places where the place of origin of the neophytes is sometimes noted.

The Bishop of Durango reported in 1751 that Babonoyaba had only a few Indians. He personally had not visited this spot but said he had been shown the parish records by the priest of the town (UTD 1742–1754). This may have been faulty information, for in 1765 Bishop Tamarón reported that Babonoyaba possessed a population of 203 Indians, making up 50 families; one visita, Guadalupe, had 100 persons (40 families), and the other, La Concepción, had 90 people (28 families) (Tamarón 1937: 139). While later reports cited Babonoyaba specifically as a Tarahumara town, Lafora, in 1767, made a curious statement: he cited no population figures for the mission, but said that it was inhabited by some "civilized" people and Tepehuan Indians (Kinnaird 1958: 133).

The census taken at the time of the inspection tour of the Bishop of Durango in 1789 denoted Babonoyaba as a Tarahumara mission with 142 persons – 116 adults and 26 children (BL 1789a; 1789b); according to a military census of two years earlier, the Indian auxiliary detachment numbered 47 persons (the list included the men, their wives, and their families) (BL 1787). In 1793, Babonoyaba was said to have 192 people (Bancroft 1884: 657, fn. 39). Six years later, in 1799, the census recorded a population of 28 men and 35 women (a total of 63 persons), with the note that there were no Spaniards or persons of other classes (*castas*) in this town; however, the total population was stated to be 160 persons (BL 1799), which was probably a more accurate figure, in view of the previous censuses and the apparent omission of children from the stated numbers of men and women. The 1816 and 1817 figures note, respectively, 43 and 53 adult neophytes, and 62 and 73 children, which give totals of 105 and 126 persons (AGN 1816).

Alabachi

Alabachi was reported in the 1650s to be a Concho settlement, located west of San Pedro in the direction of Satevó, on the border with the Tarahumara country (near Babonoyaba?). It quite clearly was a mixed settlement; on one occasion Tarahumara women were said to live here, and the Conchos living here were reported to speak the Tarahumara language (AHP 1654Aa; 1655A).

Santa Isabel

The mission of Santa Isabel (today, General Trías), lying southwest of the present-day Chihuahua City, was one of the most important of the Franciscan missions of the central Chihuahua river valleys. Urrízar records the date of its founding as 1664; and Arlegui as 1668 (López-Velarde 1964: 99; Arlegui 1851: 97). However, the spot, some eight leagues from Babonoyaba, was visited in the fall of 1649 by the Spanish governor Guajardo, and again in the spring of 1650 by Fray Lorenzo Canto, who referred to it as "el pueblo y dotrina de Santa Ysabel de nra administracion" (Hackett 1926: 166; CPP 7: 595-601; 8: 2-9, 13-7). In 1651, and again two years later, the place was stated to be a Franciscan town (AGN 1651; AHP 1653Ba; 1687Ac). One would guess that quite likely Santa Isabel had visita status at this time. Even earlier, Montaño de la Cueva in 1645 had referred to a town called Santa Isabel, lying roughly in this area (CD 1650a).

By the early 1690s, Santa Isabel was one of the largest of the missions of the Franciscan system, administering to some nine towns, although it had only one missionary in 1693 (Hackett 1926: 360; BL 1695a).

Immediately preceding the reorganization of the Franciscan missions, around 1694, information was collected concerning the state of the Santa Isabel mission. The circumference of the mission, the perimeter around all of its towns, was given variously as 50 to 70 leagues. The total population was 1,500 persons, which included newly converted pueblos in the Sierra de San Andrés and the Valle de San Rafael de Sainopa (Sainapos); apparently these pueblos are included in the maximum number of nine towns given at this time. The nine pueblos, all said to consist of Tarahumara Indians, except Nombre de Dios, were as follows: Santa Isabel, cabecera, with 70 families; San Bernardino (San Bernardo?), located five leagues from Santa Isabel, with 30 families; San Juan de la Concepción, nine leagues from the cabecera, and Santa Cruz, with a combined total of 70 families; San Bernabé, five leagues from Santa Isabel (no population figures given); Sainapos or Sainápuchi, 14 leagues from Santa Isabel, with 40 families; San Andrés, five leagues from Santa Isabel, with 120 families; Chubisca (Chu-

víscar), five leagues from Santa Isabel and four from Nombre de Dios, with 44 families; and Nombre de Dios, nine or ten leagues from Santa Isabel, with 40 families of Conchos Indians (BL 1695a).

When Arlegui wrote in the early 1730s, he noted that the mission of Santa Isabel de Tarcimares (*sic* – Tarahumares, according to 18th-century baptismal records) administered some six pueblos (1851: 97). However, in the census of 1728 only three visitas were listed. These satellite towns were La Concepción, Santa Cruz, and San Bernardo (AHP 1728Aa). In 1765 Bishop Tamarón recorded the same three visitas for the mission (Tamarón 1937: 152). In 1728, the organization of the town of Santa Isabel proper consisted of the positions of *governador, teniente de gobernador, alcalde, capitán, alguacil,* three *topiles, alférez, sargento,* five *fiscales,* ten *cantores,* and seven *sacristanes* (AHP 1728Aa).

In April 1643 there is mention of 15 Tarahumaras from a settlement called Santa Isabel (this same place?), and all subsequent references note that Santa Isabel was Tarahumara (AHP 1653Ba; 1687Ac; BL 1697-1703; 1789a; 1789b; CPP 24: 181-4; DHM 1704). Nevertheless, in 1653, when two Conchos Indians testified in Parral regarding their communication with Tarahumaras, one said he was from the town of Santa Isabel, the other from the *partido* (district) of Santa Isabel (AHP 1652D). A year later, another Concho stated while testifying in Parral that he was from the town of Santa Isabel, some 35 or more leagues from Parral (apparently, this same Santa Isabel) (AHP 1654A).

The total population of the mission in 1728 was listed as 282 adult males (AHP 1728Aa). In 1751 the Bishop of Durango reported only a few Indians dwelling here, but he also noted that there were a few Spaniards and mulattoes living scattered along either side of the river that ran by the town (UTD 1742-1754). Fourteen years later, Bishop Tamarón recorded 41 families comprising 185 Indians (Tamarón 1937: 152). In 1787, 164 Indians were listed on the garrison rolls as auxiliaries (this figure includes wives and children) (BL 1787). In the census given in the 1789 report of the Bishop of Durango, the total population of the mission (apparently including the satellite parishes, although these are not mentioned specifically), was 425 souls (BL 1789a; 1789b). Four years later, in 1793, Santa Isabel was censused at 657, an increase of more than 230 persons (Bancroft 1884: 657, fn. 39). By 1816 and 1817, the total figures had dropped to 344 and 325 respectively (AGN 1816).

The highly fragmentary extant parish records do little to clarify the situation of Santa Isabel. There is record of a few baptisms beginning in 1762. When tribal identities are stated, only Tarahumaras are mentioned; otherwise the places of origin are usually given, and these are for the most part known to be Tarahumara towns or settlements. These places included, in 1762, the visitas of Santa Cruz and San Bernardino; in 1763, La Concepción, San Bernardino, San Andrés, and Santa Cruz, the latter having the highest number of entries; in 1765, Cusihuiriachi, Santa Cruz, San Bernardino, and La Concepción; in 1767, Santa Cruz, San Bernardino, La Purísima Concepción, and Cusihuiriachi; in 1768, Santa Cruz and Comorachi; in 1783, Santa Cruz and San Borja; in 1785, San Bernardino, Santa Cruz, Santa María de las Cuevas and Santa Rosalía; and in 1786, Santa Cruz, San Bernardino, Babonoyaba, San Lorenzo, and Santa Rosalía. In these sparse records for the 18th century, a few non-Indians also show up – Spaniards, Negroes, mulattoes, and mestizos.

A quick survey of some of the 19th-century parish records (1829-1832 and 1846-1848) revealed just two basic classifications for ethnic identity. About three-quarters of the entries cite the persons involved as *vecinos,* and the remaining one-fourth record *indígenas.* Today, the local population has about the same appearance as the general northern Mexican mestizo population.

La Concepción

La Concepción (or San Juan de la Concepción) was a visita of the Santa Isabel mission, and it remained so to the end of the colonial period. The spot was visited at least by the latter part of 1694 (CPP 7: 595-601; 8: 2-9). In 1693 La Concepción was reported to possess 70 families of Indians (although this count apparently included the settlement of Santa Cruz) (BL 1695a). The town was visited by Retana in 1701; he reported that it contained 17 families of Indians, as well as 10 more men who worked on haciendas in the area (AHP 1701). According to the 1728 mission *padrón* or census, La Concepción had a total population of 33 adult males; only 12 were reported as able to work, and 13 were classified as old men and not fit for labor. The administration of the town at this time consisted of a *teniente* [*de gobernador*], an *alcalde,* a *capitán,* an *alguacil,* and four *fiscales* (AHP 1728Aa).

In 1765 Bishop Tamarón recorded 21 Indian families, with 61 persons, for this visita. At this time, it was said to be located some 17½ leagues to the west of Santa Isabel (an earlier document stated only nine leagues – see *Santa Isabel,* above), and the Indians were living scattered about the area (*dispersos*) (Tamarón 1937: 152).

Santa Cruz

In the 1690s Santa Cruz was reported to be a Tarahumara town, visita of Santa Isabel, and located between Santa Isabel and Babonoyaba (BL 1695A; 1697-1703). The 1728 *padrón,* or census, listed the names of some 98 adult males. Of these, 34 were old men (that is, not fit for work) and 51 were capable of working; the remaining 13 were town officials. According to the same source, the Spanish organization of the town included a *teniente* [*de gobernador*], an *alcalde,* a *capitán,* two *topiles,* a *sargento,* an *alguacil,* an *alférez,* and five *fiscales* (AHP 1728Aa). In 1765, Bishop Tamarón reported that this visita of Santa Isabel had 89

families consisting of some 319 Indians. The site was said to be some six leagues south of its cabecera (Tamarón 1937: 152).

San Bernardo

San Bernardo was a satellite parish of the mission of Santa Isabel, and was apparently the same place as San Bernardino. In 1666, Governor Oca Sarmiento stated that San Bernardo was a Concho settlement (BL 1649-1700); however, later, in the 1690s, its population was reported to be Tarahumara (BL 1695a). According to the names in the *padrón* of 1728, the town possessed a population of 68 adult males, including 25 old men and 30 who were fit for work. The town organization consisted of a *teniente* [*de gobernador*], an *alcalde,* a *capitán,* a *topil,* a *sargento,* an *aguacil,* and five *fiscales* (AHP 1728Aa). In 1765, Bishop Tamarón stated that San Bernardino, which had remained a satellite parish of Santa Isabel, consisted of 34 Indian families, totaling 88 people (Tamarón 1937: 152).

San Andrés

San Andrés (today, Riva Palacio) apparently owed its inception as a principal (cabecera) mission to the reorganization of the Franciscan mission system in 1694. However, Almada gives the date 1696, citing Fray Alonso de Victorino as the founder and noting that the original name at this time was San Andrés de Osaguiqui (Almada 1968: 463). In any event, San Andrés had previously formed part of the mission of Santa Isabel. It was visited in the fall of 1649 by Governor Guajardo Fajardo, and in the spring of the following year by Fray Lorenzo Canto; the latter called it the *pueblo y doctrina de San Andrés,* five leagues from Santa Isabel (Arlegui 1851: 97; Hackett 1926: 166; BL 1695a; CPP 7: 595-601; 8: 2-9, 13-7).

According to Arlegui, San Andrés as a cabecera consisted of seven towns, but he did not give their names (Arlegui 1851: 97). However, San Bernabé (once a visita of Santa Isabel [BL 1695a; AHP 1730Ca]) and another place named Santa Rosa (possibly the same place as the Rancho de Santa Rosa, the lands of which were originally claimed in 1699 by Bernabé Márquez [Almada 1968: 494; AHP 1706]) were both stated at one time or another to be visitas of San Andrés. Most probably Sainapos (Sainápuchi) was a satellite, and possibly also San Diego del Monte; in 1701, Juan de Retana, while not stating explicitly that any towns were visitas, did note that San Bernabé, Santa Rosa, and Sainapos were associated with San Andrés (AHP 1701).

San Andrés was always a Franciscan mission for Tarahumaras (AHP 1653Ba; 1653Bc; 1723A; 1731A; BL 1789B; DHM 1704), although it was said to be located near the border of Concho country (AHP 1684Ab; CPP 9: 527-30; 15: 527-34). In 1693, San Andrés had a population of 120 Tarahumara families (BL 1695a). In 1765, Bishop Tamarón gave a fairly complete report on the mission. San Andrés was still a cabecera at this time, administered by Franciscans;

it consisted of 68 Indian families with 183 persons, plus another 210 persons *de razón* (non-Indians). He cited two satellite parishes of San Andrés: San Bernabé and another called San Buenaventura, which today seems to be unidentifiable (see Tamarón 1937: 163, fn.). San Buenaventura was said to be six leagues from San Andrés and to possess 130 families consisting of 394 Indians (Tamarón 1937: 151). In 1789, San Andrés had a population of 118 Tarahumaras (only 12 of whom were children) (BL 1789a; 1789b), but four years later the total was reported as 170, possibly including more children at this time (Bancroft 1884: 657, fn. 39). In the years 1816 and 1817 (for which no information on visitas is given), the population consisted of 178 Tarahumara Indians, about half of whom were children (AGN 1816).

San Bernabé

San Bernabé was visited in May of 1650 by Fray Lorenzo Canto, who reported it to be six long leagues from the town of San Andrés. At this time he listed it as a *pueblo y doctrina,* saying that it had a number of good (apparently, well populated) settlements. However, it did not have either church or convent, and Fray Canto designated places where these should be built. He had baptized 17 children and the wife of the son of the cacique named Bernabé. He recounted that because he began the ministering of the Holy Sacraments here, he gave the place the name of San Bernabé del Nombre de Dios (Hackett 1926: 166; CPP 8: 13-7). While not explicitly stated at this time, there is little doubt that this was Tarahumara country; in 1653, San Bernabé was referred to as if it were a Tarahumara town, together with Santa Isabel, San Andrés, and Chubisca (Chuvíscar) (AHP 1730Ca).

A 1693 report listed San Bernabé as one of the visitas of Santa Isabel (five leagues away), but no population for the place was given (BL 1695a). Later, in 1765, Bishop Tamarón stated this town was 10 leagues to the northwest of San Andrés and at the time of his report possessed 64 families of Indians, totaling 210 persons (Tamarón 1937: 151).

San Miguel

In 1685, San Miguel was mentioned together with a number of other Nueva Vizcayan *reducciones*; it was probably a satellite parish of one of the better-known cabeceras. In 1690, a rancheria of Conchos was said to reside here. The site was apparently in the area of Queparipa and Guainopa, between Bachíniva and Namiquipa (AHP 1684Da; 1688A).

Guainopa

Guainopa was possibly one of the satellite parishes that belonged either to Santa Isabel or to San Andrés. In 1690 it was reported to be a Concho Indian settlement (AHP 1688A); otherwise its history is unknown.

San Gregorio de Yaguna

San Gregorio de Yaguna (also, Ayaguna), nine leagues from San Bernabé, was cited in 1650 as a "town and mission (*doctrina*)" by Fray Lorenzo Canto when he visited the spot. Canto and his group stayed here a couple of days and were visited by most of the people from a settlement named San Diego, which lay six leagues away; they came with their cacique, Don Lorenzo. At this time 37 children were baptized, making a total of 54 baptized persons at this place, according to Canto (Hackett 1926: 166; CPP 8: 13-7).

San Diego

A place named San Diego, possibly in Tarahumara territory or on the border, was claimed by Franciscans (AHP 1653Aa; 1653Ba; 1653Bc). However, it may have been Concho, and some Conchos were apparently living here at the end of the 17th century, if documentary identifications are correct. Once in the mid-1600s, some Tepehuanes who were passing through the area reported that at San Diego they had encountered a well-dressed Concho who was recruiting Indians to work on the harvest at Spanish holdings (AHP 1655A).

The earliest mention of San Diego occurs in the reports of Governor Guajardo Fajardo, who visited the settlement in the fall of 1649. It was in the following spring that the people from San Diego made the visit to San Gregorio mentioned in the above entry (Hackett 1926: 166; CPP 7: 595-601; 8: 2-9, 13-7).

In the last decade of the 17th century, a town that was apparently the same one cited in mid-century is given the fuller name of San Diego del Monte or San Diego del Monte y la Sierra. It was listed as a Concho settlement, and at least two Concho town governors lived here; in 1695, the town governor was Juan Corma, the same man who later turned up as a Concho governor at Casas Grandes in the attempted revolt of 1697 (AHP 1695; BL 1697-1703). The Indian governor of the Western Conchería also resided here in 1692 (AHP 1692A). While no explicit statement appears in the sources, it is difficult to imagine that San Diego was not a visita of one of the missions, probably of Santa Isabel, San Andrés, or both. Today, there is a rancho or community called Morelos at the location of San Diego del Monte in the area of Cuauhtémoc, Chihuahua (Almada 1968: 481).

Queparipa

In 1690 Queparipa was reported to be a rancheria or settlement of Concho Indians, apparently in the general area of San Miguel and Guainopa (AHP 1688A). It was possibly a visita of one of the missions of the region.

Sainapos

Sainapos, or Sainápuchi, was listed as a Tarahumara town and visita of Santa Isabel in 1694. It was located 14 leagues from its cabecera and 9 leagues from San Andrés, which was on the same road.

According to the 1694 report, Sainapos had just recently been missionized and had 40 Indian families. Later on, it most probably fell within the jurisdiction of San Andrés when the latter became a separate cabecera mission. Unfortunately, no other references to the history of Sainapos are extant (AHP 1701; BL 1695a).

Nombre de Dios

The mission of Nombre de Dios was located about one league from the spot where the city of Chihuahua was later founded, and it now lies within the limits of the greatly expanded capital city. Arlegui recorded that Nombre de Dios was founded in 1697 (Arlegui 1851: 98); however, before this date, in 1694, it had been cited as a satellite of the mission of Santa Isabel (BL 1695a), but it is uncertain when missionization actually began in this immediate area. Almada notes, however, that Nombre de Dios was founded (in the sense of some kind of formal Spanish recognition) in 1678, when governor Sierra y Osorio named Captain Juan de Portillo as protector of the Conchos Indians located at this spot (Almada 1968: 363).

The population of this mission was made up of Conchos Indians; people of this nation were reported here in 1690 (AHP 1688A), in 1693 (BL 1695a), in 1698 (AHP 1697Aa), and in 1712 (BL 1709–1715). In 1716, some Chinarras living at Nombre de Dios moved to Santa Ana de Chinarras (CPP 24: 150-1). Later, the ethnic composition of the population changed, as is noted below. The Concho name for Nombre de Dios was Navocolaba (AHP 1688A).

At least from the 1730s into the 1760s, Nombre de Dios possessed three visitas. The Bishops of Durango, in 1751 and 1765, stated that San Cristóbal del Nombre de Dios, one and a half leagues from San Felipe el Real (Chihuahua City), administered the satellites of San Gerónimo, San Antonio de Chuvisca, and San Juan de los Alamillos, the latter possibly some eight leagues north of San Gerónimo (Arlegui 1851: 98; Tamarón 1937: 154, 166; UTD 1742–1754).

In 1765, Bishop Tamarón reported that at the cabecera, Nombre de Dios proper, the population consisted of 18 families, totaling 100 Indians. These people, however, lived away from the mission, near their fields, and consequently the mission site consisted only of the church and the missionary's house. The visita (here said to be a *sitio*) of San Juan del Alamillo had only 28 Indians at the time of his inspection (Tamarón 1937: 154). Unfortunately, neither Tamarón nor Lafora two years later recorded what kind of Indians inhabited the mission. Lafora only noted that Nombre de Dios was an Indian town (Kinnaird 1958: 70). However, previous to this, at the beginning of 1751, Nombre de Dios was said to have both Tarahumaras and Conchos in its population (UTD 1749b).

In 1789, the Bishop of Durango reported that the mission possessed a total of 194 souls, made up of Norteño and Tarahumara Indians (BL 1789a; 1789b). Four years later, in 1793, this number had jumped to 262 (Bancroft 1884: 657, fn. 39). In the 1816 and 1817 censuses, the figures were 138 and 158, respectively; again the ethnic identification was given as Tarahumara and Norteño (AGN 1816). The fact that Norteños are reported here into the 19th century indicates that La Junta peoples continued to settle in the Chihuahua area much as they had in the early 1730s, according to Arlegui's remarks on the Chihuahua convent (Arlegui 1851: 100).

Chuvíscar

Chuvíscar,* still in existence today a few miles west and slightly south of Chihuahua City, was originally an Indian settlement, apparently of Tarahumaras. In 1653, there is a reference to the rancherías of Chuvisca that were governed by a Don Bernabé, and the settlement is treated, though not explicitly identified, as a Tarahumara place (AHP 1653Ba; 1653Bc); later, in 1684, a Tarahumara is cited as being from a place called San Antonio Chubisca (AHP 1684Db). Nevertheless, Chuvíscar seems to have been about at the edge of the Tarahumara, bordering on Concho territory. In 1710, a number of Conchos met here for a junta, and Chuvíscar, together with a number of Concho rancherías, was reported to have admitted "evil talks" from the Tarahumara country (AHP 1710a).

Before 1694, Chubisca was a visita of Santa Isabel; sometime after this date it was transferred to Nombre de Dios (Arlegui 1851: 98; BL 1695a). In 1693, the settlement had a population of 44 families; 72 years later, in 1765, Bishop Tamarón reported 42 families, totaling 123 persons (Tamarón 1937: 154). Unfortunately, the Bishop of Durango in 1751 merely noted that San Antonio de Chuvisca was an Indian town, and a visita of Nombre de Dios; no data on population or ethnic identity of the populace were given (UTD 1742–1754). Chuvíscar is not mentioned again with respect to Indians, as a visita or otherwise, except in 1787. On a military census for this year it is recorded that there were some 61 Indian auxiliaries at Chuvíscar; this number included 12 children (BL 1787).

San Gerónimo

San Gerónimo (today, Villa Aldama) possessed a Franciscan mission in the early years of the 18th century, but the area was settled and the site named considerably earlier. In 1671, Captain Pedro Cano de los Ríos claimed land here, four leagues below the hacienda of Tabalaopa. Ten years later the lands of San Gerónimo, including water rights, were sold to the Apresa y Falcón family. A town was founded at San Gerónimo by 1707, and somewhat before 1717 the Franciscans established their mission of the same name there, as a satellite of Nombre de Dios. In 1717 the Jesuits founded their own mission of Santa Ana de Chinarras nearby (AGN 1725; AHP 1684Aa; Almada 1968: 25)

Practically no information on the parish exists until the latter part of the 1700s. After the Jesuit demise in 1767, San Gerónimo acquired the mission of Santa Ana as part of its

---

*The early rendering of this name is usually Chubisca or Chuvisca, the terminal "r" becoming more frequent in later times. In 1710, it was recorded once as Chiguisca (AHP 1710a).

own establishment. According to Almada, San Gerónimo was then abandoned two years later, in 1769, when Apaches killed 49 persons and carried off another 10 from here and from Santa Ana. San Gerónimo was not (officially) refounded until 1783, when a commission from the General Commander of the Provincias Internas was issued for this purpose (Almada 1968: 25). Unfortunately, such official documentation does not reflect the stability in the local population (or even a possible increase) that seems to have obtained during this interim, to judge from other sources.

In 1765, Bishop Tamarón y Romeral recorded that this *visita* of Nombre de Dios had its own missionary. The population consisted of 121 persons, in 23 families, and the people were quite scattered about the area (as they were at Nombre de Dios), apparently dwelling near their fields (Tamarón 1937: 154). In 1789, according to the report of the Bishop of Durango, the population of San Gerónimo had increased to some 201 Indians (BL 1789a; 1789b); however, Bancroft (1884: 657, fn. 39) seems to give 189 for this same year. Two years earlier, in 1787, 67 Indians (24 men, plus their wives and families) were listed as auxiliaries; they served at the royal presidio of San Carlos, which had been erected nearby (BL 1787). In 1817, the native population was recorded as 205 persons; the total population for the immediate area, however, was 2,887. This last number included 1,181 Spaniards and 1,501 people of other *castas* – mestizos, Negroes, and mulattoes (BL 1817). Apparently owing to the small number of Indians, the mission portion of the San Gerónimo jurisdiction had been secularized in 1791 (AGN 1816).

Statements made in 1716, at the time of the founding of Santa Ana de Chinarras, indicate that San Gerónimo was located in traditional Chinarra and/or Concho territory. At the same time, it was noted that some Tarahumaras were living at San Gerónimo proper, and a year later, possibly with exaggeration, it was referred to as a Tarahumara mission by the Jesuit Antonio Arias (CPP 24: 132-4, 181-9). In 1767, Lafora also recorded that there were Tarahumaras dwelling here (Kinnaird 1958: 70-1). The Bishop of Durango stated in his 1789 report that the ethnic affiliation of the indigenous portion of the populace was Tarahumara and Chinarra (BL 1789a; 1789b).

Only a few fragmentary church records dating from the 18th century remain at the parish church at Aldama. These, however, may not cover exactly the same population as the above reports, since they refer to the church of the San Carlos presidio and to the *santuario* of Guadalupe (just to the west of the present-day parish church). Burials at the Guadalupe chapel begin in 1741; one Mesquite Indian from the Rio Grande is recorded for this year and another for the following year. In 1743 an Apache is recorded. In the 1760s, five Cholomes, one Cíbolo, one Mesquite, three Pulicas, six Tarahumaras, and seven other persons – identified as from the Río del Norte or as Norteños – appear in the parish books. For the place called San Antonio de Chorreras, roughly to the northeast, toward La Junta, Cholomes

are mentioned in 1774 (twice), 1775 (this year, together with a Chiso woman), 1777, 1779 and 1787. In 1790 two Apaches were buried at San Carlos.

Baptisms at the San Carlos presidio record a Cholome in 1775, a Comanche from the settlement of San Antonio de Chorreras in 1785, and an Apache in 1798 (Villa Aldama Parish Records). These records do not support the general reports cited above, which state that the native population of the local San Gerónimo area consisted of Tarahumaras and Chinarras.

Santa Ana de Chinarras

Santa Ana is the only Jesuit cabecera mission in the Concho River drainage region that fell indisputably within the Conchería. Its full name was Santa Ana y San Francisco Xavier. It was founded in 1716 for some Chinarras and Concho Indians who had been living around Las Salinas, Patos, El Ojo de San Martín, El Ojo de San Miguel, and Ojo Caliente, all in the desert area between Encinillas and El Paso. At least some of these people had previously been residents of San Pedro de Conchos and Nombre de Dios, but they had left these places and had been doing some raiding in the El Paso area. Others had been living at La Candelaria, 50 leagues from San Francisco Cuéllar, near El Paso. Their chiefs' names were Don Santiago, whose rancheria was later said to be Chinarra, and Don Esteban. When the mission was established, Santiago requested that his people be settled near San Gerónimo, where their parents, grandparents, and ancestors had had their territory (he himself had been born at a *ciénega* between the entrance of the town and Tabalaopa) (AHP 1718Ae; 1723; AGN 1725; CPP 24: 120-240).

By June 14 of 1716, 77 of these Indians, plus more than 35 from Nombre de Dios and Tabalaopa, were at the Santa Ana site. By December 4, the first stone of the church had been laid. Then came a delay in getting all of the Chinarras in from the interior, because of a smallpox attack, and there arose a rumor about an Indian at Santa Ana who was accused of being a witch (*hechizero*) and of having sent the plague, and who was subsequently killed by the *teniente* of the newly established pueblo (CPP 24: 120-240).

By March 5, 1717, after a number of persons had died of this epidemic, 144 people were listed in the total population: 31 married couples; 30 widows, widowers, and unmarried adults; and 52 children, 28 of whom were girls. Later, on April 30, Arias wrote that the population had continued to increase and that the people were making progress both in school and in music. On November 27 he noted that there were still some rancherias of Chinarras that had not yet been settled. However, by December 5, 1717, he reported that there were more than 200 Chinarras living at Santa Ana. In 1717, the local Indian officials consisted of a town governor, a *teniente* [*de gobernador*], an *alcalde,* an *alguacil,* and a *fiscal* (CPP 24: 120-240).

Church of the presidio of San Carlos at Aldama, Chihuahua

Interior of the presidio church of San Carlos

Another report on the population of Santa Ana comes from the pen of the Jesuit *visitador,* Guendulain, in 1725. The mission had had only one missionary, Father Antonio de Arias, whose length of stay is unknown. After Father Arias, it had been under the rector or a missionary of the Jesuit College at Chihuahua City, some six leagues away. Guendulain reported also that Santa Ana was only a quarter of a league to the north of the Franciscan mission of San Gerónimo. On the east, north, and west were the Jesuit haciendas of Tabalaopa and Dolores. At the time of his visit the church was not yet finished, and the walls were only about two *varas* high (it was later completed and still stands today). A room in the missionary's small house was serving as a church at this time (Almada 1968: 25, 491; AGN 1725).

In 1725, 38 families were listed on the mission roster. However, Guendulain found only seven present; the others had absented themselves from the mission to look for food. This list noted several nations and languages at the mission – Conchos, Tobosos, Sumas, and Chinarras (AGN 1725).

Slightly more than a quarter of a decade later, in 1758, the Jesuit missionary of Santa Ana, Dionysio Murillo, remitted a brief but fairly complete account of the mission population. There were, at the time of his writing, 106 Indian families living at the mission. Since 1753, he reported, he had baptized 108 infants, had carried out marriages for 18 couples, and had buried 49 persons of all ages. He went on to note that in the previous year four gentile Indian women had been baptized and then had decided to take up residence at Santa Ana. One of the women, who was very old, died within a few days of her arrival; the other three were still at the mission and one had married a local Indian. At this time, he stated, most of the natives were far enough along with their Christian doctrine to be able to receive the Holy Sacrament of the Eucharist (AGN 1751–1757).

In 1765, Bishop Tamarón noted that Santa Ana had 25 families, totaling 74 Indians (Tamarón 1937: 148), a considerable drop since Murillo's report. Two years later, the military engineer Lafora, while omitting population figures, stated that the Indians at Santa Ana were Conchos (Kinnaird 1958: 70).

Tabalaopa

In the latter part of the 17th century and in the 18th century, Tabalaopa, four leagues from San Gerónimo and slightly downriver from Nombre de Dios, was the site of a Spanish hacienda of considerable importance. It was in existence at least by 1684, belonging at that time to the *fundidor* Domingo de Apresa y Falcón, but Almada seems to indicate that the hacienda of Tabalaopa was cited as early as 1671 (Almada 1968: 25; AHP 1684Db). In 1718 the Jesuits took possession of Tabalaopa, holding it until their expulsion in 1767 (AGN 1725; BL 1746; Almada 1968: 511). (Although much reduced in size, it is still a hacienda, or called such; the present main or big house – *casco* – bears a date of 1801.) (See also Arlegui 1851: 91.)

There may be a slight possibility that Tabalaopa was the same spot referred to in earlier documents as a Concho Indian settlement. Nicolás de Zepeda, in his general report on the 1644–1645 hostilities, may have referred to Tabalaopa when he noted that the rebels congregated at a place called Japalahopa (perhaps a misprint?), located on the San Pedro River (*sic*?) and on the road to New Mexico (DHM 1645). The name also occurs as Tavalaopa, and a 1684 source renders it as Tabalahopa (AHP 1684Db). In 1716, at least one of the workers at the Tabalaopa hacienda was Concho, and a number were Chinarras (CPP 24: 132–4, 150–1).

Convent of Chihuahua

The Franciscan convent of Chihuahua was established in 1715, some six years after the founding of San Felipe el Real (today, Ciudad Chihuahua) (Almada and others 1959: 39–40; Arlegui 1851: 90). Unfortunately, little is known of its role in Indian assimilation in northern Mexico, and I could locate no local parish or other records pertaining to this establishment.

In 1730, El Coyame settled here with a number of Cholomes from the Ciénega del Coyame. These people had been living on the San Pedro River at San Lucas, where some 40 families had arrived with El Coyame in 1726. These Cholomes were still administered by the convent of Chihuahua at the time of Arlegui's writing (about 1730), living along the river (Chuvíscar?). Arlegui stated that many other *norteño* families were also coming to Chihuahua to settle, attracted by their kinsmen who were already there (Arlegui 1851: 90–1, 100).

Bachíniva

To the west, and moving northward down the Santa María River, the first mission to be established was Santa María de la Natividad (Navidad, Nativitas) de Bachíniva.* It was founded in 1660, according to Arlegui, or in 1677, according to Urrízar (Arlegui 1851: 97; López–Velarde 1965: 99). Although Bachíniva enjoyed a long existence as a mission, lasting until the end of the colonial period, its history is relatively obscure. In 1694 it was called one of the "New Conversions," but it is unknown how the reorganization of the mission system at this time might have affected it (Hackett 1926: 358–60).

From its inception, Bachíniva seems to have been a Tarahumara establishment; documents concerning the 1684 hostilities of Conchos and others imply this (AHP 1684Db), and in 1698 and 1701, it is explicitly stated that Bachíniva was Tarahumara. Arlegui described the mission as administering five large towns, but left these settlements unnamed; however, he probably included Bachíniva proper in his count (Arlegui 1851: 97; CPP 24: 181–4; DHM 18thb). Of the remaining four, one was San Luis Obispo (AHP 1701; 1728Aa),

---

*Occasionally *Bachíniva* is rendered as *Bachimba,* which is not to be confused, however, with the Bachimba southeast of Chihuahua City (see p. 72).

Facade of the Jesuit Church at
Santa Ana de Chinarras (near Almada, Chihuahua)

Interior of the Jesuit Church at
Santa Ana de Chinarras

and a second was possibly the later Cossiquemachi (however, these two names may refer to the same place; see below). What other pueblos were satellites is a matter of conjecture, but since the Franciscans apparently left few settlements unministered to and outside their system, another candidate was perhaps San Diego del Monte. By 1728, however, apparently only one visita, San Luis Obispo, remained. The report for this year noted that the local organization of Bachíniva proper included one man for each of the following posts: *general, gobernador, teniente de general, alcalde, alguacil, topile, sargento, alférez, capitán, albañil, fiscal,* and *carpintero* (AHP 1728Aa).

The same 1728 census lists the names of some 193 persons living at the mission at this time. In 1765, Bishop Tamarón reported 100 Indians in 30 families at the mission,

plus another 79 natives (in 26 families) at its visita of Cossiquemachi (San Luis Obispo?) (Tamarón 1937: 149-50). Later, in 1789, Natividad de Bachíniba was said to be a cabecera mission of the jurisdiction of Cosihuiriachic; it was a Tarahumara town and consisted of 166 persons, only seven of whom were children (BL 1789a; 1789b). A report in 1793, however, gives 200 people, possibly now including more children (Bancroft 1884: 657, fn. 39). In the years 1816 and 1817, the place was listed as a Tarahumara mission, with population totals of 242 and 243, respectively (AGN 1816). While these figures indicate an overall increase in population, the numbers of adults for these years are only 126 and 124, a drop of some 30 persons since 1789. Why there should be so few children reported for the 1789 date is unknown.

The earliest extant parish books of the mission at modern Bachíniva date only from the early part of the 19th century. The books are extremely fragmentary, and the years collected run from 1806 to 1823. In these records, Indians appear to be a minority in the immediate area. In the burial records from 1806 to 1810, there is a total of 14 entries, eight of which are unclassified as to ethnic or class group; only three Indians are explicitly noted, plus one other person who is said to be half Indian and half mestizo. From 1811 to the latter part of 1815, there is a total of 31 entries, 13 of which are *indios*; the remainder are unclassified. In the baptisms for the period from 1809 to May 20, 1812, there are 29 entries, and 13 of these are said to be Indians from Bachíniva; among the latter there is one child who had an Indian mother and a mestizo father, and another whose parents came from Papigochi and were apparently Tarahumaras − although the mother's name was Serafina Suma. The baptisms for the year 1823 totaled 30 entries. Seven of those baptized were natives of Bachíniva, another was an Apache child whose parents were gentiles, and the parents of one came from San Bernabé. The remaining 21 entries included 10 Spaniards, eight mestizos, and three persons of unstated affiliation (Bachíniva Parish Records).

San Luis Obispo

The town of San Luis Obispo was a visita of the mission of Bachíniva. From the names that appear on the 1728 census, there were 173 persons living at the town at this time (this figure may be somewhat in error since some of the names taken as single names may actually be double). According to the same source, the Spanish organization of the pueblo consisted of a *teniente de gobernador,* an *alcalde,* a *capitán,* and a *cabo* (AHP 1728Aa).

Namiquipa

The mission of San Pedro de Namiquipa (called Santa Cathalina de Namiquipa once in 1666 [BL 1649-1700]) was founded in 1663, according to Arlegui, or in 1677, according to Urrízar. It administered five large Indian towns ("copiosísimos pueblos de indios"). While Arlegui leaves these settlements unnamed, he was probably including San Pedro proper; a second was Santa Clara (BL 1695a), and a third was almost certainly Las Cruces (see entry below) (DHM 18thb). According to Arlegui's account, Fray Andrés de Mendoza from Casas Grandes went to the *sierra*; after about six months of toil, he brought back some 200 families with whom he founded the Namiquipa mission (Arlegui 1851: 96-7; López-Velarde 1964: 99).

Early documents (which render the name variously as Namiquipa, Batnamiquipa, Anamiquipa, and Amiquipa) state explicitly that this was a Concho town bordering on Tarahumara country. In the 1650s, before the founding date given by Arlegui, it was called a Concho settlement, and in 1666 several rancherias of Conchos were reported living at Namiquipa proper, while others were located nearby (AHP 1653Bb; 1653Bc; BL 1649-1700). Conchos from Namiquipa are cited in 1690 (AHP 1688A), and again in 1691, when 40 Concho military auxiliaries were recruited here and sent to Commander Juan de Retana (BL 1693b); Conchos were also sent from Namiquipa in 1695 to participate in the campaign into the area of present-day Arizona and Sonora (AHP 1695). In 1697, some of the Conchos involved in the abortive revolt led by Juan Cormas, a Concho from Casas Grandes, were also reported to be from Namiquipa (AHP 1697Aa; BL 1697-1703). In 1704 Namiquipa was again called a Concho settlement (AHP 1704Ba).

As time goes on, Tarahumaras begin to show up at Namiquipa. Three are reported in 1690, and in a petition dated 15 September 1692, Fray Simón Marcos states that a number of these Indians had moved into Namiquipa after the 1690 Tarahumara revolt. In 1693 antagonism between Conchos and Tarahumaras was so grave that it almost broke out in open conflict (CPP 17: 69-72). In the course of the 18th century, this town came to have more and more non-Conchos and non-Indians in it.

One report lists Namiquipa as secularized in 1753, 90 years after the date Arlegui gives for its founding (AGN 1816). However, in 1765 Bishop Tamarón still classed Namiquipa as a mission, administered by a Franciscan. At this time it had 13 families of Indians, comprising 42 persons, plus another nine families of non-Indians, comprising 70 persons (Tamarón 1937: 150). In any event, the mission was soon to become defunct, although it is possible that the settlement was never entirely abandoned.

Thirteen years after Tamarón's account, on November 15, 1778, Don Teodoro de Croix, Comandante General of the Provincias Internas, ordered that five towns be established, with presidios, in what is now the northwestern portion of Chihuahua. One of these was Namiquipa,* which was to be formally refounded (the order reads, "in the ancient abandoned mission of San Pedro de Alcántara de Namiquipa") (document supplied by Sr. José María Cano, Namiquipa, Chihuahua; Janos Municipal Archives). However, since 1772, Namiquipa had already been serving as headquarters of the Second Flying Company, whose commander was also the chief civil administrative officer (Almada 1968: 353). A few scraps of still-existing parish records from about 1780 begin, "En esta nueba Poblazon de S.n Pedro Alcantara de Namiquipa. . . ."

In the parish records, the majority of the Indians, some explicitly called "Indian settlers," are identified as Tarahumaras or as coming from Tarahumara towns − such as Yepómera, Santo Tomás, Temósachic, Papigochic, San Borja, and Tomochic (see Map 1) − a reflection of a continuing trend of Tarahumara migration into the immediate vicinity. A few non-Tarahumara Indians show up designated as *indios norteños*; several Apaches are cited in 1780, and again in

---

*The other four were to be at Las Cruces, San Buenaventura, Casas Grandes, and Janos (see entries below).

Ruins of the church of the Santo Niño de Atocha at Casas Coloradas, Namiquipa, Chihuahua

1803, 1804, and 1805 (after which time the priest ceased to note ethnic affiliation). During the 1780s Indians occur in somewhat less than one–half of the entries; in the above-cited three years of the 19th century, Indians are listed in about 10 percent of the entries, while mestizos account for well over half of the entries (Namiquipa Parish Records).

Santa Clara

The town or settlement of Santa Clara, just east of Namiquipa, is first referred to in 1684. It was called a place (*puesto*) where Indians lived and where some Spaniards had settled, and in this year it was assaulted by a combined group of Chinarras and Janos (AHP 1684Ab; 1684Db). It already was, or it soon became, a visita of the mission of San Pedro de Namiquipa; in 1692, a statement reads, "puesto de Santa Clara, administracion del pueblo y mission de Namiquipa," 12 leagues to the east of its cabecera (BL 1695a).

As noted above, the site of Santa Clara was originally an Indian settlement. Several times around 1690 Indians were said to be living here, and Conchos were specifically cited on one occasion (AHP 1688A); in 1693, some 20 Concho families were reported to make up the population of Santa Clara. A year earlier, the place was said to have both Tarahumara and Concho Indians, although the Tarahumara lived three leagues from Santa Clara proper. It is highly probable that these Tarahumara had settled here after the 1690 Tarahumara rebellion, as was reported for Namiquipa (BL 1695a).

Las Cruces

Las Cruces was a Concho town, north of Namiquipa and also on the Santa María River (AHP 1695; 1697Aa; 1704Ba; BL 1697-1703). In 1704 it was stated expressly that Las Cruces possessed an Indian governor and that the town itself was very close to Tarahumara country ("mas vecino a Tarahumares") (AHP 1704Ba). Apparently it was always a visita of Namiquipa, as Bishop Tamarón reported it to be in 1765 (1937: 150). In the late 1600s, one source noted that the Indian officials of Las Cruces were subordinate to those of Namiquipa (AHP 1695), and Lizasoin later gave strong indications that this town was a satellite of Namiquipa (DHM 18thb).

The founding date of Las Cruces as an Indian settlement under the jurisdiction of Namiquipa is obscure, although a title to lands at Las Cruces was given to Captain Ignacio López de Gracia in 1686 by the Nueva Vizcayan governor Neyra y Quiroga. Almada states that later, in 1689, Indians who had been dispersed were ordered by the Spanish governor Pardiñas to congregate at Las Cruces in order to form an Indian town; unfortunately, nothing more is reported about ethnic identity or settlement (Almada 1968: 126).

In 1765, Bishop Tamarón noted that Las Cruces had 35 families comprising 86 Indians (1937: 150). He did not cite the ethnic affiliation of these people, but it is entirely possible that they were Tarahumaras who had migrated into this locality. In 1778, the Caballero Teodoro de Croix ordered that a presidio and a town be founded at this settlement, and that the name be changed to Santa Cruz (document supplied by Sr. José M. Cano, Namiquipa, Chihuahua). The present-day inhabitants usually refer to the place as Las Cruces or simply as Cruces.

Santa Ana del Torreón (San Buenaventura)

The historical record contains a small amount of information on a short-lived mission, called variously Santa Ana del Torreón or San Buenaventura del Torreón, in the general region of the Casas Grandes district (e.g., Arlegui 1851: 43; AHP 1685Dc).

Very little has come to light regarding the history of the mission itself, but if Arlegui is correct in characterizing the place as having had at one time four satellite towns, it began its existence with the prospect of obtaining some importance. The same writer states that the mission was destroyed sometime between 1685 and 1700 by some people he called Apaches, who, he adds, were apparently joined in the attack by the Indians from the mission, judging from the fact that they took flight after the destruction (Arlegui 1851: 43, 95).

Arlegui gives no founding date for this mission, but López-Velarde cites Urrízar as giving the year 1677 (the same year Urrízar gives for several other missions of the Conchería area) (López-Velarde 1964: 99). Since the main effort of missionization in this general region appears to have begun in the 1660s, Urrízar's date seems to be rather late. In any event, Santa Ana was a head or cabecera mission, presumably in an important location, and it was referred to a number of times in the 1684–85 period – once as possessing a *convento,* 10 leagues from Casas Grandes, with a population of both Sumas and Chinarras (AHP 1684Da; 1685Dc; 1686Bb; CPP 23: 13–5). After 1686 Santa Ana is occasionally mentioned in the sources (sometimes under its alternate name, San Buenaventura), but not as a mission (e.g., AHP 1695). Given the great number of hostilities in this region during the late 1680s and the 1690s and presumably some corresponding depopulation, it would seem that the demise of this mission took place closer to 1685 than to 1700 (see Arlegui's statement above), probably between 1684 and 1686.

While none of the documentary sources give the specific location of the Santa Ana mission, they do indicate that it was in the Casas Grandes-Namiquipa region (AHP 1684Da; 1684Db; BL 1693a). In 1686, the area of this mission site was said to be the Valle del Torreón (AHP 1686Bb). A more exact location would seem to have been just south of the present town of Galeana, at a place still called El Torreón (see Map 1), which I visited in July of 1969 in the company of Sr. Carlos Caraveo. In the mid-18th century, Santa Ana del Torreón was an hacienda belonging to Pedro de Almoyna, four leagues from the town of El Valle de San Buenaventura (the present Buenaventura) and 10 leagues from the hacienda of San Antonio de Casas Grandes (CPP 35: 329-36, 364-76). For what is almost certainly the same place, Almada gives the name as El Torreón de Almoloya (Almoyna?) (Oconor 1952: 12, fn.), and again as Santa Ana del Torreón (Almada 1968: 491). On an 1891 map (Valenzuela 1891), this spot is designated as Santa Ana del Torreón.

The above interpretation of the location of the mission is supported by the 1778 document detailing Teodoro de Croix's orders for the establishment of five towns, with presidios, in this area. One of these, to be called San Juan Nepomuceno, was to be located at the settlement which until this time had been designated variously as El Sitio de Chavarría, Villa del Torreón, or San Buenaventura (document supplied by Sr. José M. Cano, Namiquipa, Chihuahua; Janos Municipal Archives). Again, however (as at Namiquipa), a presidio had already been established – in this case, as early as 1767 (Almada 1968: 213). Records from the presidio church for the latter 1700s, which were found in 1963 at the Buenaventura parish church, carry the title "Iglesia de San Juan Nepomuceno y Real Presidio de San Buenaventura." This presidio was located at the present site of Galeana, and in the 1960s the small church of the town was still remembered to have had San Juan Nepomuceno as its patron in the last century.

In the early years there is occasionally an indication that the names El Torreón and San Buenaventura refer to the same location, but sometimes these appear to be two places, possibly quite close to each other. Probably this is an early distinction between the site of the mission of Santa Ana Buenaventura (at the spot called El Torreón, just south of the town of Galeana) and the site of the town of El Valle de San Buenaventura (today, Buenaventura; see Map 1). In 1695, in an attempt to get a group of Janos, Jocomes, Mansos, Sumas, and Chinarras to render peace, the Europeans promised that each band could have its own town; while citing which places were abandoned and therefore available for the Indians, they mentioned these two spots separately ("disiendoles que el pueblo de Carretas el de casas grandes el torreon el de sn buenaventura estaban despoblados") (AHP 1695).

Several sources dating from the 1690s, especially from the first half of the decade, when citing other settlements of the region such as Namiquipa, Santa Clara, Las Cruces, and Casas Grandes, omit reference to either Santa Ana or San Buenaventura (e.g., AHP 1692A; BL 1695a; 1695b; 1697–

Presidio church of San Buenaventura at Galeana, Chihuahua

1703). An exception occurs in 1697, during the trouble with the local Concho populace, when the place of San Buenaventura is cited (AHP 1684Db; BL 1697–1703). Despite this apparent evidence for depopulation of the Santa María valley in the late 1680s and early 1690s, later information indicates continuous settlement in the region in the 18th century, during the time when the Casas Grandes valley to the west and north was undergoing considerable depopulation (see *Casas Grandes,* below); indeed, in 1751 El Valle de San Buenaventura was said to be the breadbasket (*granero*) for the mines in the immediate region (CPP 35: 338–42, 528–32, 587–93).

For El Valle de San Buenaventura, Almada notes that the first Spanish land claim was made in 1678. The request was made by Doña Catalina Sánchez de Villela to the Nueva Vizcayan governor, Don Lope de Sierra y Osorio. The property was later sold (dates not mentioned) to Don Antonio González de la Parra family. By 1710, the lands were again vacant and another claim was put forth, this time by Don Nicolás Ponce (Almada 1968: 75). A few years earlier, in 1703, the parish church (non-mission) had been founded, which apparently is an indication of resettlement of the immediate area around the turn of the century (Buenaventura Parish Archives: Libro No. 1, Bautismos y un inventario de Objectos de la Parroquia – 1703 a 1748). Indeed, it is my guess that some people, including Indians, had remained in the Santa María valley during the troublous 1680s and 1690s.

In 1684 the mission of El Torreón was reported to have both Sumas and Chinarras (CPP 23: 13-4). In 1685 one individual, Hernando Cafueminaaucu, who was sentenced with the large group of Suma who were executed in this year, was recorded as being from this mission and was presumably also a Suma (AHP 1685Dc). Somewhat later evidence, from 1690 and 1697, indicates that Conchos were living at Santa Ana del Torreón (Sauer 1934: 61; AHP 1688A; BL 1697–1703). Probably some of these Conchos were actually immigrants into the valley, as they were at Casas Grandes (see entry below). It is also possible that the Franciscans brought in some Sumas from the Casas Grandes area or from farther north in the Santa María valley and mixed them with the original Concho or Chinarra population. However, this may not be the explanation for the presence of the Sumas, for the Nueva Vizcayan governor, Gorráez Beaumont, noted as early as the 1660s that there were many Yuma (Suma) Indians at the places of Casas Grandes, Carretas, and El Torreón (DHM 1668). In any event, the sources do seem to show that Santa Ana was essentially a Suma mission, located on the Sumas' border with the Conchos and Chinarras. This is supported by two letters written August 15, 1651, by Fray Gerónimo de Birvés and Juan de Munguía y Villela, who were leading an expedition from Sonora into central Chihuahua in the area of the valley of San Martín and the Sierra del

Sacramento. They indicated that they could see or had seen two large buildings with two towers (*torreones*), and they signed their letters from the "rio del Torreón, land of the first sumas" (CPP 8: 323-6).

None of the early mission books seem to be in existence, although some of the 18th-century secular establishment records are stored in the present parish church of Buenaventura. These consist of baptismal records from the settlement of El Valle de San Buenaventura, and they cover the 18th century from the founding of the secular parish in 1703. A number of other records, from the old presidio of San Buenaventura, include burials and marriages and are very incomplete and fragmentary. Together, however, these sources afford some notion of the population situation in this part of northern Mexico during the last century of the colonial period.

The baptismal records reflect the considerable upset in the local native populations that had already taken place by the beginning of the 18th century. Also to be noted over this period is the increasing intermixture of ethnic groups and biological races, along with the drop in the number of specific Indian groups after the first two decades, leaving principally Apaches and Tarahumaras.

Taking the documentary sources at face value, it would appear that up to the 1680s there had been considerable Indian population in the region of the Santa María valley, but that by the early 1700s this population had been reduced quite radically. Unfortunately, the extant church records are not very clear in indicating the make-up of this native population. The great number of people who were left unclassified with regard to ethnic or *casta* group may mean that there were more Indians living at this place than it appears. Since the church at El Valle de San Buenaventura was not a mission in the 18th century, it is little surprise that specific ethnic identity is noted for so few Indians.

Table 6, summarizing the baptismal records of El Valle de San Buenaventura, shows several trends that probably reflect in some measure the population changes for this general region during the 18th century. In the main, the number of persons classified as Spaniards tends to increase, as does the number of mixed bloods such as *coyotes,* mestizos, and the like. The number of "Indians" reaches a high plateau during the second quarter of the century, and then dwindles off to almost nothing by the end of the period. A number of Indians are designated as "Apaches," and some of these are also said to be "gentiles"; in fact, in almost all entries listing both an ethnic identification and the term "gentile," the former is given as "Apache." There are quite a few entries between 1720 and 1754 in which the person receiving the baptismal rite is cited merely as the child of "gentile parents" (these are shown in Table 6 as Indians, no affiliation stated); most probably, a large percentage of these were also Apaches.

In the baptismal records from El Valle de San Buenaventura, after about 1725 the number of different Indian

groups dwindles (with only three exceptions) to two nations – Apaches and Tarahumaras. The burial and marriage records from the San Buenaventura presidio, although much less complete and commencing considerably later than the baptismal records from the nearby town, tend to support them. However, the burial records, which by their nature record many more adults (very few of the persons baptized were said to be adults), show that some ethnic diversity continued into the latter part of the century. Between 1775 and 1780, the death records include six Indians from El Paso, a married couple from Yepómera (the husband was a military auxiliary, and presumably both were Tarahumaras), and an Indian man from the mission of Santa Cruz de Tapacolmes. Also listed are 15 other persons stated to be either Tarahumaras or from one of the Tarahumara missions, most often Yepómera; others cited are two Norteño Indians (one an auxiliary soldier), two New Mexican Indians, and four Sumas (three said to be from El Paso).

Other information concerning the characteristics of the San Buenaventura population indicates that the residents came from a fairly wide geographical area. Places of origin noted in the church records are El Paso, the presidios of Janos and San Francisco de Conchos, Chihuahua, the Florido River, San Miguel el Grande, Durango, and Querétaro. From a rough count of the entries in these records for the years 1775 through 1780, some 348 persons were noted to have died, while during the years 1775 through 1779, only 115 were baptized. Thus it would seem that during this period the population of San Buenaventura was being maintained in large part through immigration.

In 1765 Bishop Tamarón recorded 30 Spanish families, with 479 persons, at San Buenaventura (he made no distinction between the presidio town and El Valle) (Tamarón 1937: 150). The marriage records between 1775 and 1785, 10 to 20 years later, show that most of the people were classified as either Spaniards or mestizos, and that the majority of the men were soldiers; occasionally it is stated that they belonged to the Fourth Military Company, stationed at the presidio. Between March 21, 1779, and November 22, 1780, the entries for some 13 persons who were buried state that they were killed by enemy Indians; where identified, these enemies were Apaches.

El Carmen

The records at the Hacienda de Nuestra Señora del Carmen de Peña Blanca (today, Flores Magón), to the east of San Buenaventura, support the San Buenaventura data fairly well. The baptisms between August of 1759 and November of 1775 cite some 213 persons, while the burial entries from July 28, 1759, through the year 1776 indicate that about 278 people died. Thus the population apparently decreased by about one-fourth during this period.

Tribal identification of Indians in the local baptismal records is quite infrequent; there are only two entries noting

TABLE 6

El Valle de San Buenaventura: Ethnic Groups Cited in Baptismal Records, 1703–1799

	Castizos	Coyotes	Lobos	Mestizos	Mulattoes	Negroes	Spanish	Unclassified	Apache	Tarahumara	Other	Total Indians
1703–1706						1	2	9			1 Concho, 1 Jova, 1 Mexico, 1 New Mexico, 3 Opatas	9
1707–1711							1	11	1		1 Opata, 1 Chinarra	3
1712–1715							1	25	2		1 Opata, 1 Sonora	4
1716–1718		2					11	15			1 Concho, 1 Panana, 1 Sonora	11
1720–1724		4		3			23	44	6	4	1 Concho, 3 Jovas, 1 Panana	33
1725–1729		2					2	19	1	1		9
1730–1734				2			16	16	15	2(?)	1 Jumana	26
1735–1739		1		1	1		32	40	7	4	1 Sonora	17
1740–1746		3	1	9	1	6	22	34	8	8		25
1746–1750	1	4		13	5	1	8	19	23	5		36
1750–1754		2		17	6		29	15	6	5		27
1755–1759		2		27	11		51	27	1	2	1 Opata	19
1760–1764		5		31	12		36	15		3		14
1765–1769		3	1	28	5		55	5	1	2		15
1770–1774	1	8	1	34	12		46	26	1	7		18
1775–1779				40	11		35	22		1		5
1780–1788				41	6		61	13		4		9
1791–1799				14	4		70	19		1		1

Source: Parish Church, Buenaventura, Chihuahua.

Apaches and six recording Tarahumaras, and no other native groups are listed. However, the marriage and burial records deal with the adult population for roughly the same span of years, and these note a much higher degree of ethnic diversity. Cited in these are one Ute, one Pawnee (Panana), one Concho, one Suma, three Apaches, one Indian (apparently Opata) from Nácore, five Indians from El Paso, 16 Tarahumaras, and six Norteño Indians – three from the town of Guadalupe, one from San Juan, and one from San Francisco.

There was a high number of mixed bloods at this hacienda. Well over 50 percent of the people listed for this period were said to be *mulatos,* and about 20 percent were mestizos; Indians, Spaniards, and such other mixed bloods as *coyotes* and *lobos* were only a handful (only seven Spaniards and nine Indians out of the total of 213 entries, which included only 11 unclassified). There is, however, a question of what *mulato* might mean here, since no Negroes as such are listed. El Carmen records also note Indians from other haciendas – El Corral de Piedra, El Carrizal, San Isidro, and de Mala Noche – while the records of San Buenaventura mention only that a number of Indians were servants of specific individuals. Nineteen persons cited in these chapel records were said to have died at the hands of enemy Indians – that is, Apaches.

In 1765, Bishop Tamarón stated that the people of El Carmen were *sirvientes,* and that there were 118 persons in 26 families; he offered no further breakdown by ethnic or caste group (Tamarón 1937: 150). Two years later, Lafora stated that there were 291 souls at the El Carmen hacienda; at least 35 of the men, he guessed, were Spanish (Kinnaird 1958: 96).

San Lorenzo

In the last years of the 17th century, two Conchos were reported to be associated with a place named San Lorenzo, apparently not the visita of the Jesuit mission of Satevó (BL 1695). In 1684, a Bachicyolic Concho was said to be from a spot named San Lorenzo (AHP 1684Aa). In 1690, in a junta of Indians at Las Encinillas that involved Conchos or some type of Concho confederation, two of the participants were reported to be from the town of San Lorenzo. While it remains unknown which San Lorenzo these citations refer to, it is likely that in at least some cases it is the place by this name on the El Carmen River, which apparently was a Concho settlement. It seems less likely that they refer to the San Lorenzo said to be Tarahumara in 1684 (apparently the Jesuit visita) or to the spot visited by Retana in 1701, roughly in the vicinity of Santa Isabel (AHP 1684b; 1701).

Casas Grandes

San Antonio de Casas Grandes, which lay within Suma country, is the last major Franciscan mission on the eastern edge of the Sierra Madre to be treated here. The place was first visited by Francisco de Ibarra in the early 1560s, but it was not until the middle of the following century that missionary efforts were carried out in the region. Arlegui gives a date of 1640 for the founding of the Casas Grandes mission; however, other information indicates that the mission was established in the 1660s (Arlegui 1851: 95-6; see DiPeso 1974, especially 900-902).

According to Almada, Spanish Casas Grandes was begun in 1661 by Captain Andrés Gracia under a commission granted by Governor Gorráez Beaumont. Gracia, with other members of his family and with Father Andrés Páez, began to settle the area. Apparently a mission was founded at this time, since Almada states that it was abandoned in 1667, but was refounded the next year on orders from the Nueva Vizcayan governor, Oca y Sarmiento. In any event, Franciscans had been working in the general area before these later dates, having established themselves just over the mountains in Sonora by 1649. In the 1660s, several Spanish civilian holdings, including mines, were reported for the immediate Casas Grandes area; in 1684, however, it was noted that there were only six or seven Spanish *vecinos* at Casas Grandes (Almada 1968: 93; Bancroft 1884: 364; Mecham 1927; Spicer 1962: 232; West 1949: 122, fn.; BL 1649-1700; CPP 10: 321-32; 23: 13-4; DHM 1666; 1667a; 1667b; 1667c; 1667d; 1668).

For a number of years after the 1684 rebellion, there were some Indians living at Casas Grandes. In 1687 some of the Suma there complained that their lands were being encroached upon by Spaniards. In one of their petitions, they described the Indian lands as they existed at that time, lands that had been granted to them formally by the Spanish authorities, although they had always belonged to the Suma. The petitioners stated that "these lands and waters of all this valley which at present are subject to dispute (*partes*) used to be ours, of our fathers and ancestors, on which we have been born and raised, and we request as loyal vassals of His Majesty that they be given and granted to us by the Justices in His Name" (AHP 1687Ad).

The Suma lands at this time consisted of one league of ground downriver, to the north of the mission, for corn and wheat, plus four *caballerías* for sheep and goats (*ganado menor*) and four *sitios* for cattle. The Indians also had rights to three additional leagues, located farther down the river, for the collection of firewood (*leña*) and for fishing and deer hunting. One and one-half leagues from the Indian pueblo there also existed a hot-water spring that the natives utilized; out of this spring there ran a ditch (*asequia; zanja*) from which the Indians obtained water and which at the same time served as a boundary marker between Indian and Spanish lands. All the land upriver, to the south, belonged to the Spanish settlers (AHP 1687Ad).

The remaining history of Casas Grandes is rather sketchy. Arlegui reported that in the early years it had been a cabecera with three visitas. One of these was Janos, but the sources are silent regarding the names and locations of the other two (Arlegui 1851: 95-6). While Casas Grandes existed in name as a mission until it was formally secularized in 1758 (AGN 1816), the composition of the Indian population some 30 years earlier would seem to indicate that it was close to being defunct even in the 1720s.

Documents of the 1680s clearly indicate that this was a Suma mission, and it was in 1687 that the Sumas made the claim, noted above, that they had dwelt in this region from time immemorial (AHP 1687Ad). In the 1690s, some Conchos were reported living at Casas Grandes, but they do not seem to have been native to the place. During the abortive uprising of 1697, when the Concho population of the town together with its governor, Juan Corma, was implicated in the trouble, it was explicitly stated that Corma and at least some of his people were originally from the town of San Diego del Monte (BL 1697-1703).

By this last decade of the 1600s, Casas Grandes was already becoming a multi-ethnic community. It is not too surprising to find Conchos here, and apparently there were also some Apaches residing in town at this time (BL 1697-1703). It is unknown how large an Indian population lived at this place in the 1600s, either before or after the revolts and executions of the 1680s. However, by 1716 the mission was reported to consist of only 11 or 12 Indian families (probably totaling some 35 to 50 persons), together with one resident missionary (AHP 1716A; UTD 1715a). Twelve years later, in 1728, the mission had only 23 people; most were either over 60 years of age or under 16, which apparently indicates an outmigration of the able-bodied young adults to areas of greater activity. This group consisted of seven Conchos, five Sumas, three Opatas, one Apache, one Sonora, one person who was half Jano and half Suma, and five persons with no ethnic identity given (AHP 1728Aa).

There are no more reports covering Casas Grandes until its demise as a mission in 1758. When Lafora passed through the area in 1767, he mentioned no people at this site – apparently it had now been abandoned. However, some 11 years later, Teodoro de Croix commanded that a *villa* be

Ruins of the *convento* of the first mission at Casas Grandes, Chihuahua

established here with the name of San Antonio, following the usual practice of assigning a previously used name to a new establishment (Janos Municipal Archives; document in the possession of Sr. José M. Cano, Namiquipa, Chihuahua). Presumably, by this time the indigenous population of the area had been extinct for many years – except for the marauding Apache.

It is not clear how soon Teodoro de Croix's orders of 1778 had any effect, but at least by around 1790 a new effort to resettle and develop the Casas Grandes district was being made. At the end of the year of 1792, new settlers (*pobladores*) were mentioned for Casas Grandes (no population figures given), and they apparently had located near the ancient and abandoned Indian settlement of Paquimé, several miles upstream from the early mission site, at present-day Casas Grandes Viejo (UTJ: F8, S2). In April of 1795, a report noted some 60 persons at Casas Grandes; this group was composed of Spanish *vecinos* and their families, together with some nine servants (UTEP: Reel 2). Censuses for August, September, and December indicate that the total number of inhabitants had risen to about 100 people, with a category called *agregados* accounting for most of the increase, although a few more servants were also included. During this year, all of the reports list a detachment of 51 men from the Janos presidio who were stationed at Casas Grandes;

a mill is also mentioned, and in August it was noted that four houses had been constructed (UTEP: Reel 2; UTJ: F11, S1).

In 1799, the total population for Casas Grandes was 144 souls (UTJ: F15, S2). A year later, in December of 1800, the total was listed as between 123 and 148 (UTJ: F15, S3). While I could locate no other reports specifically citing the population of Casas Grandes and immediate vicinity, what does exist for this period clearly indicates that there was considerable discontinuity with the earlier population here, and that the local base of the modern population was formed during the latter part of the 18th century. Original native inhabitants apparently contributed little directly at Casas Grandes itself, even less than in the Janos and Santa María River valley districts.

Janos

The Janos establishment, a satellite parish of the Casas Grandes mission, was said to be about 15 leagues from the latter and was called Nuestra Señora de la Soledad. It retained visita status during the entire time of its existence (Arlegui 1851: 95-6; AHP 1728Aa; CPP 23: 528-32). In 1684, one writer designated Janos as a *nueva conversión,* in contrast to Carretas – apparently indicating that Janos was founded after Carretas, and also no doubt after Casas Grandes (CPP 14: 98-102; see DiPeso 1974, especially 902-3).

View of the town of Janos, Chihuahua, from the neighboring hill called El Cerro de la Espia ("lookout hill")

The Janos parish was presumably set up for Janos Indians in Jano territory, and some information indicates that this was so. However, in the 1680s Sumas were reported to be living at this mission with the Janos (AHP 1684Db; CPP 23. 5–13). In the testimonies taken in Casas Grandes in 1685, a number of Sumas were said to be from this spot, and one of them had been governor of the Indian pueblo at Janos (although he may have been governor only of the Sumas residing there) (AHP 1685Dc). In 1692 it was explicitly stated that this settlement was in the territory of the Janos (BL 1693a), but it may well have been just on the border between the Sumas and the Janos.

After the Indian troubles of 1684–85, a presidio named San Felipe y Santiago de Janos was founded at the Janos settlement (Kinnaird 1958: 100). While the later documentary sources do not abound with information about the Indian population, some of them do afford a general idea of trends during the 1700s.

First, in the spring of 1717, the Indian town of Nuestra Señora de la Soledad, which had been destroyed during the Indian rebellions of the 1680s, was formally refounded. This refounding included orders for the construction of a church and a public building, possibly located three leagues from the presidio (it is unknown whether this was carried out); these were to serve 155 Janos and Jocomes (a number that was said to include all individuals, although two years

previously this same group was reported to consist of 100 families; other reports mentioned 90 to 100 *indios*). The settlement of these Indians in 1717 was the result of some two years of effort made by the Spaniards to get them to locate at Casas Grandes, where there was already a mission. However, these Janos and Jocomes had refused, saying that the Janos site was in their territory, but that Casas Grandes was not. These same Janos and Jocomes had earlier made peace at El Paso, but some 13 years had now passed by the time they were finally brought back to their original homeland in the Janos district (AHP 1716A; CPP 24: 243–4, 271).

These people, or some of them, apparently stayed on at Janos for at least a decade or so, and some stayed for a longer time. In 1724, the Spanish commander of the Janos presidio, Antonio Bezerra Nieto, after recounting that he had encountered some 2,000 Apaches in the Sierra de Enmedio (northwest of Janos), stated that he had sent 25 men and 40 Janos Indian auxiliaries to reconnoiter the region. This would seem to mean that a fair portion of the 1717 population was still at Janos (AHP 1722Ba). Two years later, in 1726, Bezerra Nieto reported that 143 Sumas had come to settle at the presidio, and he added that fortunately these Sumas had not allied themselves with the Apaches. At this time Bezerra employed both Sumas and Janos as auxiliaries (AHP 1727Ab). He did not state where these Sumas came from, and he gave no further information on this group.

TABLE 7

Janos Presidio: Ethnic Groups Cited in Baptismal Records, 1688–1723

Year	Affiliation Unstated	"Casta" Groups						Indian Groups																			Total Indians	TOTAL
		Spaniards	Mestizos	Coyotes	Negroes	Mulattoes	Slaves	Indians, Group Unspecified	Janos	Jocomes	Sumas	Jumanos	Chinarras	Conchos	Opatas	Sonoras	Piros	Pananas	Mansos	Apaches	Apache-Concha	Opata-Apache	Opata-Suma	Manso-Jana	New Mexico Indians	Unknown Parents		
1688								14			1				1												16	16
1689	3												7	2	1												10	13
1690	2													1	1												2	4
1691	10										2				1					5							8	18
1692	5	2				1		2			3						1			2						1	9	17
1693	5	1			1	1		2							1					1						2	6	14
1694	4	3									1	1			2					5							9	16
1695	6	1						1			3									4						1	9	16
1696	12	2								4			1	2	1					2						1	11	25
1697	5			1				1		4	1				2					1							9	15
1698															1								1				2	2
1699	6	1						2	16	1	9				3												31	38
1700	2	5		2							1				3												4	13
1701	2	4			2						2				2												4	12
1702	3	3		1				1																			1	8
1703	2	2						2																	1		3	7
1704	— missing —																											
1705		2		1																							0	3
1706	2	2	2																	1							1	7
1707	2	2		1				1						1													2	7
1708	2	1	1					1	1					1						1							4	8
1709	5	4	3							2												1					3	15
1710	6	1				2		1												4							5	14
1711	8	5							1											2							3	16
1712	1	10	3					1	1		1	1								2			1				6	21
1713	2	5	4	1		1									1	1			5	5					1		13	26
1714	1	7	2	1																8							8	19
1715	2	2	3						1	1									1	12							15	22
1716	5	6		1				3			2																5	17
1717	4	1						4			1				1												6	11
1718	4																										0	4
1719	3	1								3					1												4	8
1720	2	4	1																								0	7
1721	2	7	1	1				3		4										1							8	19
1722		8	2			1		2		2					1					4							9	20
1723		3		1				1																			1	5

Source: Book from Archives, Casas Grandes Viejo, Chihuahua.

The extant church records fill out the population picture somewhat. Baptismal records for the presidio are fairly complete between 1688 and 1723, a span of some 35 years (see Table 7). For the next 40 years, until about 1765, they are quite fragmentary (nothing exists for some years), and as a matter of convenience these data have been grouped into three-year periods in Table 8. Even with these limitations, some very general and tentative conclusions can be drawn, and in the main they support the trends noted for other parishes in the region.

TABLE 8

Janos Presidio: Ethnic Groups Cited in Baptismal Records, 1723-1765

| | Spaniards | Mestizos and Other Mixed Bloods | Unidentified, Parents' Names Given | Unidentified, No Parents' Names Given | Indians | | | | | TOTAL |
					Janos	Sumas	Apaches	Group Unstated	Total Indians	
1723–1725	16	8	5	4	13	1	9	7	30	63
1726–1728	6	1	3	1	----	--	--	1	1	12
1729–1731	6	2	2	--	----	--	--	--	0	10
1732–1734	9	2	2	3	----	--	--	--	0	16
1735–1737	6	----	16	6	1	--	2	--	3	31
1738–1740	2	----	3	1	----	--	--	--	0	6
1741–1743	5	6	18	4	2	--	6	--	8	41
1744–1746	5	5	3	--	1	--	--	2	3	16
1747–1749	4	2	1	5	----	--	4	1	5	17
1750–1751				– missing –						
1752	3	1	2	--	----	--	--	--	0	6
1753–1755	11	2	17	7	----	--	--	2	2	39
1756				– missing –						
1757–1759	12	3	5	3	----	--	8	2	10	33
1760–1761	6	5	5	2	----	--	--	1	1	19
1762–1763				– missing –						
1764–1765	6	14	2	4	----	--	--	2	2	28

Sources: UTEP: Reel 2; UTJ: F1, S1; Casas Grandes Viejo Parish Archives.

For the period reported, which falls mainly within the earlier portion of the 18th century, three points can be noted: (1) the number of persons classified as Spaniards appears to remain about the same; (2) the number of people classified as mestizos or other mixed bloods (*coyotes, lobos, mulatos*) seems to increase somewhat; and (3) the number of Indians of every kind but Apaches decreases. The history of specific Apache contacts at Janos (and elsewhere) during this period still needs to be worked out, as does the use and extension of the word "Apache" at different times; this last point will be commented on below.

The fragmentary marriage and burial records for approximately the same time span support the above generalizations. They too indicate that some members of the population were apparently distinguishable as Apaches, Sumas, or Janos, a few of the last group being noted into the early 1750s. None of the three types of records, however, indicate on what basis Janos, Sumas, and Apaches were distinguished, or how different they might have been culturally from each other. There is also a tendency, noted in other places, for children of unknown parents to be listed as Apaches. In Table 8, the individuals have been entered under the most specific category possible; in some cases, however, the records give other, less specific information. For example, of nine Apaches listed for the year 1724, seven are also said to have unknown parents; this is the most extreme example, but the same pattern occurs in other years also. In one year, 1733, one child of unknown parents is said to be a *coyote* (entered in column 2 of Table 8); otherwise, children with-

out known parents are said to be Apaches or no affiliation is given. This would seem to indicate again that the term "Apache" was being employed somewhat loosely, whereas the other tribal names were applied more specifically. On one occasion (June 1758), an Apache woman was said to belong to the "Navaxo" nation; otherwise nothing more detailed is given concerning the specific affiliations of Apaches (UTEP: Reel 2; UTJ: F1, S1; Casas Grandes Viejo Parish Archives).

In August of 1697, the Bishop García de Legaspi y Velasco visited the Janos presidio and made a number of confirmations. Of a total of 150 persons listed, almost half (74) were Spaniards, and somewhat fewer (61) were Indians. The remaining 15 comprised seven mestizos, four *mulatos,* three *coyotes,* and one Negro. At the nearby settlement of Ojo de Ramos, at this same time, 13 persons were confirmed – 12 Indians and one mestizo (Casas Grandes Viejo Parish Archives).

The marriage records are quite incomplete, but what entries exist contribute to the general picture of ethnic mixing occurring at the time. Following is a sampling from these entries. In 1698, aside from one Spanish couple, two Opatas married, and a Concho from San Diego del Monte married an Apache. The next year, a mestizo from New Mexico married a Piro Indian woman from the same place. Two Suma couples also married; one of the husbands was from Isleta, El Paso, and his wife was from Carretas. A fifth Suma, a woman, married an Opata, and one Opata couple also married during this year. In 1700 an Opata married a Concho woman, and in 1701 one Opata man married a Suma while another married an Apache. In 1704 an Apache woman and an Opata man both married persons of unstated *casta* or ethnic affiliation, and an Opata couple were married the following year. In 1706 a Sonora Indian couple and an Opata couple married, in 1707 a Manso man married a Jano woman, and one Opata couple was married in each of the next two years. In 1710 one Opata man married a mulatto woman, and another a Suma. In 1712 a Sonora man married a Concho woman, and a second an Opata woman. In 1714 a Suma married an Apache woman, and a Sonora Indian man married an Opata.

In the year 1723, four couples of Janos Indians married, one Apache woman married a *lobo,* and a Suma girl married a man of unstated *casta.* In the following year, Antonio Venadito, a Jano man, married an Indian woman. In 1725, five Janos couples married, and another couple consisted of a Manso man and a Jano woman (UTJ: F1, S1). No Indians are listed again until 1733, although records exist for 1726, 1727, 1728, and 1730 (the other three years are lacking). In 1733 two Janos couples married, and again Indians go unmentioned until 1737, when another Janos couple married. In the following year, 1738, a man classified simply as an *indio* married an Apache woman. In 1741 a Jano by the name of Juan Antonio married the Apache Juana Micaela, and in 1747 one Janos couple got married. Seven years later, in 1754, there appears a listing for an Indian man, a *sirviente* of the captain, who married a woman listed as María Jano, apparently a Jano Indian. This is the last time the name "Jano" occurs in the records consulted, although the terms *indio* and *Apache* continue to show up from time to time. In 1760 an Apache couple are listed, along with two other couples of Indians and an Indian man from El Paso who married a woman of unstated affiliation. After this, both *Apache* and *indio* are extremely infrequent.

The burial records give similar information. Of a total of 21 burials recorded in 1723, almost half (10) were of Indians: four Apaches, one Jano, two Sumas, and three of unlisted affiliation. In the following year, of a total of 18 buried, 10 were Indians: five Janos and five Apaches. In 1725, out of 17, nine were Indians: two Janos, one Suma, four Apaches, and two of unnoted identification. Again the records are fragmentary, but in 1737, two Apaches were buried, and the next year five Apaches were laid to rest. In 1747, or the next year, four Apaches and five *indios* were buried.

While this picture is not unlike that for other parishes in the general region, more data on the indigenous population may eventually show up and change it slightly. In the burial records for 1725, nine Indians are recorded, but one of the Apache entries is crossed off with a note that refers to the "book of the Indians." Possibly more detailed information was kept on the indigenous population. At Janos in 1730, during an inspection tour, Benito, the Bishop of Durango, made reference to the "administration of the Janos

Indians," but he gave no more details on what this "administration" might have consisted of (UTEP: Reel 2).

Data on the later overall demographic history of Janos is better than for most communities. In 1767, the Bishop of Durango, Tamarón y Romeral, simply listed the total population as 434 souls, in 91 families; he gave no breakdown for Indians or non–Indians (Tamarón 1937: 151). Lafora's report of two years later gave a total of 455 persons in 101 families, including mestizos and mulattoes (Kinnaird 1958: 100).

A general population increase is later noted beginning around the last decade of the century and persisting to the end of the colonial period; this trend, however, was not continued, at least at Janos, after the beginning of the Mexican period. These demographic changes were clearly correlated with changes in the Spanish military organization, which was strengthened on the northern frontier, only to fall apart soon after Mexican independence. The buildup included an increase in the size of the garrison at Janos from 50 to some 125 to 150 men and an active policy of resettling the general area, including the Casas Grandes valley. Also, in 1778, Teodoro de Croix commanded that a *villa* be formally established here with the name of Santiago de Janos (document supplied by Sr. José M. Cano, Namiquipa, Chihuahua; Janos Municipal Archives). While this order, covering five towns (see *Namiquipa,* above), also called for the establishment of presidios, in the case of Janos a presidio had remained in existence since the late 17th century.

In December of 1792, some 500 persons, including the military and their families, were reported at Janos (UTJ: F8, S2). In January of 1796, the number had increased to 592 (UTJ: F12, S1). In December of 1799, the number was given at about 789 (UTJ: F15, S2), with another 68 at the Estancia de Becerra, a ranch that had apparently been continuously occupied since early in the century, some five leagues from the presidio on the San Antonio River. A year later, in December 1800, the total was between 670 and 695 (UTJ: F15, S3), with no apparent reason for the loss of almost 100. About four years later, however, the number was given as 907 persons (this figure might have included Casas Grandes, but apparently it did not) (UTJ: F17, S2). In December of 1807, the total population of the *puesto* of Janos was given as 1,300 persons, consisting of 517 Spaniards, 592 mestizos, and 191 servants (UTJ: F18, S3); in December of 1812, the total number of persons reported for Janos was 1,348, now with 556 Spaniards, and with the remaining 792 persons belonging to a single, combined category of *Negros, Mulatos, y Mestizos* (UTJ: F20, S4). By December of 1818 the population total was given as 1,453 (UTJ: F23, S3), although another census report of February, 1819, only two months later, listed only 1,116 persons (UTJ: F24, S2).

These figures indicate a general rise in the population of the Janos district* similar to that in the Casas Grandes

---

*A closer analysis of the history of Janos and its population is being prepared for separate publication.

district (see entry above) at the end of the colonial period (it is always possible that some of these later figures include people at other settlements such as Santa Rita del Cobre in present-day New Mexico, although this is not explicitly stated). However, native Indians are simply not mentioned after the 1750s, with the exception of Apaches; for example, one report, while specifically including Apaches as *Yndios Gentiles,* also notes explicitly that there existed no *Yndios del Pueblo* at Janos (UTJ: F20, S4 – December 1812).

From the early 1790s until after the beginning of the Mexican period, Janos was one of the principal spots where Apaches at peace were maintained, in line with the general reforms in Indian policy and practice that were instituted during the last decades of the 18th century (the Mexicans attempted to keep the "peace establishment" organization, but with practically no success after 1832). The number of gentile Chiricahua and other groups camped in and around Janos varied from about 100 to as many as 800, and these Apaches often operated as scouts and auxiliaries for the Spanish forces (UTJ; UTEP: Reels 1 and 2). While theoretically these Indians were administered to by the Franciscans, Janos was said to be quite distant from the Franciscan missions that still survived; apparently the chaplain at the presidio was the only resident religious available – if indeed he was needed at all by these Apaches, who were generally considered gentiles (CIV 1795; Park 1962).

Carretas

Santa María de Gracia de las Carretas was the westernmost of the Franciscan missions in this region of Nueva Vizcaya. It was located roughly at the juncture of the southern portion of the Chihuicahui (Chiricahua) mountains with the plains (*llanos*) of San Francisco, apparently where there still is a settlement called Carretas; it was 14 leagues from the Janos presidio and 30 leagues from Casas Grandes (Arlegui 1851: 131; AHP 1684Da; BL 1693a; 1695b; CPP 17: 200-5; DHM 18thc). In the mid-1660s, and again in 1684, Carretas was said to be a mission for Suma Indians (CPP 23: 13-4; DHM 1668).

Carretas was founded sometime during the 17th century, apparently after 1660; Urrízar gives 1677 (López-Velarde 1964: 99), but the mission may well have been established considerably earlier. During its existence it administered as many as three settlements or pueblos; one was no doubt Carretas proper, but the names of the other two seem to be lost to history. According to Arlegui, the mission was destroyed between 1685 and 1700 by Apaches, with the local mission Indians apparently assisting the attackers (Arlegui 1851: 43, 95). Arlegui's statements are not very precise, but other documents do indicate that Carretas was attacked at the time of the 1684 revolt, when the Indians desecrated many holy objects. Later, in 1692, a town was reported in existence at Carretas, but it was not said to be a mission (CPP 14: 98-102; 17: 200-5).

The La Junta District

In the northern part of the eastern Conchería, down-river from the town of Julimes on the Conchos River, there existed a number of Indian rancherias and pueblos. Apart from Santa Cruz de Ochanes, these settlements ran from the area of the present-day town of Coyame to the confluence of the Conchos River with the Rio Grande (La Junta proper), and for some distance up and down the Rio Grande (see Map 1). These were the last of the settled native communities in the northeastern Conchería, and the Spaniards called the inhabitants variously the people from La Junta, the people from El Río del Norte, or, in later years, simply Norteños. Working as laborers on haciendas and other Spanish establishments, and serving as auxiliary military personnel for the Spanish forces, they were the last of the mission Indians of the Conchería who played a part in the development of Nueva Vizcaya.

The La Junta district, comprising several different named groups or settlements, is treated here as a single unit, in keeping with the way the Spanish usually considered it. From the earliest time of European penetration into northern Nueva Vizcaya, there was some contact with the La Junta peoples. By the time of the Rodríguez and Espejo expeditions in the early 1580s, other Spaniards had already been in the region seeking slaves. During the 1644 and 1684 revolts, the Spanish military campaigned as far as the La Junta area (the 1684 expedition was under Juan de Retana and was apart from the better-known Mendoza visit).

It is unclear whether Spaniards themselves actually entered the region during the interim between 1644 and 1684 – one report in the mid-18th century states that La Junta was missionized by two Franciscans from 1670 to 1672, when the Indians rose up and expelled their missionaries. In any case, during this period Indians in the service of the Europeans, such as the Eastern Conchería governor, Hernando de Obregón, often went to the La Junta district either on labor-recruiting or military business. In 1689 and 1693, General Juan de Retana made two more expeditions into the area. After the 1715 Trasviña Retis entrada, Spanish priests remained at La Junta until 1718, when they were expelled by the Indians. From 1720 until about the 1750s, some missionaries resided there at least part of each year. In the mid-18th century, there were several expeditions to La Junta – Aguirre came in 1726, Berroterán in 1729, Rábago y Terán in 1746-47, Idoyaga in 1747-48, Vidaurre in 1747-48, and Rubín de Celís in 1750-51.

In 1715-16, six missions, with an equal number of missionaries, were established at La Junta. These were Nuestra Señora de la Redonda at Coyame (given by Hackett as "Nuestro Señor la Redonda del Collame"), Nuestro Señor Padre San Francisco, San Pedro del Cuchillo Parado, San Juan Baptista (Los Cacalotes), San Cristóbal, and Nuestra Señora de Guadalupe (Los Polacmes) (Hackett 1937: 408). In 1748, at the time of Idoyaga's visit, there were two missionaries at La Junta, Fray Lorenzo Saabedra and Fray Francisco Sánchez. Saabedra, *lector vice custodio,* lived at San Francisco but also administered the town of San Juan Baptista; Sánchez kept his residence at Nuestra Señora de Guadalupe and ministered to the satellite parishes of San Cristóbal and Los Puliques (BL 1746). In 1765, Bishop Tamarón (in the last report I have been able to locate on the La Junta missions) recorded that only four mission towns were left. The first was San Juan Baptista, which by this time had lost its former two visitas, El Mesquite and Conejos; the inhabitants of these satellites had moved into the cabecera. The other three mission pueblos were San Francisco, Guadalupe, and San Cristóbal; Puliques had been abandoned by this time.

Several of these Spanish contacts with La Junta have yielded a fair amount of information on the area. Pieced together, the records indicate that this was one of the more heavily settled areas both aboriginally and in colonial times into the 1700s. However, by the end of the 18th century, the La Junta district appears to have been for the most part depopulated of its native inhabitants (Hackett 1937: 407ff; Hammond and Rey 1927; 1929; Kelley 1952a; 1952b; 1953; AHP 1684Aa; 1715Ac; BL 1695a; CPP 24: 101; DHM 1645; 1715; 1748; UTD 1715B).

The following pueblos of La Junta have already been reported on in the excellent work of J. Charles Kelley (1952a; 1952b; 1953), and I have not tried to duplicate it. Instead, relying heavily on Kelley's work, I have included a short summary of these towns and missions merely to give a more comprehensive view of native settlements and their abandonment or amalgamation into the Spanish colonial system. Occasionally, where some additional documentary information has been encountered, it has been included.

Santa Cruz de Ochanes

The settlement of Santa Cruz de Ochanes was located in the area of the modern town of Pueblito, on the Conchos River down from Julimes, about in the middle of the stretch between the Chuvíscar and the Rio Grande.* It was probably at this place that the 16th-century expeditions noted a number of Concho rancherias.

Later the spot was called Santa Cruz de Ochanes, and apparently a Spanish-Indian type of town was eventually established here. It had been mentioned in 1684, but by 1715, when Trasviña Retis traveled through the region, Santa Cruz had been abandoned. By 1715, the Auchanes who had been living here were settled in the town of Julimes, and a few show up in the church records of Julimes and Santa Eulalia.

Idoyaga, in 1747, recorded 299 persons who had just located at Santa Cruz (owing to Apache attacks farther north); these consisted of Cholomes, Conejos, and Tecolotes – 120 from Cuchillo Parado, 60 from La Ciénega del Coyame,

and 71 Tecolotes from the north of La Junta, across the Rio Grande. This was apparently the same place as Santa Cruz de los Cholomes, where 97 families, 16 unmarried adults, and some gentiles (all of unstated ethnic affiliation) settled in 1746. However, four years after Idoyaga's visit, Rubín de Celís found only a few small Indian rancherias here; presumably within a short time after this the site was abandoned for good, and some of the people, at least, apparently returned to their own pueblos (Kelley 1952b; 1953; AHP 1715Ac; CPP 35: 364-76; DHM 1715).

Coyame

Coyame was located in Cholome country. In 1715, the Trasviña Retis expedition called this spot La Cieneguilla, and the Spanish governor later that year gave it the name of Nuestra Señora de la Redonda y San Andrés. At this time, it was reported to have a population of some 180 persons. Two other pueblos were associated with it (*allegados*) – San Pedro and Cuchillo Parado (see entries below). Beasoain, in his version of the Trasviña Retis expedition, said that the head of the town was Don Andrés Coyame; he was called the Captain General of the Cholomes and said to be "Concho Prinzipal del Pueblo de la Zieneguilla." Later, when testimony was taken from Don Andrés (July 27, 1715), his position was reaffirmed and formalized by the Spanish governor, San Juan de Santa Cruz ("le mando despachar titulo de Gral de los referidos tres Pueblos le pusso al prinzipal nombrado le sieneguilla Nuestra Senora de la Redonda y San Andres") (AHP 1715Ac).

A mission was established here in 1716; in 1724, it was called Santiago de la Redonda. The general of the Indians was now said to be Juan Cíbola, a Cholome Indian (AHP 1722Bb). The site was abandoned by 1747, but it was still designated as La Ciénega del Coyame; Idoyaga reported that 60 of the colonists at Santa Cruz de Ochanes came from here. In 1751, Rubín de Celís met 40 Indians and their chief who said that they were from Coyame but were now living at Santa Cruz. The place at this time was referred to as "Santa María la Redonda, alias el Coyame" (Kelley 1952b).

San Pedro

San Pedro was apparently the place called Santa Teresa by Mendoza in 1684, and reported to possess many rancherias of Indians. At the time of the visit of Trasviña Retis, in 1715, the population of the settlement consisted of 190 Cholomes, some of whom worked on the hacienda of Juan Cortés in the Parral district. It was a satellite of Coyame, and the *capitán* of the town was one Don Santiago, subordinate to Don Andrés Coyame at Coyame.

Apparently the site was continuously occupied into the mid-18th century. There were people living here when Aguirre passed through in 1726, and while Idoyaga did not make it to San Pedro, Rubín de Celís recorded that this was a large town populated by Conejos Indians (the same as Cholomes, or perhaps there had been population replacement?). He also reported that some apostate Sumas from a

---

*Santa Cruz de Ochanes was not usually considered part of La Junta proper, but it is included here as a matter of convenience.

mission on the Rio Grande south of El Paso had recently joined the settlement (Kelley 1952b; AHP 1715Ac; DHM 1715; UTD 1710-1738a).

Cuchillo Parado

Almost due east of Coyame, on the Conchos River, was the town of Cuchillo Parado. In 1715, Trasviña Retis reported that there were 44 Conejos Indians inhabiting this town – a satellite of La Cieneguilla (Coyame) – and he called it Nuestra Señora de Begonia de Cuchillo Parado. This was probably the same spot where there were several rancherias that Mendoza in 1684 called Santa Polonia, and apparently it was the location of the Cabris or Passaguates Indians mentioned in the early 1580s by Gallegos and Luján, respectively. Cuchillo Parado was abandoned by the time of Idoyaga's visit in 1747 (Kelley 1952b; AHP 1715Ac; DHM 1715).

El Mesquite

In 1715 El Mesquite was reported to be the first town in the valley of La Junta de los Ríos on the south side of the Conchos River. It often went by the name of El Pueblo del Mesquite, but the Trasviña Retis expedition gave it the Spanish designation of Nuestra Señora de Loreto. This is apparently the place linked with San Juan Baptista as "Santa Catalina" by Mendoza, who said in 1684 that it consisted of "many people."

In 1715, the town had 80 souls. In 1747, Idoyaga reported 77 inhabitants, plus another 78 Indians, including 40 Conejos, who were refugees from another pueblo (the remaining 38 were apparently Cholomes). Rubín de Celís noted only a few dwellings in the area in 1751, as well as some huts on the north bank of the Conchos, somewhat downriver. In 1765, Bishop Tamarón noted that El Mesquite, now abandoned, had been one of the two visitas of the town of San Juan (see *Los Cacalotes,* below).

In the 17th and 18th centuries, the Indians from El Mesquite were often simply called Mesquites. These were, however, apparently the same people who, in the early 1580s, were named the Amotomancos by the Rodríguez expedition and the Otomoaco (or Patarabueyes) by Luján (Kelley 1952b; Tamarón 1937: 155-6; AHP 1715Ac; DHM 1715).

Los Conejos

The town of Los Conejos, the location of which is in some doubt, was named Nuestra Señora de Aranzazu by Trasviña Retis in 1715; it was said to possess a population of 71 Conejos Indians. Kelley believes that this was probably a temporary pueblo, founded about 1700 and abandoned by 1747, and that the 40 Conejos among the 78 refugees at the Mesquite pueblo may have been from Aranzazu; also, some of these Conejos could have gone to Cuchillo Parado, where the number of Conejos increased from 44 in 1715 to 120 in 1747. In 1765 Bishop Tamarón reported that Conejos was a defunct visita of the mission of San Juan (see *Los Cacalotes,* below) (Kelley 1953; Tamarón 1937: 156; AHP 1715Ac; DHM 1715).

Los Cacalotes (San Juan Baptista)

The pueblo of Los Cacalotes was located some four leagues from the confluence of the Conchos River and the Rio Grande, and about one league from El Mesquite. It was visited in 1582 by Espejo, who called it La Paz, and in 1684 by Mendoza, who apparently coupled it with the Mesquites pueblo under the name of Santa Catalina. Retana in 1693, Trasviña Retis in 1715, Aguirre in 1726, and the mid-18th-century expeditions of Idoyaga, Rábago y Terán, Vidaurre, and Rubín de Celís all passed by Los Cacalotes.

In 1715 Los Cacalotes possessed 165 persons, according to the information given by Trasviña Retis; at this time it was designated San Juan Baptista, the name by which it was known as a cabecera mission in later years. In 1747 the population included 143 Cacalotes Indians, who were native inhabitants of the pueblo; there were also 40 Conejos who had moved into the town from elsewhere because of Apache attacks, as well as 38 Cholomes who were living either here or at El Mesquite. Four years later, in 1751, the population was reported to be 40 families. However, in 1765, Bishop Tamarón noted that there were 84 families, with 309 Indians; this count apparently included people from the two defunct satellite parishes of Conejos and Mesquites, who had now been reduced to the cabecera of San Juan (Kelley 1952b; Tamarón 1937: 156; AHP 1715Aa; BL 1746b; DHM 1715).

San Francisco

San Francisco was located immediately west of the Rio Grande-Conchos River confluence. No other name seems to have been employed for this pueblo in the late 17th and 18th centuries. However, this was apparently the place called Santo Tomás by Luján, who recorded a population of some 600 souls belonging to the nation called the Abriaches. In 1684, Mendoza left the place unnamed, but said that it contained a number of rancherias of Julimes Indians living on both sides of the Rio Grande; 31 years later, Trasviña Retis described three separate pueblos about 300 yards apart, the one in the middle possessing a church, in need of considerable repair, located outside the settlement itself.

In 1715, San Francisco had a population of 180 persons under the governor Don Pascual de Ortega. Idoyaga reported in 1747 that there were 217 people living at the place, but these included 50 Tecolotes from up the Rio Grande; the rest were "Julimes (or Oposmes)," according to Kelley. In 1765, Bishop Tamarón stated that there were 165 persons, making up 42 families. Although by ethnic identification the people of this pueblo may have been Oposmes (or Julimes, which appears somewhat more doubtful), the Beasoain version of the Trasviña Retis expedition seems to read Po[salmes] (?), as does the report of Retana's 1693 entrada, which is quite unclear (Kelley 1952b; 1953; Tamarón 1937: 156; AHP 1715Ac; BL 1695; DHM 1715).

San Juan Evangelista

The pueblo of San Juan Evangelista was located a short distance from San Francisco, on the opposite or eastern bank of the Rio Grande. It was abandoned apparently sometime between Luján's reporting of it in 1582 and the Trasviña Retis expedition of 1715. There is no further mention of it in the documentary sources. Espejo does not identify the nation that inhabited this place, but Kelley thinks that it was possibly the Conejo Indians, who later moved to the settlements of Cuchillo Parado, Mesquites, and Santa Cruz (Kelley 1953).

San Bernardino

San Bernardino, located some five leagues up the Rio Grande from La Junta, on the west side of the river, was visited and named by the Espejo expedition in 1582. The López-Mendoza entrada of 1683 and that of Idoyaga in 1747 both passed through this settlement.

Luján stated that the inhabitants were Otomoacos, and Idoyaga called them by the 18th-century name "Tecolotes." The custodian of the mission at San Francisco, Fray Lorenzo Saabedra, also considered them in 1747-48 to be Tecolotes. The Espejo party noted that the people of San Bernardino were similar to the Otomoacos of the Mesquite-San Juan Baptista settlement. A number of other Otomoacos lived up the Rio Grande, but apparently not in towns as did those of San Bernardino. At any rate, by the time of Idoyaga's visit in 1747, San Bernardino and the upriver settlements were abandoned; the populace had moved into the other La Junta towns, including the pueblo of San Francisco and the new town of Santa Cruz (Kelley 1952b; 1953; BL 1746).

Los Polacmes (Nuestra Señora de Guadalupe)

In 1715, Los Polacmes – also called Nuestra Señora de Guadalupe at this time – was reported to be the largest pueblo of all the La Junta settlements. It consisted of 550 persons, including some Cíbolos Indians who lived here with the Polacmes. The gathering together of the two groups was apparently recent, and there were two plazas, one for each group. This was possibly the same town that Espejo visited and called Santiago, whose chief all the other towns respected; however, it is perhaps more likely that Santiago was San Cristóbal (see entry below), farther down the Rio Grande on the Texas side.

From the population of 550 in 1715, Los Polacmes declined to only 172 Indians in 1747. At least some of these people consisted of Cíbolos; Pescados Indians were said to live immediately downriver from the settlement and were not included in this figure. In 1765 Bishop Tamarón stated that the place had 194 persons, making up 66 families, and these figures may or may not have included the Pescados.

In 1747, despite the reduced population, Guadalupe was a cabecera with a church, a priest, and a plaza large enough for a fair-sized Spanish party to camp in. Later, in 1759-60, a presidio called "El Presidio del Norte" was established here. In 1765 Bishop Tamarón reported that this presidio possessed 133 persons, making up 50 families, plus five Spaniards. Two years later, in 1767, the presidio was moved to Julimes, but in 1773, it was relocated again at Guadalupe. Today, the town of Ojinaga is located at about the same site. It is unknown precisely what became of the remaining native population after 1765 (Kelley 1952b; 1953; Kinnaird 1958: 73; Tamarón 1937: 157; AHP 1715Ac; BL 1746b; DHM 1715).

San Cristóbal

The town of San Cristóbal was located between the settlements of Guadalupe and Puliques (both on the southwest side of the Rio Grande downriver from La Junta), but on the northeast bank of the Rio Grande. The population in 1715 was reported at 180 Poxalmas (Posalmes) Indians. At this time the town was simply called San Cristóbal, and it is very likely the same place called San Cristóbal in earlier records (AHP 1685Db).

This was most probably the town of Santiago visited by the Espejo party in 1582; it was then described as the largest pueblo of the area, and its chief was said to be respected by all the other La Junta pueblo leaders. If this identification of Santiago with San Cristóbal is correct, and if its general prominence among the La Junta pueblos was not exaggerated by Espejo, this may explain why in 1684 the nativistic leader Taagua chose the church at San Cristóbal for his activities (see Chapter 2) (AHP 1685Db).

In 1747 San Cristóbal had 154 persons. In 1765 Tamarón reported 117 persons, making up 30 families; the settlement of Puliques, by this time abandoned, had been a visita of the San Cristóbal mission. San Cristóbal itself was probably abandoned during the last quarter of the 18th century (Kelley 1953; Tamarón 1937: 157; AHP 1715Ac; DHM 1715).

Los Puliques

Los Puliques was situated on the southwest side of the Rio Grande, about one league downriver from Los Polacmes. In 1715 it had a population of 92 persons, and was called San Joseph.

In 1747 Idoyaga called it San Antonio de los Puliques. Its population at this time was 271 persons, including 156 refugees – 96 Cíbolos and 60 Pescados (leaving, therefore, only 115 native Puliques). The Cíbolos had apparently lived north of La Junta in their own town before moving to Los Puliques. In 1765 Tamarón recorded that Los Puliques had been a visita of the town and mission of San Cristóbal, but was now abandoned (Kelley 1952b; 1953; Tamarón 1937: 156; BL 1746).

Pueblo of Conchos at La Junta

This settlement was near the towns of Los Polacmes, Los Puliques, and San Cristóbal. In 1715 Trasviña Retis reported that the population of the town, which he called San Antonio de Padua, consisted of 87 Conchos Indians. Kelley, however, makes a case for "Concho" here to mean "Cíbolo," since "Concho" was occasionally used generically (i.e., to refer to people of the Conchería) for at least some of the La Junta peoples, and because Trasviña Retis did not always have reliable information. The Cíbolos had abandoned their town in the Chinati mountains north of the Rio Grande (see *Los Cíbolos,* below) slightly before 1715, apparently moving in with the Puliques, or at least onto land of the Puliques, across the river. This town is not mentioned by earlier or later expeditions (Kelley 1953; AHP 1715Ac; DHM 1715).

Los Cíbolos

The pueblo of Los Cíbolos was located northeast of San Cristóbal, about 13 leagues away from the Rio Grande. In 1747 the place was in ruins; the expedition in this year found traces of farming, adobe houses, and possibly the ruins of a Catholic chapel.

In 1688 it was reported that the Cíbolos would come to La Junta to trade, and these traders may well have been from this town, but they could have been plains Indians who traded for the agricultural produce and Spanish goods at La Junta. Some of these people, at least, apparently wintered at La Junta. Kelley thinks that the data indicate that they may have had some particular affiliation with the people of Puliques and San Cristóbal because of the statement "Cíbolas of Puliques and San Cristóbal," and because some had joined each pueblo. A few may also have been at Guadalupe, according to Trasviña Retis. In 1747 Cíbolos at La Junta stated that they (their ancestors) had come from this town (Kelley 1953; BL 1746).

Los Tapacolmes

Tapacolmes was located on the northeast bank of the Rio Grande, some 11 leagues down from San Cristóbal, in what is today the Redford Valley. By 1747 the settlement was abandoned; however, some 60 Pescado Indians, who at this time were living at Puliques, were reported to have dwelt here previously. Presumably, this site was also the place of origin of the Tapacolmes Indians who migrated to the Santa Cruz mission on the San Pedro River, and the place where the Chiso bands, Batayoliclas and Suninoliglas, were settled in 1693 by Retana (Kelley 1953; BL 1695a; 1746).

7. CHANGING INDIAN SETTLEMENTS AND POPULATION

In the early 1560s, there were no major, and practically no minor, Spanish settlements north of the city of Zacatecas. Within 200 years, the Spanish frontier had spread into all of the Nueva Vizcayan river valley area concerned in this report. Spaniards had established a great variety of settlements, from haciendas and mines to towns and cities, and had drastically affected the native populations of the entire region.

Tables 9 through 12 present in summary form the data on population and ethnic groups that form the basis of this paper. However, some additional comments are necessary to round out the picture of population changes during the colonial period in this sector of northern Mexico – population changes that proceeded at different rates at different times and places, depending on the specific conditions that prevailed.

The Franciscan mission system, one of the principal contact institutions, quite clearly followed the same pattern of development that was characteristic of the rest of Spanish settlement. In general, Spanish movement into and development of the region got off to a slow start, during the first eighty years or so of the colonial period. Then in the early 1630s came the rapid expansion of the Parral mining district, and it was not long before the mission system itself began to extend over a considerably wider area (see Table 9).

From the time of the earliest Spanish settlement of San Bartolomé, there was a religious establishment that ministered to the native population there. For many years, a

TABLE 9

Dates of Existence of Conchería Missions

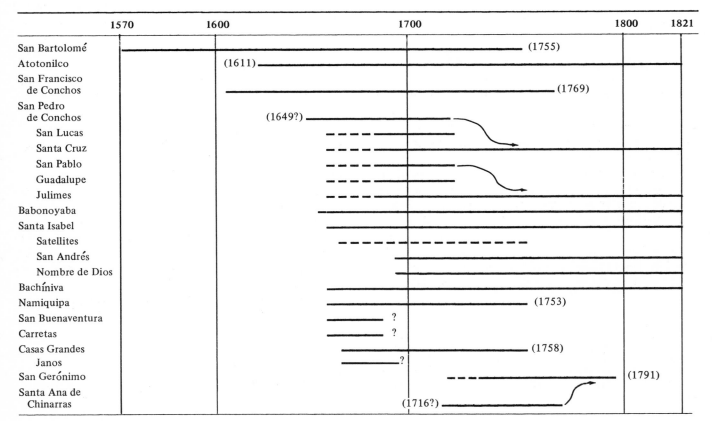

- - - - Evidence for existence is circumstantial.

few men of the order of Saint Francis worked the northern mission frontier from this administrative center. After some 30 years, in 1604, the mission of San Francisco de Conchos was founded, and within a decade, about the year 1611, Atotonilco was also established. Still, the expansion of Spanish holdings seems to have been slow, in comparison with later years. It was apparently not until about the 1630s and 1640s (taking the earliest dates indicated in the sources) that other religious establishments were founded – by Jesuits in the Tarahumara as well as by Franciscans in the Conchería (Dunne 1948). Several new Franciscan missions were then established within the two or three decades following the 1650s. By the end of the 17th century, the Franciscans had some dozen missions and many satellite parishes in operation. The following century, however, saw the demise of a number of these places, so that by the beginning of the 1800s, when the colonial period was ending, only eight missions remained, and these with few or no satellites.

Despite the lack of quantitative data for the 16th and 17th centuries, there is no doubt that from the time of first contact the Indian population of the Conchería, particularly the Conchos proper (that is, excluding the Jumano speakers), suffered a heavy reduction in numbers. This is indicated by the noticeable decrease in the occurrence of the name Concho during the 1600s (Table 10), although in 1677 it was said that the Concho nation (including La Junta?) was (still) among the most numerous of the peoples on the northern frontier (CPP 39: 292–309). There is some evidence that disease, in the early period of contact, exacted a high toll, and the overworking of laborers, especially in the mines – but also on farms – probably did its share.* In any event, there is no direct information (such as census reports or surveys) regarding population trends until the 1700s. What figures are available at this later time indicate an expected and continued reduction in the native population, although for the last 28 years of the colonial period the figures seem to show a slowing down in the rate of decrease. By this time, the remaining Indians were a very small percentage of the total population of the region.

Very little information exists on the populations of the individual Franciscan missions for the period prior to the last half of the 18th century. The San Bartolomé establishment itself never included many Indians, since the people it ministered to lived on haciendas; Atotonilco and San Francisco de Conchos had somewhat spotty ethnic and population histories because so many of the groups that were settled at these places later fled or moved away. Likewise,

there are practically no data for Santa Cruz de Tapacolmes, Namiquipa, Casas Grandes, or other mission holdings farther north that had greatly declined or become defunct by the early 1700s. The few figures that exist for these places for the 17th and early 18th centuries cannot provide a coherent picture.

There are only a few exceptions to this general dearth of information. In 1693, Julimes, with two visitas at that time, had a population of 124 families, totaling possibly as many as 400 individuals. The decrease to 88 persons at this mission in 1765 (see Table 11) is notable. Santa Ana de Chinarras also suffered a considerable decrease (although in a shorter time span), going from 200 persons in 1717 to only 74 in 1765. The mission of Santa Isabel, for which there are also some extant records, went somewhat contrary to this pattern, apparently owing in large part to an inmigration to this general area; since Santa Ana was within this same area of immigration, it would be interesting to know more of its history during this period.

In 1694 Santa Isabel was reported to have nine visitas totaling 1,500 persons (see p. 74). In 1765 nine sites* (now distributed among three different missions – Santa Isabel and its former satellites of San Andrés and Nombre de Dios) contained a total population of some 1,663 people. This would seem to indicate a certain amount of stability in overall numbers for the population of this area at this time.

On the surface, this same stability does not appear to hold, however, for the intervening years when more specific comparisons are made. It is possible to estimate the population in 1728 for Santa Isabel and its then three current satellites of Santa Cruz, San Bernardino, and La Concepción. The total number of adult males censused in this year for these four towns was 282 (AHP 1728Aa). Calculating that the average number of persons per family would be around 3.62 (the average number in 1694, when 414 families comprised a total of 1,500 persons in the nine towns of the entire mission of Santa Isabel), and that these adult males can essentially be considered to be heads of families, the total for the four towns in 1728 would be 1,021. For the sake of exposition, assuming that in 1728 these four mission towns comprised around one half the population of all the Santa Isabel mission towns as constituted in 1694 (by 1765 their proportion was actually about 40 percent rather than one half), then the total population in 1728 for all the earlier Santa Isabel mission towns would have been 2,000 persons or more, an increase of 25 percent since 1694. While these interpolated estimates may be high, they possibly indicate that over this 71-year period there was a peaking of population around 1728 for these mission towns. This pattern, of

---

*A petition for an encomienda of Indians, made by Diego del Castillo in the early 1640s, stated that the natives on his hacienda (one of the oldest in the area) had died off because of diseases (CD 1643). See also West (1949: 73, 125, fn. 71), who records that by the 1690s the shortage of local native labor (mostly Concho), owing to the high death rate, was being acutely felt.

---

*One visita, Sainapos, is not mentioned after 1701, and another, San Buenaventura (possibly the same place), is added in 1765.

TABLE 10

Summary of Tribal Groups at the Conchería Missions Outside La Junta, 1600–1817

	Early 1600s	Later 1600s	Early 1700s	ca. 1765	1789	1816–17
San Bartolomé	Conchos Julimes Mamites	increasingly more La Juntans	Conchos La Juntans	?	?	?
Atotonilco	Tobosos	Tarahumaras		Tarahumaras	Tarahumaras Conchos	Tarahumaras
San Francisco de Conchos	Conchos plus some Julimes Mamites	Conchos Chisos Tobosos	*1723* Conchos Chisos Tobosos Tarahumaras	Chisos Tarahumaras	?	?
San Pedro de Conchos	Conchos	Conchos		Conchos	?	?
Santa Cruz de Tapacolmes	Conchos plus some Julimes Mamites	Conchos Tapacolmes	*1724* Conchos plus all nations from La Junta		Cholomes Conchos Tapacolmes Tarahumaras	Conchos Tapacolmes Tarahumaras
Julimes	? probably Conchos	Julimes Conchos?	*1710* Conchos *1715* Auchanes	?	Cholomes Tarahumaras Julimeños	Tarahumaras Julimeños
Nombre de Dios	? probably Conchos	Conchos	*1730* number of Cholomes moved into area	Tarahumaras Conchos	Norteños Tarahumaras	Norteños Tarahumaras
San Gerónimo	probably Conchos	probably Conchos		Norteños Tarahumaras	Norteños Tarahumaras Chinarras	Norteños
Santa Ana de Chinarras			*1725* Conchos Tobosos Sumas Chinarras	probably some Norteños	?	?
Babonoyaba	Conchos plus Tarahumaras?	Tarahumaras	—	—	—	Tarahumaras
Santa Isabel	probably Tarahumaras, possibly a few Conchos at *visitas*	Tarahumaras	Tarahumaras	Tarahumaras	Tarahumaras	Tarahumaras
San Andrés	Tarahumaras, possibly a few Conchos at *visitas*	Tarahumaras	Tarahumaras	Tarahumaras	Tarahumaras	Tarahumaras
Bachíniva	probably Tarahumaras	Tarahumaras	Tarahumaras	Tarahumaras	Tarahumaras	Tarahumaras
Namiquipa	probably Conchos	Conchos	Conchos plus some Tarahumaras	Tarahumaras	Tarahumaras	
San Beunaventura del Torreón	?	Sumas	?	?	?	?
Casas Grandes	probably Sumas	Sumas plus some Conchos	*1728* practically defunct — much mixed: Conchos, Opatas, Sumas, Apaches, Sonoras	?	?	?
Janos		Sumas Janos?	Janos	Janos	Apaches	
Carretas		Sumas Janos?				

TABLE 11

Summary Population Figures for Native Groups at Major Conchería Missions Outside La Junta, 1765–1817

		1765	1789	1793	1816–1817 (Averaged)
Atotonilco		280	227	331	187.5
San Francisco de Conchos		289	0?	0?	0?
Santa Cruz de Tapacolmes		69	76	100	142
San Pedro de Conchos		74	?	?	?
San Antonio de Julimes	52 ⎫	88	76*	112*	61*
San Pablo	36 ⎭				
Babonoyaba	203 ⎫				
Guadalupe	100 ⎬	393	142*	192*	115.5*
La Concepción	90 ⎭				
Santa Isabel	185 ⎫				
San Bernardino	88 ⎬	653	425*	657*	334.5*
Santa Cruz	319 ⎬				
La Concepción	61 ⎭				
San Andrés	183 ⎫		118	170	178
San Bernabé	210 ⎬	787			
San Buenaventura	394 ⎭		[*visitas* apparently not censused]		
Bachíniva	100 ⎫	179	166*	200*	242.5*
Cossiquemachi·	79 ⎭				
Namiquipa	42 ⎫	128	?	?	?
Cruces	86 ⎭				
Nombre de Dios	100 ⎫		194* ⎫	395	148* ⎫ 351
San Gerónimo	121 ⎬		201 ⎭		203 ⎭
Chuvíscar	123 ⎬	372		262*	
El Alamillo	28 ⎭				
Santa Ana De Chinarras		74	?	?	?
Totals		3,386	1,625	2,024	1,612

*Including visita(s)?

course, may not have been true for any of the other missions of the area. For the four towns in question it will be interesting if future research is able to show whether the apparent increase was real, and whether it was due to immigration from other Tarahumara towns or due to natural increase.

For the later 1700s, the summary figures of Tables 11 and 12 can be considered at best only approximate, and as very general indicators of events occurring at the major missions of the Conchería during this time. In the entries for 1765 (Table 11), quite possibly more satellites were included in the censuses than in the later years, something that must be kept in mind when evaluating the evidence presented below. For example, the two visitas of San Andrés were included in its 1765 total, but almost certainly they were not counted in later years (contrary to what appears to have been the case for Santa Isabel). While the remaining evidence is only that of omission, for reasons of convenience and the lack of contrary positive evidence it is assumed that satellite parishes were not listed in 1789, in 1793, and in 1816–17 because they had in effect become defunct.

In 1765 the overall population for the Conchería missions (excluding those of La Junta, which are discussed below) was 3,386 persons. By 1789, after a period of 24 years,

this figure had dropped to 1,625 – a reduction of some 1,761 souls, or more than 50 percent. A slightly different interpretation can be made if the visitas of the San Andrés mission are excluded from these calculations, since apparently they were never censused again after 1765. Excluding these visitas in 1765, the total population of the Conchería would amount to 2,782 people. The loss between 1765 and 1789 would then be 1,157 persons, or about 42 percent.*

The census of 1793 registered a total increase of 397 persons over the 1789 figures, although at least for some of the sites considerably more children were included in the 1793 count. Thus the 1793 list might be a better census than that of 1789, and if so, a more accurate portrayal would

_____

*Diseases and epidemics were common during this period and no doubt account for some of this decrease in local population, despite the lack of direct historical evidence. A large epidemic had hit the Valley of Mexico area in 1779, and had moved northward into Sonora, New Mexico, and other northern territories by 1781. While no documents have turned up that mention an epidemic at this time for the Nueva Vizcayan region, it is reasonable to expect that an epidemic of such major proportions was also felt here (Dobyns 1966).

span the 28 years between 1765 and 1793 and would show a decrease of 758 people, or only 27.2 percent, excluding the San Andrés satellites; alternatively, the decrease would be 1,362 persons, or 40.2 percent, including the San Andrés satellites. For the remainder of the period, the 24 years up to the 1816–17 censuses, the loss was 412 people, or just under 20.4 percent. Thus from 1765 to 1816–17, a span of slightly more than half a century, the reduction was 42 percent, or 1,170, if the San Andrés satellites (totaling 604 people) are excluded from the 1765 total. If these satellites are included in the 1765 total of 3,386 persons, then the loss in population is 52.4 percent, or 1,774.

In summary, accepting here what seems to be the best information (omitting the San Andrés visitas in 1765, and using the 1793 figures rather than those of 1789), the population loss for the Franciscan missions outside of La Junta for the last 50 or so years of the colonial period indicates that the rate of decrease was about 27 percent for the first half of the period and about 20 percent for the second half. For the La Junta missions, the rate is unknown for this period because the places were not censused again after 1765. However, for the previous half century, from 1715 to 1765 (Table 12), these missions decreased from 1,819 people to some 787, or 56.7 percent. This is a loss of 435 persons, or 23.9 percent, over the period of 32 years from 1715 to 1747. Over the next 18 years, to 1765, the decrease was 597 persons, or 42.8 percent, almost four times the rate of the preceding period. Extrapolating from these crude figures, the La Junta establishments were losing people at an increasing rate; consequently, it could be expected that within a very few years after 1765, they would be practically devoid of people. The documentary evidence supports the conclusion that these missions indeed disappeared not long after 1765, probably within the next 20 years.

Returning to the missions outside La Junta, several factors that probably affected the above figures and the general rate of decrease should be mentioned. First, some of the fluctuations that occur in the counts can probably be attributed to faulty census taking (as in the difference between the 1789 and 1793 lists, mentioned above). Also, the total numbers of Indians at the missions concerned are so small that any slight deviation or error in absolute figures would radically shift the percentages.

More fundamental is another factor which, from the evidence available, had an important effect upon the rates of population loss at different sites – the more or less continuous migration into several of the mission settlements (and no doubt into other types of settlements also).

The data from the several church and parish archives, as well as from the censuses and other general reports (see individual site entries in Chapter 6), record a movement of Indians into the existing Franciscan missions during the 17th and 18th centuries. In the latter part of the colonial period, at the more northern missions still surviving, there were increasing reports of the appearance of Tarahumaras and what

were generically classed as Norteños (from the general La Junta and Rio Grande area). Thus, while most of the missions lost at least some population between the years 1765 and 1816–17, this was not the case for Bachíniva, Santa Cruz de Tapacolmes, Nombre de Dios, and San Gerónimo (Table 11). Bachíniva, which was traditionally in Tarahumara territory, continued to receive Tarahumara immigrants – it had lost population between 1728 and 1765, down from 266 souls to 179 (including its visita Cossiquemachi), but was almost back up to the earlier figure in 1816–17. The other three towns that gained population between 1765 and 1816–17 – Santa Cruz, Nombre de Dios, and San Gerónimo – were absorbing Indians mainly from La Junta, but also a few from the Tarahumara country. Probably the remaining missions for which figures are available – Julimes, San Andrés, Santa Isabel, Babonoyaba, and Atotonilco – would have shown a loss of even more persons than they did during this period but for this same factor of inmigration.

Some colonial writers also noted this process of immigration. In 1748 Saabedra, one of the two missionaries at La Junta, reported that the old people in the area remembered that at the time of first missionization (1715?), these pueblos had contained many people; however, at the time of his writing the population had been reduced to about 200 families because of either sickness and plagues (*peste*), or emigration (*fugas*) (BL 1746) – many of the emigrants no doubt having moved to the area of Chihuahua City. Some years earlier, in 1728, Jesuits recorded that some of the Tarahumaras from their missions were moving into the Chihuahua region (AHP 1728Ab). In the early 1730s, Arlegui reported the arrival of Cholomes in the same place. He also summarized the history of the Indian groups of the central river valley area, noting that "anciently the Conchos occupied much territory and many pueblos [but] today the Tarahumaras are the majority," with the Tarahumaras slowly resettling the towns that the Conchos (and others?) had abandoned ("y los que en los pueblos que desamparon van poblando" [Arlegui 1851: 100–1]).

In effect, the "Concho" population at the time of Arlegui's writing is likely to have been fairly low, at least at the missions. Jumping ahead a few years to the early 1760s, of the Franciscan missions outside La Junta listed by Bishop Tamarón, at least three were traditionally Tarahumara places – Santa Isabel, San Andrés, and Bachíniva – and one, Babonoyaba, had been taken over by Tarahumara. The population at these four establishments alone came to 2,012 persons, just under 60 percent of the total of 3,386. At the same time, other mission sites such as Atotonilco, San Francisco de Conchos, and San Gerónimo were reported to have a number of Tarahumaras. Indeed, by this time it would seem that the Franciscan mission system was predominately Tarahumara, with the non–Tarahumara Indians in central Chihuahua possibly not amounting to more than 1,000 to 1,200 at the very most, and the majority of these being Norteños or La Juntans whose roots were along the Rio

TABLE 12

Summary Population Figures for Native Groups at La Junta and Vicnity, 1715–1765

	1715	1747	1765
La Junta Proper			
El Mesquite/NS de Loreto	80	abandoned(?)	abandoned
Los Cacalotes/San Juan Bautista	165	143 Cacalotes 40 Conejos ——— 183 + 38 Cholomes either ——— here or at Mesquite 221	309 including persons from Mesquites and Conejos
San Francisco/Posalmes?/Oposmes?	180	167 (natives) 50 Tecolotes ——— 217	167
Guadalupe/Polacmes (includes some Cíbolos)	550	172 persons	194 may or may not include some nearby Pescados
San Joseph/Puliques	92	115 Puliques 96 Cíbolos 60 Pescados ——— 271	abandoned
Pueblo de Conchos	87	0?	0
San Cristóbal/Posalmes	180	154	117
Conejos/NS de Aranzazu	71	120	abandoned
San Bernardino/Tecolotes	(no figures)	abandoned	0
San Juan Evangelista	abandoned	0	0
Pueblo of the Cíbolos	(no figures)	abandoned	0
Tapacolme Pueblo	(no figures)	abandoned	0
Subtotal	1,405	1,155	787
Vicinity of La Junta, Upriver Conchos Area			
Santa Cruz de Ochanes	abandoned	299 refugees Cholomes Conejos Tecolotes plus others	in process of abandonment
Coyame/La Cieneguilla/ Santiago la Redonda	180	abandoned	0
San Pedro Cholomes	190	(no figures) (1751, said to be a large town with Conejos and some Sumas)	?
Cuchillo Parado/Conejos	44	abandoned	0
Subtotal	414	299+ (?)	0 (?)
Grand Total	1,819	1,384+	787+

Grande. Even when the population of the La Junta missions, some 787 people, is added to the total, bringing it up to 4,173, more than half are Tarahumara. It would appear without much doubt that by the mid-18th century very few of the descendants of the original Concho population remained, at least in a cultural sense.

The process of migration probably continued for a considerable time. However, as the La Junta zone became more depopulated in the latter half of the 18th century and as the ethnic boundaries of the Tarahumara were withdrawn westward and southward toward the higher mountain country, Indian immigration into the old Conchería would have slowed down more or less commensurately. If population figures were available, they would no doubt show a great decrease in the numbers of natives at the old Franciscan missions and settlements during the 19th century. Today the only Indians in the region are the occasional Tarahumara who come down from their mountain dwellings to do some trading and begging.

In summary, then, the greatest reduction of the native population for this area of Nueva Vizcaya occurred before 1765. The 1700s present a picture of merely a few remnant pockets of native population (not all, of course, at missions) – the results of a couple of centuries of European-Indian interaction within the context of the conditions set up on the frontier by the Spaniards. In considering 18th-century sites, allowing a reasonable margin of error for the population censuses, what might at times appear to be population stability or a slow rate of decrease is, at least in part, the result of immigration into the central zone of the old Conchería. Considering the La Junta area alone (see Table 12), if one assumes that a fair portion of the reported population (1,819 persons in 1715, 1,384 in 1747, and 787 in 1765) had indeed moved southward into the area during the 18th century, then there does seem to have been considerable assimilation of the aboriginal population by this time.

Comprehensive census material from administrative sources for this period would help give some perspective to this summary. Unfortunately, what little exists, aside from its unknown reliability, does not break down the population precisely enough for meaningful comparisons. For one report, dated at the beginning of 1730, it is impossible to determine with any accuracy what proportions apply to Conchería Indians. The total, excluding Tarahumaras, was 14,387 persons, listed under 29 tribal names: Choras, Tepehuanes, Xiximes, Xixies, Tubaris, Boroxios, Pimas, Nuris, Babosarigames, Atapobandas, Conchos, Chizos, Otaquitatomies, Mammetes, Julimes, Tapacolmes, Janos, Xocomes, Sumas, Mesquites, Cacalotes, Conexos, Poxalmes, Chinarras, Poaracmes, Hoposmes, Sibulos, Puclicas, and Zizimbres. Probably only the last 19 of these, beginning with the name Concho, were from the Conchería, the others dwelling farther south, either in the Sierra Madre country down into Nayarit or in the coastal lowlands.

Given the depletion of many of the native groups at this time, a conservative population estimate for 1730 would be about 1,500 to 1,600 persons for the La Junta groups (assuming a more or less constant rate of depletion between the census years of 1715 and 1747, shown in Table 12), and possibly another 1,300 to 1,400 (a rough estimate) for non-Tarahumara peoples at the remaining Conchería settlements – a total of 2,800 to 3,000. Subtracting these from the general non-Tarahumara total of 14,387, cited above, would leave a remainder of some 11,000 to 12,000 people for the other, non-Conchería groups in the general Nueva Vizcaya area, a good many of whom occupied part of the Sierra Madre country. The Tarahumara are listed in the 1730 report as consisting of 37,523 souls, and addition of the 14,387

listed as non-Tarahumaras brings the total native population of Nueva Vizcaya to 51,910 persons (CPP 151-72).

Another census 80 years later, in 1810, gives the total Indian population of Nueva Vizcaya as 63,890, with Spaniards numbering 35,992 and the several *castas* 77,303 (Porras Munoz 1966: 257). These figures would seem to be rather high, and in any event it is unknown what population might actually have been counted. Perhaps Bancroft's estimate (taken mostly from Bishop Tamarón's early 1760s report) is more meaningful since he restricts his coverage essentially to the area of the present-day state of Chihuahua. Aside from the 4,000 or so natives living at Franciscan missions, he calculates another 18,000 (probably mostly Tarahumaras) at Jesuit establishments, plus an additional 5,000 Indians dwelling in non-mission pueblos. This gives a total of 27,000 natives, out of 50,000 persons inhabiting this portion of Nueva Vizcaya (Bancroft 1884: 597-8).

Some additional data might be presented here for comparative purposes, to help show what position within late colonial Spanish society was occupied by those who had remained culturally Indian (or who were at least classified as Indian). Bancroft's figures for northern Nueva Vizcaya indicate that around the year 1760, Indians made up about 54 percent of the total population. However, two-thirds of this native population lived at Jesuit missions, almost all of which were located at some distance from the major centers of Spanish settlement in the lower river valleys. It was in the latter region that the Franciscans had their missions and that those people classified as Indians were a minority. And it was here that the Indians were subjected to considerable acculturation pressure from the hispanic population.

For example, in the early 1760s, Tamarón's report included the fact that there were some inhabitants who were culturally non-Indians (*gente de razón*) living within the jurisdictions of some of the mission parishes, or at least quite close by. Atotonilco was all Indian, but the neighboring Guajoquilla had something like 1,400(?) persons classified as non-Indians. The less than 300 Indians at San Francisco de Conchos were engulfed by 1,330 non-Indians (and later, between 1815 and 1822, Indians listed in the parish records here constituted only 18 percent of the population). Babonoyaba had 109 *gente de razón*; Santa Cruz had no Indians listed by Tamarón, but according to the parish records there were several Spanish holdings and a number of non-Indians in the immediate area. Santa Isabel was reported as all Indian, but in 1751 it had been noted that there were some Spaniards and mulattoes dwelling there. San Andrés had 210 persons *de razón* and the nearby mines of Cusihuiriachi had 1,353; Bachíniva was Indian but Namiquipa had almost twice as many non-Indians as natives. The remaining old mission sites to the north had lost their native Indian populations and had become defunct as missions long before this – San Buenaventura had 479 persons *de razón* and nearby El Carmen had 118, while Casas Grandes had no population of any kind mentioned and Janos had more than 400 non-Indian persons (Tamarón 1937: 120-23, 139-40, 150).

Some of the larger non-mission sites should also be noted as hispanic centers that would hold some attraction for Indians. Chihuahua City before the mid-18th century was one of the largest; Bishop Tamarón listed 4,652 persons there, and a number of other *gente de razón* were reported for surrounding settlements. The cathedral of the city was founded in 1709, and the present archives contain several books dating from the 18th century, beginning with 1721. Very few Indians appear in the entries. Most persons are mixed bloods and Spaniards, and the few Indians whose ethnic or tribal identification is given are Yaquis, Sonoras, and an occasional Indian from New Mexico (Tamarón 1937: 152-3; Chihuahua Cathedral Archives).

The mining town of Santa Eulalia (today, Aquiles Serdán), a few miles to the southeast and formally founded in 1707, two years before Chihuahua City, was slightly larger in population than the latter, but it lacked its governmental and commercial complex. Tamarón recorded 4,755 persons there, without specifically mentioning Indians (1937: 153-4). During the 1720s, about one-third of the baptismal entries in the parish records refer to Indians; most are Tarahumaras, but a few Julimes, Norteños, and Sonoras or Sinaloas (e.g., Yaquis) are noted also. In the entries for the years 1745 and 1766, the number of Indians specifically mentioned is down to about 23 out of 100, although there is a higher number of entries with no ethnic identity stated. The remaining entries list Spaniards and mixed bloods (classified as mestizos, *mulatos, coyotes, lobos,* and *castizos,* as in other parishes, but impossible to define precisely from the local data). By the 1780s and 1790s, there are only two classes of persons listed in these baptismal records – mestizos and Spaniards. The extant marriage records of Santa Eulalia for the 18th century follow a similar pattern (Aquiles Serdán Parish Archives).

Farther south is Santa Rosalía (today, Camargo, Chihuahua), located downriver from San Francisco de Conchos on the present-day highway that runs between Ciudad Delicias and Jiménez (the ancient Guajoquilla). The only surviving records date from late in the colonial period, after the last reestablishment of the town in 1797 (Almada 1968: 83), but they do provide another glimpse of the population of the region at this time. In a census of 1821, the town possessed 1,506 inhabitants, but no division by ethnic or caste grouping was given (BL 1821). However, the earliest extant parish records, in a book running from 1818 to 1828, do include a breakdown by *casta* for the years 1818 through 1822. There were only a few people recognized as Indians, and most were mestizos and Spaniards, in about equal proportions. The numbers of Indians in the baptismal records for the five years cited above were as follows: in 1818, 83 entries, with no aborigines noted and only six entries that do not classify the person being baptized; in 1819, 129 entries, with only two Indians recorded and seven people left unclassified;

in 1820, 121 entries, with one Indian and one unclassified; in 1821, 103 entries, with one unclassified and one Indian, said to be an Apache, who was adopted by her godmother on this occasion of her baptism; and in 1822, 144 entries, with only one Indian and seven unclassified (Camargo Parish Archives).

In the general Parral district, the old nuclear area of northern Nueva Vizcaya, Bishop Tamarón reported some 5,546 persons for the three major settlements – Parral (2,693), Santa Bárbara (1,020), and San Bartolomé (1,833). Another report, dating from 1766, gives 4,751 persons for the greater San Bartolomé district (consisting of 21 haciendas), although it is not clear how such a figure should be evaluated or compared with the one given by Bishop Tamarón. While there is no internal breakdown of the population in either report, it seems quite clear that Indians were a small portion of the total number of inhabitants (Bancroft 1884: 598; Tamarón 1937: 121).

Other materials on Parral give a better notion of the structure of the local population, and how this changed over time. In a census of 1788, which yielded a figure considerably higher than Tamarón's 2,693 of a quarter of a century earlier, the following proportions were listed. For Parral proper, Spaniards (873 persons) made up 36.9 percent of the population, mestizos (435 persons) made up 18.4 percent, people classified as *color quebrado* (776 persons), who today would also be called mestizos, 32.8 percent, and Indians (260 persons), 10.9 percent. The remaining 20 persons, less than 1.0 percent, were slaves. In the neighboring settlements of the district – Huertas, Hacienda de Almanza, Santa Rosa and ranches, San Cristóbal, and Minas Nuevas – the population was as follows: 5.6 percent Spaniards (56 persons), 35.4 percent mestizos (355 persons), 42.1 percent *color quebrado* (423 persons), and 15.3 percent Indians (154 persons); 1.6 percent (16 persons) were slaves. In summary, for the total Parral district censused, Indians made up about 13.1 percent of the population, Spaniards about 21.3 percent, and those who today would be classified as mestizos or mixed bloods, some 64.4 percent (AHP 1788Ad).*

By contrast, some 155 years earlier, in 1635, only a short time after the founding of Parral, this city (or district?) was said to have around 1,000 Spaniards and 4,000 Indians and slaves (Porras Munoz 1966: 298). In 1649 the governor of Nueva Vizcaya noted that the population of Parral (district?) comprised some 400 families (probably totaling around 1,500 persons), all large (*numerosas*), and consisting of Indians, Negroes, mestizos, and mulattoes who worked in the mines and on the haciendas; in addition, there were some 500 people who were constantly coming and going to and from Parral (CPP 7: 551-2). Some 25 years later, in 1674, it was reported that the mixture of *mulatos*, Negroes,

---

*The total of the individual population entries comes to 3,428 persons. The census report, however, states at the beginning that there are 5,001 people in the Parral district. The reason for this discrepancy is not clear.

mestizos, and *coyotes* was very high in the San Bartolomé area, but no breakdown with specific figures for these groups was given (CPP 39: 203-16).

In 1669, when Bishop Gorospe visited the Parral district, he recorded that at the "mines of Parral" he confirmed over 4,000 individuals, most of whom were Indians recently converted to Christianity. He also confirmed another 3,000 at the mining towns of San Diego de Minas Nuevas, San Francisco del Oro, and Santa Bárbara, as well as at Valle de San Bartolomé, where the Indians came in from their rancherias. He went on to say that he would have been able to confirm even more people if there had been more food and other necessary items (CPP 10: 315-32). Five years later, in 1674, it was reported that Parral had 80 Spanish *vecinos* (probably heads of families, making a total of 250 to 300 Spaniards?) (CPP 39: 203-16).

The proportions of different kinds of people changed somewhat, and it would appear that the population of the Parral district diminished during the 100 years prior to Bishop Tamarón's visit of the 1760s. However, the Chihuahua mining district and that of Cusihuiriachi, which had been developed during the intervening period, had absorbed some of this southern population.

Finally, in the northeast outpost of the old Conchería, at the chapel of the presidio of La Junta de los Ríos del Norte y Conchos (founded or refounded in 1773), only a few Indians are cited in the late 18th century. For the years 1775 through the mid-1780s, some 79 baptisms are recorded. Only six of the persons listed are identified as Indians; the rest comprise nine Spaniards, 17 *mulatos,* four *coyotes* (one of whom had a Spanish father and an Indian mother), and 41 unclassified. One of the latter, however, was said to have a Cholome mother, and several of the other entries are likely to have concerned Indians, for they involve individuals from towns such as Julimes and Santa Cruz de Tapacolmes, which contained some Indians at this time. One entry noted that there were Indian auxiliaries stationed at the presidio but did not state their tribal affiliations. Presumably at this time the native La Junta population was rapidly diminishing, but this is not necessarily indicated by these records since there is no certainty that they include the native nonmilitary population.

At Ojinaga in 1963 there existed a few scraps of parish books that record baptisms done at Nuestra Señora del Pilar del Presidio del Principe, the presidio church at the town of Coyame. These records touch on the years of 1792, part of 1807, into 1808, and a portion of 1813 through 1815. Of 44 entries counted, 38 do not mention the ethnic identity of the persons involved. Of the remainder, one was a mulatto and five were Apaches (two of gentile parents). Two of the Apaches were baptized in 1792, and two in the period 1813-1815 (Ojinaga Parish Records).

In summary, the number of people classified as Indians during the latter part of the colonial period was only a small proportion of the total population of the old Conchería, an administrative unit now long defunct. By no means did all of the persons called *indios* live at settlements formally classified as missions; unfortunately, present data do not indicate what proportion of the aborigines dwelt in the essentially hispanic communities. At the same time, the greatest proportion of the "non-Indian" population possessed some Indian ancestry, and many, no doubt, were predominantly Indian genetically, although culturally they belonged to a nonaboriginal way of life that was almost totally hispanic, except for a few dietary traits, probably some house construction, and the like.

Conversely, even those persons who were called Indians, either by the Spanish system of social classification or by their own identification, were probably for the most part hispanicized. The hispanicization of at least some individuals began soon after the Europeans entered the area, and as early as the 1650s a number of Conchos and Julimes Indians were said to be *muy ladinos* – that is, they spoke the Spanish language (in many cases, the term *ladino* also implied the acceptance of other items of Spanish culture, such as dress). In 1723, the Indians living at the town of Julimes were described as very hispanicized ("de mucha razon y espanolados"). Indeed, peoples as far away as La Junta, in the period around 1715 to 1730, were characterized by Spaniards as having accepted a number of hispanic culture traits (because of the many years they had worked for Spaniards in the Parral district), despite the fact that they still carried out their own dances and indulged in peyote intoxications. A number were said to speak Castilian and to wear the Spanish dress (the women specifically were said to wear *enaguas* and *camisas*; the Tapacolme governor from Santa Cruz de Tapacolmes was described as dressed in the Spanish style with a cape and shoes and was fluent in the Spanish language) (Bolton 1930: 325; AHP 1653Ad; 1715Ac; 1722Bb; 1723A; 1730Cc; UTD 1710-1738a).

8. CULTURAL PROCESSES AND ASSIMILATION

Within 250 years after the Spaniards entered the river valleys of the Nueva Vizcayan region under consideration here, the native Indian population had suffered tremendous reduction. By the beginning of the Mexican national period, the number of distinct, ongoing ethnic groups was only a small fraction of the great number of differently named bands, rancherias, and settlements that had once existed; indeed, the small number of ethnic group names that still occurred around the beginning of the 19th century apparently referred more to traditional designations of people from certain locales than to any viable, distinctive native sociocultural systems (Apaches and Tarahumaras excepted).

Much of the summary that is given below is of necessity quite preliminary. Many studies concerning a number of topics important for a thorough analysis of the factors of acculturation and assimilation will be needed before more definite conclusions can be reached. Specifically needed are better population figures and better information on the number of places such as towns, haciendas, mines, and other kinds of settlements that formed part of the colonial scene, as well as analyses of the economic, political, and general social import and influence of these social units. However, a general picture can be sketched that will summarize the present data.

In the 1560s, Spaniards began to penetrate the southern portion of the area, establishing mines, ranches and haciendas, and small towns. The major period of development of Spanish Nueva Vizcaya seems to have occurred after the large silver strikes at Parral in the 1630s, and it then progressed at a much faster pace than it had during the first 60 years or so. However, from the earliest decades, in the 1560s and 1570s, the native populations of northern Mexico had begun to feel the influence of the arrival of the Spaniards. Everywhere these Europeans entered and remained, they created a demand for labor that soon began to have repercussions upon the local native peoples, as well as on populations that dwelt farther away.

The slowness of early Spanish penetration into the northern hinterland seems to be reflected in the fact that, according to Miranda (1871), it was not until 1575, some seven or eight years after the Spaniards founded Santa Bárbara, that they contacted the Conchos Indians living only some 15 leagues north of that settlement. However, within the next seven or eight years the Europeans had already gone as far north as the La Junta country, looking for Indian recruits for their labor force (i.e., on slave-raiding expeditions). By this time, if not considerably earlier, the processes of change leading to a reduction of the native populations had already commenced. These earliest changes, which began to affect the general ecology of the region and the biological populations residing there, came in the form of many new diseases (viruses and bacterias), some new plants and animals (wheat and horses, for example), and no doubt some material cultural items that human portions of the regional ecosystems could use in their adjustments to their changing niches in the general ecological picture. Unfortunately, little or no data exist at present on these most fundamental questions, answers to which will eventually be needed if the northern Mexico case is to make any contribution to a general theory of culture change.

While the Spaniards brought with them their own basic institutions, these institutions at different places and times had varying effects upon the native Indian population. Not only was there a different array of contact social units in the several areas or regions of northern Mexico, but there were also some important variations in the focus of their pressure upon the native ways of life.

Missions, with which this paper is principally concerned, were involved mainly in the education or instruction of the natives. Often this activity could fit into the native enculturation systems when the priest or his assistants could begin to teach the young Indian children before they had arrived at the usual state of adult socialization as defined by the local native social system. The mission's particular emphasis upon the socialization-enculturation processes led to the introduction of many innovations in material culture, techniques, and thought patterns that began to skew the sociocultural systems of the Indians. Included in these new and alien influences were new forms of social organization on the levels of the community (new officials) and the family (godparents, marriage customs, and so on), as well as new customs and values in the religious, the ideological, and other intangible spheres of life. The policy and practice of the missionaries was to use community reorganization and development as means toward their goal of civilizing and Christianizing the natives in order to make them effective participants in the Spanish colonial society. In a very real sense, the emphasis of the mission was one of community cooperation.

Other Spanish contact institutions, such as the hacienda,

the mine, and the military contingent, had different aims with respect to native behavior and, ultimately, the native culture. These social units were focused much more upon specific task accomplishment that required the cooperation of individuals, often from different communities and cultures, in new social groupings or contexts; the emphasis here was not upon changes in community organization, cooperation, and ideology, but rather upon getting a job done. Teaching in these non-mission contexts was probably minimal (and may have been carried out in the context of applying negative sanctions); probably it involved only enough instruction to demonstrate the way the task should be done and the specific value of completing the job for the *patrón*, hacendado, or military commander.

The mission, therefore, was much more holistic in its intent than was the hacienda or mine. However, despite the fact that the missionaries did work on several aspects of Indian acculturation simultaneously, from new specific tasks to community reorganization, mines and haciendas were probably more thoroughgoing in their breakdown of native life than were the missions. While little is known of the specific conditions under which the Indians lived, mines and haciendas were responsible for uprooting individuals and, at times, entire families and placing them into new social contexts for greater or lesser periods. Here the natives were often forced to associate with individuals from other ethnic and language groups, some from a considerable distance away. Such intimate contact gave great opportunity for the exchange of cultural behavior, for intermarriage, and for the working out of other common social patterns in more radically new conditions than those that existed at the mission towns. In the latter the missionary attempted consciously to alter native practices, but in a more gradual fashion. Indeed, at the mission the Indians probably had greater opportunities to resist, or to modify in their own fashion, the innovations made by the Europeans.

In all of the contact social units the Indians were eventually forced to learn another language so that they could communicate with their fellow workers and associates, as well as with their Spanish masters or teachers. This was, of course, most often and in the long run Spanish, but in the 17th century it was sometimes Nahuatl (see Griffen 1969: 133-4). This seems to have been as true of the Franciscan missions as it was of the non-mission contexts (though it was in contrast to the situation at some Jesuit missions). Aside from the evidence that the Franciscans were not interested in learning the native vernaculars, the fact that people living at a mission often belonged to more than one language group would have inhibited the Franciscans' employing the native tongues for the catechism and for other types of instruction.

This multi-ethnicity was partly due to the proximity of the Franciscan missions to the principal areas of Spanish settlement. Indians were often induced away from the missions by hacienda and mine operators, and new natives would then be brought in to replace them. The result, at missions and at other contact social units, was a tremendous mixing of peoples, including Indians from widely spaced geographical areas – from as far south as central Mexico, the west coast, and New Mexico, and from many different groups in the Nueva Vizcayan province – as well as some Spaniards and Negroes.

Concurrent with this great amalgamation of peoples and cultures, and partly as an outgrowth of it, came the development of a common, widely shared colonial "Indian" subculture (and low social class, according to the *casta* system). As the native patterns broke down through a process of cultural leveling in the various aspects of the native culture (e.g., belief and ritual) the replacement patterns generally followed hispanic models, although some alternatives were no doubt on occasion available. Indian customs were eroded away in a process of cultural leveling in aspects of the native life for which alternative models were eventually presented. One example of this pattern would be what seems to have happened in the religious sphere. When native curers and ceremonial specialists were by and large unattainable at the mine or hacienda, or when native practices were pushed underground, the Indians either learned to go without the benefits of the rite sought, or they learned to recur to a religious specialist not of their own culture – whether this was another Indian, a folk curer of the developing colonial hispanic cultural system, or a priest of the formal Spanish religious system. In any event, these social units afforded the opportunity and the necessity for the Indians to learn a new *modus operandi* and eventually to forge a more or less common culture.

It is possible to draw a fairly clear picture of the gross population movements and shifts that took place as the processes of acculturation and assimilation were set in motion by the imposition of Spanish colonial society on the north Mexican frontier. First, as in other parts of Latin America, there was a general decrease in the original native population of the region. Second, and concurrently, as Spanish society developed it brought into the province a rather large influx of peoples from various other areas. A good number of these newcomers were Indians, but there were also many mestizos, mulattoes, and other caste groups. This gave opportunity for, and indeed resulted in, a great deal of biological intermixing of peoples of different ethnic groups and racial stocks (Indian, Spanish European, and some Negroes).

Third, those portions of the local native population that happened to reside closest to, and were therefore most accessible from, Spanish settlements and areas of development (with certain exceptions due to terrain) were affected more quickly than were the peoples of the hinterlands. Consequently, not all regions were affected equally, and, to be sure, some areas that were distant from the places where Spanish settlement flourished were never depopulated of their aboriginal inhabitants. These were (and are) the regions – such as the high mountain Tarahumara country – that Aguirre

Beltrán (1967) has called "zones of refuge" (*regiones de refugio*), where the biological and cultural continuity may be very high, albeit with some change. Although the Tarahumara highlands are one of these refuge zones, the eastern and northern borders of Tarahumara country have suffered some contraction, by hispanicization, since the beginning of the colonial period. However, in a somewhat paradoxical development, during much of the colonial contact period the Tarahumaras actually moved eastward and northward rather than contracted their borders. While sometimes the Spaniards intentionally colonized certain abandoned Concho and Tepehuan settlements with Tarahumaras, much of Tarahumara movement was a slow occupation of the border areas left vacant by the Conchos as these became acculturated or assimilated or died off.

Possibly, or even probably, many of the Tarahumaras who did infiltrate these border areas were already somewhat acculturated, or were at least sympathetic to the Spanish way of life; others were captives taken in Spanish slave-raids. The result was that the people and the cultural configuration along this Tarahumara border zone became shuffled and hispanicized during the colonial period.

A similar pattern characterized the northern regions of Nueva Vizcaya. There occurred a general movement of population southward, first to the Parral district, when Spanish activity was concentrated there, and later to other centers of Spanish activity such as Cusihuiriachi and Chihuahua City. This process is particularly striking with regard to peoples of the La Junta district; at times whole communities, or at least segments of communities (e.g., Cacuita-taomes, Cholomes, Tapacolmes), moved southward in order to live closer to the haciendas and other places of work, and because of ecological pressures, to some extent including raiding nomads such as Apaches. Indeed, the apparent stability of the mission population during the last 50 or so years before Mexican independence was in large measure due to the influx of La Junta peoples into the river valley missions.

This process is indeed noticeable over the whole of the northern area. A number of the nomadic, desert-dwelling peoples were brought in from the north expressly to settle at missions, although many simply moved southward of their own volition because of the attraction of the Spanish system (or because their own by this time may have been broken down and their population decimated).

While the data indicate that the major population shifts were in the nature of a centripetal movement toward the areas of Spanish settlement, there was at the same time a distinguishable centrifugal shift of people. This seems to have been a fairly minor process, and one much more difficult to document, with individuals and sometimes groups

moving away from Spanish settlement – often to join the uncontrolled desert nomads, as some Conchos did in the 1600s, or to settle at La Junta, as the reference in 1715 to a Concho town at that place perhaps indicates. The Julimeños who moved to Coahuila may also be a case in point.

In general summary, as the colonial period drew on, there were fewer and fewer Indians settled in the hinterland who could or would come to the Spanish holdings to work, or for other reasons. At the same time, the communities proximate to the Spaniards, from which they obtained workers, came increasingly to be composed of half-acculturated, semi-detribalized Indians. This process continued through the colonial period, creating a low-class, hispanicized worker group, until the Indian ways had essentially disappeared.

Looking at this picture of increasing development of a culturally non-Indian, hispanicized "mestizo" population in the 18th century (biology aside for the moment), it appears on the surface that the role of the Franciscan missions that remained at this time was to create little islands of Indian population in a rising sea of mestizos. This may be only partially correct, however, since the cultural characteristics of these small pockets of natives are for the most part unknown (see the end of Chapter 7 for a few statements on acculturation) and consequently cannot be compared with those of the surrounding population (also unknown in sufficient detail).

The Indians who ultimately joined the Spaniards (the major exceptions being those who resided in the "zone of refuge" of the highland Tarahumara) became for the most part genetically and culturally extinct, although first they may have joined the nomadic desert raiders in the back-country. However, this route did not necessarily lead to total extinction, for incoming Apaches (some of whose descendants were eventually settled in the United States) absorbed some of these people.

Finally, the shifts in geographical focus of both the Spanish mission system and Indian revolts and raids reflect these trends in population movements and in assimilation and acculturation. As the area of Spanish settlement grew outwards from the original district of Santa Bárbara and as the Indians who dwelt within this area became more assimilated, the contact border zone inhabited by the less-acculturated natives was moved farther into the hinterland. Although raiders continued throughout the period to penetrate into the heavily settled Spanish areas, by the period around the turn of the 18th century both Indian revolts *per se* and some of the more intense mission activity (e.g., in the Casas Grandes district) were taking place at a considerable remove from the area of original Spanish contact around Santa Bárbara and Parral.

REFERENCES

DOCUMENTS

AGN: Archivo General de la Nación, Mexico City

1617 Historia Vol. 308. Francisco de Arista, Relacion de La guerra de los Tepehuanes este mes de dic.e de *1617.*

1618 Historia, Tomo 308, Francisco de Arista, Relacion delo succedido en la guerra de tepehuanes este mes de febrero de 1618.

1640 Misiones Leg. III–7. Autos, 4 y 5 de enero, 1640, gobernador Francisco Bravo de la Serna, Parral.

ca. Misiones Leg. III–7. Guadiana; Pareseres q el sr
1640 G.l Don franco bravo de la serna govor y cappan General deste Reino de la nueva Viscaya ymbia al exmo sr Marqs de Cadereita Virrey de la Nueva espana el uno sobre la entrada de los Padres de La compania de Jesus a la nueva Comberssion de los yndios de la nacion Taraumar, Y el otro del descubrimiento que se a echo de una laguna de sal Muy Considerable a su Mag.d y a sus Rs quintos en las Naciones Tepeguanes y Tobosos.

1651 Misiones Leg. III–7. Gob. Diego Guajardo Fajardo, Parral, abril 24 de 1651, al rey.

1653 Misiones 26. Mision de San Francisco Javier, 1653.

1662 Misiones 26. Letter from Pe Franco de Mendoza, Zape *6 de junio de 1662,* to visitador grl Hernando Cavero.

1677a Misiones 26. Thomas de Guadalajara, Triunfo de los Angeles, y Julio 20 de 1677 anos, to Provincial.

1677b Leg. III–7. Jose Tarda al Pe Provincial, San Bernabe, 22 de julio de [16]77.

1677c Leg. III–7. Thomas de Guadalajara al Pe Provincial Thomas de Altamirano, Los Angeles, noviembre 5 de 1677.

1678 Misiones 26. Relacion de las Missiones que la Compania tiene en el Reyno y Provincias de la Nueva Viscaya en la Nueva Espana echa el ano de *1678* con ocasion de la Visita General dellas que por orden del Pe Provincial Thomas Altamirano hizo el P. Visitador Juan Hortiz Capata de la misma Compania.

1684 Misiones 26. Juan de Almonazir, Noviembre de 1684, visitador de las misiones de Sinaloa, Sonora, y Californias de la Compa de Jesus and Petition from Juan Antonio Estrella, sin fecha.

1691a [auto] D Diego de Vargas y Zapata Lujan, 22 de marzo 1691, El Passo del rio del norte.

1691b Diego de Vargas al Conde de Galve, 14 de agosto, 1691. El Passo del rio del nortte.

1691c Diego de Vargas to Juan Ysidro de Pardinas, El Passo, Agosto 14 de 1691.

1691d Diego de Vargas to Conde de Galve, El Paso, Octubre 4 de 1691.

1691e Diego Vargas Zapata lujan Ponze de Leon deste precidio Nrra Sra del pilar y el Gloriosso San Jose, y abril 29 de 1691, al Cappn Cabo y Caudillo Juo fernandez de la fuente.

1691f Juo fernandez de la fuentte, Janos, abril 19[?] de 1691 al Gov y capn Genl dn Diego de bargas zapata y lujan.

1692 Juan Fernandez de la Fuente, Presidio de San Phelipe y Santiago de Xanos, 29 de abril de 1692.

1725 Juo de Guendulain, Cocorin, Dicieme 22 de 1725 al Pe Provincial Gaspar Roder.

1730 Juan Mar^tz del Hierro to P. Prov^l Juan Antonio de Oviedo, Yepomera, Septiembre 24 de 1730.

1751– Estados de las missiones q adentro se espresan,
1757 sus familias, Casamtos Baupmos y entierros desde el ano de 1751 a 57, Dionysio Murillo, Sta Anna de los Chinarras y Febrero 23 de 1758.

1790a Misiones 13. Noticia de todas las Misiones que hay en el Reyno segun las instancias del expediente P. Y. n° 126, con expresion de las Provincias de Regulares y colegios Apostolicos que las administran . . . Mexico, 5 de octubre, 1790.

1790b Misiones 13. Relacion del numero de Misiones que hay en esta Provincia de San Luis Potosi. 7 de noviembre de 1790.

1790c Misiones 13. Estado Puntual de los Signodos que Se satisfazen en esta Yntendencia de Durango a Misioneros. 23 de noviembre de 1790.

1793 Historia Tomo 42. 27 de diciembre de 1793, Mexico, Exmos.r — El Conde de Revilla gig — do Exmos s.r D.n Pedro de Acuna [includes a report of the missions of Nueva Vizcaya].

1816 Misiones 11. Estado abreviado de las Missiones de esta Provincia de N.S.P.S. Franco de los Zacatecas; Ano de 1816, Ano de 1817, Ano de 1818. Lista de los conventos vicarios y Misiones q cumbieron a cargo de la Provincia de N.S.P.S. francisco de los Zacatecas y se han entregado a los Mnros Pres obispos en la Secularizacion hecha de orn del Rey N.S.

AHP: Archivo de Hidalgo del Parral, Parral, Chihuahua (microfilm, University of Arizona Library, Tucson)

Note: Capital letters A, B, C, and D following the date indicate the microfilm reel designation of that year, and lowercase letters indicate separate items on the same reel. The first number in the citation refers to the document number on the reel.

1637B   G-4. Criminal contra Franco Hernandez por robo.

1640C   G-108. Criminal, Averiguacion practicada por el Alcalde Don Francisco de Escobar Trevino, con motivo de las muertes y heridas que hubo al pelear indios Conchos, sinaloas y otras nacines [*sic*], despues de haber hecho un Saseme — Parral –.

1641A   34. Expediente sobre las doctrinas mandadas observar en este Real de San Jose de Parral.

1644A   No. 13. Ynformacion que rinde Fernando Gardea [*sic* — Garcia] para que se vea que su Hda esta muy inmediata alas naciones de los indios rebeldes.

1645Aa   104. Expediente formado con motivo de la paz de los yndios Tobosos por el Maestre Francisco Montano de la Cueva.

1645Ab   102. Autos para acordar lo conveniente a la seguridad y al recibimiento de los Yndios que se mandaron traer de tierra adentro para la cosecha detrigo.

1652A   No. 33. Expediente sobre la guerra que se hizo contra las naciones indias alzadas.

1652B   G-75. Expediente pa q se hagan unos pagos y continue la guerra contra los Indios Tobosos.

1652D   G-12. Criminal Contra Juan yndio en averiguacion de si fue de los indios sublevados.

1653Aa   G-101. Administrativo y de Guerra, Autos de guerra hechos por el gobernador Diego Guajardo Fajardo sobre la campana contra los Tarahumares.

1653Ab   No. 25. Autos de guerra sobre la paz de los indios retirados de los Tobosos.

1653Ac   No. 10. Autos sobre la paz de los Yndios Salineros.

1653Ad   No. 5. Autos de Guerra contra los Yndios Tobosos por Diego Guajardo Fajardo.

1653Ae   No. 43. Informacion a pedimento de Juan Mansso para poder vender unos Yndios apaches.

1653Ba   No. 22. Autos sobre la paz que se otorgo a varios Yndios.

1653Bb   No. 4. Autos sobre la venida de los Yndios Tarahumares para la guerra de los Tobosos.

1653Bc   No. 3. Autos de guerra contra los Yndios alzados seguidos por Cristoval Nevares en el pueblo de San Felipe.

1653Bd   No. 1. Autos formados con motivo de la venida de Hernando Obregon y de la Junta de Guerra contra los Yndios.

1654Aa   No. 2. Autos De Guerra hechos por el Gobernador General don Enrique Davila y Pacheco contra los indios Conchos y Tobosos que roban y matan a un carbonero de Santiago de Minas Nuevas 28 de Enero.

1654Ab   No. 5. Expediente relativo a la paz que se hizo con los Yndios Tobosos.

1654Ac   No. 72. Informacion Original hecha en este Reyno de la nueva Vizcaya de las muertes, robos, y danos que los Yndios naturales de ella hacen.

1655A   No. 5. Autos de guerra con motivo de las frecuentes abusos que cometen los indios enemigos de la Real corona.

1656A   No. 3. Autos y Diligencias originales practicadas con motivo de la guerra que hacen los indios enemigos de la Real Corona.

1657B   N 113. Criminal iniciado en Durango por el Gobernador Davila Pacheco sobre asalto q en el paraje de cerrillos serca del rio de Nazas cometieron los indios al tres de carros [?] de matiasde Hinojosa q resulto herido.

1658Aa   N 6. Diligencias practicadas con motivo dela guerra que hacen a la real Corona por los indios alzados.

1658Ab   G-10. Expediente de Averiguacion de unos indios que se sacaron de sonora [*sic*].

1669B   103. Autos practicados con motivo de dar paz a los indios enemigos.

1673A   No 152. Expediente sobre la Poblacion y misiones de los alsados de Don Pablo Yndio Tarumar en la tierra adentro.

1684Aa   No. 106. Expediente formado con motivo de la guerra que hacen los indios alzados a la Real Corona.

1684Ab   No. 113. Autos de guerra contra los Yndios alzados en Conchos.

1684Ac   No. 114. Autos de guerra contra los indios rebeldes a la Real Corona –.

1684Da   No 140. Criminal en averiguacion de las muertes y demas danos que hicieron los indios rebeldes en San Antonio de Casas Grandes.

1684Db   No 147. Criminal en averiguacion de las muertes que hicieron los Yndios rebeldes.

1684Dc   G-154. Criminal, De los Indios rebeldes Conchos y Taraumaras.

1685Da   No 46. Criminal contra un Indio de nacion Concho por presunciones de ser uno de los que asaltaron los Carros de Diego de Andavaso.

1685Db   N 45. Criminal contra Domingo Indio por presuncion de ser de los alsados.

1685Dc   49. Criminal En averiguacion de la sublevacion de los Indios Sumas.

1686A   N 3-A. Ocurso de don sebastian governador de los naturales de julimes pidiendo un religioso para que administre dho pueblo.

1686Ba   N-23. Criminal, En averiguacion del asalto y muerte que dieron los indios en los Sauces cerca de Santiago Papasquiaro en ese asalto mataron 7 personas y se llevaron 350 mulas de una recua que se dirigia a Durango.

1686Bb   N-25. Criminal, Contra Domingo de los Reyes mulato libre de la baqueria del capitan Domingo de Apresa y falcon sobre muertes de indios hechos en jurisdiccion de San Antonio de Casas Grandes.

1686Bc   No 19. Criminal contra un Yndio llamado Canuto por haber sido traidor a la Real Corona.

1687Aa N 11. Guerra, Informacion hecha a peticion de Bartolome Vazquez sobre el asalto que a una recua y carros que Venian de Mexico para este Real dieron los indios en la Boquilla del Gallo e informacion del Gov de Neira y Quiroga, para ver si cumplieron con su deber los jefes de los presidios.

1687Ab Num 8. Autos, Acordados por el Gobernador referentes a la guerra con los Yndios rebelados contra la Real Corona.

1687Ac No. 6. Autos de guerra formados a los indios revelados contra la Real Corona.

1687Ad N 13. Dununcio y adjudicacion de unas Caballerias de terria en favor de los naturales de San Antonio de Casas Grandes.

1688A 105. Diligencias practicadas con motivo de unos Yndios enemigos de la Real Corona los cuales fueron aprendidos por el Capitan Juan de Salaices.

1688Ca N 129. Criminal en averiguacion de si cuatro Yndios que aprehendieron son o no de los enemigos —.

1688Cb No. 128. Criminal contra un Yndio llamado Alonso, por traicion a la Real Corona.

1692A N 5. Autos de guerra contra los indios reveldez a la Real Corona.

1695 n 1. Testimonio de los autos de guerra que se practicaron con motivo de la guerra que hacen los enemigos de la Real Corona.

1697Aa 34. Informes de Guerra levantados por el Gral Juan Fernandez Retana, sobre sublevacion de los Tarahumaras.

1697Ab No. 35. Testimonio de los autos que se practicaron con motivo del alzamiento de los Yndios de la nacion Taraumar seguido por el Gral Juan Fernandez.

1697Ac G–33. Autos practicados con motivo de la Sublevacion de los Yndios Seguidos por Don Andrez de Rezabal.

1697Ad G–32. Autos de Guerra, Autos de Don Gabriel del Castillo cerca la guerra de las Tarahumaras y Pimas de Batopilas y la provincia de Sonora.

1699a N 123. Criminal en averiguacion si tiene o no culpa Nicolas Castaneda por encontrarse entre los indios enemigos.

1699b N 104. Gestion de D Jose Neira y Quiroga como apoderado Diego Alvarez Salgado para que se le remitan 15 indios de Nacion Concha por trabajo de su Hacienda.

1699c N 101. Administrativas, Autos de Guerra en Janos.

1700a n 122. Criminal contra Juan Antonio indio por haberse puesto de acuerdo con los indios rebelados contra la Real Corona.

1700b G–142. Queja de los indios de Babonayaba.

1701a N 103. Autos de Guerra practicados por el capitan Juan Fernandez de la Fuente contra los enemigos de la Real Corona.

1701b G–125. Administrativo, Folios 42 a 88 sobre cuestiones de guerra.

1704Aa No. 103. Autos practicados con motivo de la guerra que hacen a los enemigos de la Real Corona.

1704Ab No. 137. Guerra, Autos hechos por Dn Gregorio Alvarez Tunos y Quiroz en Sta Rosa de Coadeguarachi, Teniente de la Provincia de Sonora sobre robos de los indios pimas y su persecucion. Cartas del P. Juan Bautista de Escalante y de los Capitanes Antonio leal y Andres del Castillo.

1704Ba G–142. Criminal, Sublevacion contra la real corona.

1704Bb No 133. Criminal en averiguacion de la fuga de unos indios.

1706 G–13. Administrativo, Autos hechos por el Genl. Juan Fe. de Retana en la visita de la nacion de Indios Tarahumares.

1708a N 5. Diligencias practicadas con motivo de la paz que piden los Yndios de Nacion Acoclames.

1708b N 34. Administrativo y de Guerra, Autos de Guerra y diligencias practicadas contra los enemigos de la Real Corona.

1710a N G–24. Criminal contra el indio Diego Rafael por falsedad.

1710b G–8. Expediente por el que se vee que se concede licencia para la formacion del Pueblo de Julimes [sic].

1715Aa N 106. Guerra, Expediente relativo a la campana hecha por el governador don manuel san juan de santa crus contra los indios Cocoyomes y Acoclames.

1715Ab N 108. Informacion sobre las muertes y robos que han cometido los enemigos de la Real Corona.

1715Ac G 134. Administrativo, Diligencias practicadas con motivo de la orden para que vuelvan los indios que estaban en el Valle de San Bartolome a sus pueblos de la junta del rio del norte, y contradiccion que hicieron los labradores del valle.

1716A G–101. Autos Sobre la Reduccion de los Yndios Janos y la Mission de Sn Antonio de Cassas Grandes, y Administracion de Unos y Otros — Siendo Govor y Capn Grl el sr Dn Manuel sn Juan de sta Cruz, Cav[ ] del Orden de sntiago.

1716B G–116. Criminal en averiguacion secreta por no haber dado algunos Gobernadores de Pueblo de indios cumplimento al decreto que previene que los indios trabajen en las haciendas.

1718Aa No 7. Comunicaciones y autos de guerra contra los enemigos de la real Corona.

1718Ab No 9. Guerra, Testimonio de un Despacho de Virrey Duque de [Alburquerque] de 1656 para hacer la Guerra a los Tobosos.

1718Ac N–7. Comunicaciones y autos de guerra contra los enemigos de la Real Corona.

1718Ad N 5. Autos sobre remision de una Yndia llamada Juana que solicita Antonio Arias Visitador de la tarumara.

AHP: Archivo de Hidalgo de Parral *(continued)*

1718Ae No 12. Administrativo, 1718, Autos y Providencia sobre la reducion de los Yndios de la Nacion apache que en ellos se expresan Por El ssr Dn Manuel sn Juan de santa Cruz Cavallero deel horden de Santiago Govor y Capitan General deeste Reyno de la nueba Vizcaia sus provencias y fronteras por el rey nuestro Senor.

1720A G-102. Guerra, Diligencias y documentos relativos a la paz que ofrecieron los indios Acoclames, Venidos de Sierra Mojada del Gob Martin de Alday.

1721A G-1. Administrativo, Autos de guerra de la campana hecha por el Governador Martin de Alday, en la provincia de coahuila.

1722Ba G-112. Autos de Guerra, Orden del General Jose lopez de Carbajal, gobernador de la provincia para perseguir a los indios que robaron en la hacienda de Santa Cruz pertenecientesa los lic Neiras.

1722Bb G-107. Guerra, Providencias tomadas por el Gob Lopez de Carbajal para evitar el levantamiento de los indios de las misiones que estan en la junta de los Rios del Norte, segun carta de Fray Andres Baro.

1722D G-123. Criminal contra unos vaqueros de la hacienda de Conchos por haber matado 4 indios de San Francisco.

1723A G-104. Guerra, Testimonio de los autos que su fulminaron sobre la sublevacion y pacificacion de los indios de nacion Tacuitatomes "alias" Chisos que habitaban en el Pueblo de San Francisco de Conchos por el Gob don Martin de Alday.

1725Aa No. 107a. Guerra, Orden del Gov Lopez de Carvajal para que los Capitanes de los Presidios imediatos a parral opinen sobre la campana que se iba a hacer a los indios COCOYOMES, ACOCLAMES, SISIMBLES, TRIPAS BLANCAS, Y CUAGUILENOS, San Felipe el Real, agosto 9 de 1725.

1725Ab G-104. Guerra, Representaciones que ante el Gob Lopez de Carvajal hicieron los soldados de los presidios del gallo, mapimi, pasaje y cerro gordo por el descuente de haberes ordenado por el Brigadier Pedro de Rivera visitador de Presidios y testimonio de diligencias sobre la fuga de los soldados del valle de San Bartolome, cartas del Capn de Janos y del gob de nuevo mexico.

1725B G-137. Administrativo, Documentos Varios.

1725C G-125. Administrativo, El apoderado de Dna Maria Rosa pide al Gobernador y este concede que 30 indios de San Pedro de Conchos y Sta Cruz vayan a las labores de las haciendas de lapeticionaria a trabajar por via de repartimiento o tanda. El Gov de Santa Cruz dijo que el padre hace esclavos a los indios.

1727Aa G-6. Administrativo, Testimonio de los autos hechos por el Gob. Lopez de Carvajal sobre la oferta de paz que hicieron los indios Cocoyomes y acoclames en Parral —.

1727Ab G-7. Administrativo, Cartas delgral Antonio Becerra Nieto del Presidio de Janos y del Gob. Lopez de Carvajal, sobre la sumision de los indios Sumas.

1728Aa G-107. Administrativo, Nomina de los indios que contienen las misiones que administran los Rvdos Padres Religiosos de Sr Sn Francisco, remitadas al Gob Barrutia —.

1728Ab G-106. Administrativo, Nominas de los indio[s] que contienen las misiones que administran los Rvdos Padres de la compania de Jesus, remitidas al Gob Barrutia.

1730A G-10. Administrativo, Queja de los naturales del Pueblo de Julimes contra su misionero fr. Juan de Tilarnas [?] y orden de Gob. Barrutia para que el Cap Protector de esos indios don Jose de Berroteran investigue los hechos, Diligencias practicadas por el Citado Capitan.

1730Ca G-43. Criminal formada por orden del Gob Barrutia sobre las muertes de dos indios Tarahumares herida de un sirviente de Encinillas al prender los Isidro de Vera, Mayordomo de dicha Hacienda por decir estar poblados en dicha hacienda varios indios de los que presento 15 — San Felipe el Real —.

1730Cb G-44C. Ano de 1730 — Diligencias executtadas pr Don Joseph sanz Gallano, alias Carrero thenientte del Partido en q esta la estancia de Sn Diego[,] sobre la muerte que executto un Yndio Tarumar, a otro Cholome etca —.

1730Cc G-44D. Ano de 1730 — Diligencias que se han formado para q los religiosos de Nro Padre san francisco entren a los Pueblos de los Rios del Nortte y Conchos a Chattequizar a los Yndios etca. —.

1731A G-53. Administrativo, Carta de Gob Lucas Flores transcribiendo la queja de Gob de Pueblo de San Andres, Nicolas de la Cruz, quejandose del Padre Misionero que extorsiona a los indios —.

1779Aa G-101. Administrativo, Lista de la 1ª Compania del 2º Escuadron del Cuerpo de Dragones Provinciales.

1779Ab G-102. Administrativo, Fuerza y Destinos del Cuerpo de Dragones Provinciales de San Carlos.

1784A G-12. Administrativo, Listas de Revista Relacion Cuatrimestre y oficio de remission, correspondte al dia 4 de Agosto de 1784.

1787A No G-32. Guerra, noticias que por orden del Cavallero de Croix rendian los Alcaldes de este Real sobre las incursiones de los indios a esta jurisdicion durante los anos de 1778-1787.

1788Aa G-3. Administrativo y Guerra, Revista General del Estado y listas con Oficio de remicion concluida el 2 de Henero de 1788.

1788Ab G-6. Administrativo, Relacion de Revista Quatrimestre pasada el 6 de Abril de 1788.

1788Ac G-4. Administrativo, Relacion de Revista Quatrimestre pasada en 3 de Agosto de 1788.

1788Ad G-2. Administrativo, Padron del vecindario que tiene este Real de Minas de San Jose del Parral y su Jurisdiccion (1788).

1788B   G–11. Administracion, Pies de Lista de la 7ª compania de Alternacion y escuadron de Auxiliares de Atotonilco al cargo del Capitan Dn. Jose Ramon Diaz de Bustamante Desde la Creacion.

1794a   G–17. Administrativo, Siete Revistas Cuatrimestres — desde 3 de Agosto de 1794.

1794b   G–9. Administrativo, Relacion de Revista Quatrimestre pasada en 30 de Abril de 1794.

1794c   G–10. Administrativo, Legajo de Asuntos varios correspondientes al ano de 1794.

1795   G–3. Administrativo, 5 Revistas en Abril de 1795.

1797A   G–1. Papeles Varios.

1798A   G–6. Administrativo, Asuntos varios con 4 legajos de 91 fls.

BL: Bancroft Library, Berkeley, California

1649–   AGI: Audiencia de Guadalajara 29 (66–6–18).
1700   Simancas y Secular, Audiencia de Guadalajara. Cartas y expedientes de los Gobernadores de Durango. Ano de 1649 a 1700.

1674   Saltillo: Archibo de la Secretaria de Gobierno del Estado de Coahuila; Legajo No. 1, Anos 1688 a 1736; Ano de 1674 — Coahuila. Autos de la Conquista de la Prov.a de Coahuila.

1693–   AGI: Audiencia de Guadalajara 151 (67–4–1).
1702   Secretaria de Nueva Espana, Secular. Audiencia de Guadalaxara. Expediente sobre la guerra de los Yndios enemigos de Parral: anos de 1693 a 1702.

1693a   AGI: Audiencia de Guadalajara 152 (67–4–12). Nueva Viscaya Ano de 1693. Ynforme fho por la Prov.a de Sonora Sobre el estado en q se halla Con la guerra que remite a su Mag.d el Sarg.to m.or D. Juo Ysidro de Pardinas Villar de francos gov.r y Cap.n gen.l de este Reino.

1693b   AGI: Audiencia de Guadalajara 152 (67–4–12). Nueva Viscaya. Ano de 1693. Autos Sobre las Ynvasiones q hasen los Yndios Reveldes en este Reino Y lo q se ha ejecutado sobre la Guerra ofenciva — Tobosos Gavilanes Cocoyomes Hijos de la tierra y de las Piedras, chichitames, y otras etca. Por el Sr Sargto mor Dn Ju Ysidro de Pardinas Villar de francos Cav.o del orden de Sntiago Gov.or Y Capn Genl de la Nueva Viscaya por su Magd etca.

1694–   AGI: Audiencia de Guadalajara (67–4–12) 152.
1698   Expediente sobre los Yndios Tobosos y sus aliados. Anos de 1694–1698.

1695a   AGI: Audiencia de Guadalajara 151 (67–4–1). Govierno. Ano de 1695. Testimonio de los auttos fhos Sobre las Providencias dadas en tiempo de Dn Gabriel deel Castillo Governador de el Parral Sobre operaciones de Guerra Y otros Puntos.

1695b   AGI: Audiencia de Guadalajara 151 (67–4–1). Govierno. Ano de 1695. Testimonio de autos de Guerra Tocantes al Capitan franco Ramirez de Salazar Con los motivos y Resolucion de Junta para la formacion de la Compania Volante de Sonora Con el numero de Cinquenta Soldados que ay Sirve Dn Domingo Jironza Petris de Cruzati.

1697–   AGI: Audiencia de Guadalajara 156 (67–4–16).
1703   Secretaria de n.E. Secular. Audiencia de Guadalajara. Testimonio de autos Sobre la pacificacion y castigo de los Yndios Taraumaras, y hostilidades de los Tobosos en la Nueva Vizcaya — ano de 1697 a 1703.

1709–   AGI: Audiencia de Guadalajara 164 (67–4–24).
1715

1728   H. H. Bancroft Collection. Mexican Manuscripts, General and Miscellaneous, 1777. Mexico, 1728. Rivera y Villalon, Pedro de, Informe sobre los Presidios de las Provincias Internas; con documentos suplementarios [incomplete].

1729   AGN: Historia, Tomo 52. Diario de la Campana de 1729 por Jose de Berroteran a la Junta de los Rios.

1746a   AGI: Audiencia de Guadalajara 137 (67–3–31). Joseph de Berroteran, Joseph de Ydoiaga, Juan Antonio de Unanue, y Francisco Joseph Leisaola; San Francisco de Conchos, 21 de octubre de 1746, al virrey Juan Francisco Huemes y Horcasita.

1746b   AGI: Audiencia de Guadalajara 191 (67–3–51). Superior Governo. 1746. testimonio de los auttos fhos a ynstancia del R Pe fr Juan Miguel Menchero, sobre varias providencias que pido Pa el Restablizim,to de las Misiones del Rio de la Junta en el Govierno de el nuebo Mexico y demas q dentro se expresa —.

1748   H. H. Bancroft Collection. Mexican Manuscript 406: 13. Mexico, mayo 3, 1748. Autos Criminales que por comision del senor Governador Y capitan General deste Reyno esta siguiendo don Francisco de Ayala Vrena Contra los Yndios enemigos de la Nacion espanola.

1749–   H. H. Bancroft Collection. Mexican Manuscripts,
1750   1784. 1749–1750, Nueva Vizcaya. Governador (Puerta y Barrera). Expediente sobre la Campana de Jose de Berroteran, y los cargos que le resultaron de ella.

1751a   AGI: Audiencia de Guadalajara 191 (67–3–51). Capitania gral — 1751. testimonio de las diligencias con que el capitan del prisidio de conchos dio quenta al ex.mo Senor Virrey de este Reino de tres indioz y doz indias que Se presentaron en la Ya del Pueblo immediato de San Franco homisidas y desvastadores que havian quedado de la perniciosa quadrilla de los indios Zimbres —.

1751b   AGI: Audiencia de Guadalajara 191 (67–3–51). Capitania gral — 1751. Testimonio de los Autos que Se formaron a pedimento de Don Jph de la Sierra De los Pueblloz de los Sumas infieles y Liga que tienen con los Apaches Mescaleroz, y Salineros y los colomez por el capn y Alcalde Mayor Don Alonzo Victorez Rubin de Zeliz que lo es Vitalicio de este Rl Presidio de nra Senora del Pilar y San Jph del Paso del Rio del Norte y Su Jurisdiccion —.

BL: Bancroft Library *(continued)*

1787   H. H. Bancroft Collection. Mexican Manuscripts 1793: 2. 1787, abril 19, Chihuahua, Nueva Vizcaya. Provincia de Nueva Vizcaya, Jurisdicion de Chihuahua. Estado q manifiesta el Numero de Vasallos, Y Milicianos del Cuerpo de Dragones provinciales del Principe con sus Familias q tiene El Rey en dicha Jurisdicion con distincion de Estados, Clazes, y Castas, de ambos Sexos con inclucion de los Parvulos.

1789a   H. H. Bancroft Collection. Mexican Manuscripts, Misiones, No. 431. Estado que manifiesta las Misiones de este Obpado de Durango segun las Noticias comunicadas por los Curas y Misioneros a quienes se pidieron. Durango, 10 de Marzo, 1789. El Obpo de Durango.

1789b   H. H. Bancroft Collection. Mexican Manuscripts, Misiones, No. 431. Estado actual de las Misiones que tienea su cargo esta Provincia de N.P.S. Franco de los Zacatecas. Durango, 13 de octubre, 1789. Fr. Antono Ferndo Martinez, Mintro Proal.

1799   H. H. Bancroft Collection. Mexican Manuscripts, 1793: 3. Provincia de Nueva Vizcaya; Curato del Pueblo de Sn Franco Xavier de Sathebo; Mission de Santiago de Babonoyaba. Noticia del Curato que ocupa el Sr Cura Coajutor Dn Sabbas Porras, Clerigo Presvitero y de la Mission de Santiago de Bobonoyaba, que Ocupa el R.o P.e F. Manuel Camina, de la Regular Observancia de N.S.P.S. de dha Prov.a, sus progresos en los Numeros de Ministros, que las sirven, Sinodo, qe goza, y total de Almas Con Distincion de Clases y Sexos. 17 de enero de 1799.

1817   H. H. Bancroft Collection. Mexican Manuscripts 1793: 4. Real Presidio de San Carlos. Ano de [1817]. Estado que manifiesta el numero de Abitantes que hay en este Presidio inclusa la Tropa de la Compania que lo guarnese con distincion de clases Estados, y castas y ademas el vecindario de la Hacienda de Dolores. 13, diciembre, 1817, San Geronimo [Aldama].

1821   H. H. Bancroft Collection. Mexican Manuscripts, 1793: 5. 1821, enero 15. Santa Rosalia, Nueva Vizcaya. Padron Gral: en el que constan por mallor, en partidas: la cantidad que en el ano pazado de 1820 fallesieron en los Bivos, se estiman por Parbulos todo lo de diez a.s abajo fho por este Alluntamiento Constitusional de Este Nuevo Balle de S.ta Rosalia, en capite: el s.r Alca, de Dn Jualian Porras hoi 15 de Enero del presente ano de 1821.

CD: Centro de Documentación, Castillo de Chapultepec, Mexico City

1643   Serie Parral. 1643 Encomienda de indios en la provincia de Santa Barbara (Conchos) Expedido En Villa Durango (Julio 24, 1606) por Francisco de Urdinola. N 64. Civil, por Diego del Castillo por reclamo de unos indios contra Diego de Porras.

1644   Serie Parral. 1644, Rebelion de indios tepehuanes.

1646a   Serie Parral. N 48. Ynformacion mandada practicar por el Senor Gobernador del Reyno para saber el estado en que se haya el mismo.

1646b   Serie Parral, No. 20. Testimonio de las diligencias que se practicaron con el motivo de la reforma de Doctrinas en Atotonilco.

1646c   Serie Parral, Doc. No. 38. Mandamiento al Capitan Gomez Fernandez para que exija soldados a [los] labradores.

1648   Serie Parral, Centro de Documentacion, Rollo No. 3. Castillo de Chapultepec, Mexico D.F. N 35, Various ocursos sueltos correspondientes al ano de 1648.

1650a   Serie Parral, Documentos — Presentados por el Pbtro. Don Felipe de la Cueva Montano, referentes al Gral, Francisco Montano de la Cueva. 1650 [without number].

1650b   Serie Parral, Testimonio de los fundamentos que tuvieron los Yndios para Alzarse y como su asiento de Paz lo dio Luis de Valdez.

[1671] Serie Guadalajara. Expediente No. 7, Legajo 1, siglo XVII.

CIV: Collection of Fray Marcelino de Civezza, University of Arizona Library, Tucson

1795   Colegio Apostolico de Santa Cruz (Queretaro). Letter from Fr. Diego Bringas, Valle de San Bartolome, May 28, 1795, to Fray Francisco de Iturralde.

CPP: Colección del Padre Pablo Pastells, Audiencia de México y Guadalajara, Saint Louis University Saint Louis, Missouri

Vol. 2 Rodrigo de rrío de losa, [no place], October 25, 1591, pp. 143–156.

        Real Cédula, Madrid, May 2, 1594, pp. 194–195.

        Real Cédula, Sant Lorenzo, June 25, 1597, pp. 198–199.

Vol. 5 El Almirante Mateo de Vesga, Gobernador, Durango, April 28, 1622, pp. 26–33.

        Services of Mateo de Vezga, Durango, May, 1622, pp. 37–42.

        Mateo de Vesga, Real de Minas de Yndehe, March 11, 1621, pp. 75–82.

        Interrogatorio, Valle de San Bartolomé, March 17, 1621, pp. 82–89.

        El Gobernador Mateo de Vezga, La Ciénega que llaman de Pava, provincia de Sta. Bárbara, May 14, and Valle de Sn Bmé., May 15 and 16, 1621, Cuaderno No. 2, pp. 89–118.

        Mateo de Vezga?, Valle de San Bartolomé?, November 5, 1621, Cuaderno No. 10, pp. 137–141.

        El Gobernador Mateo de Vesga, Durango, May 17, 1624, Cuaderno No. 10, pp. 230–233.

        Razón y minuta de los Yndios que se administran en las provincias de la Nueva Vizcaya, Mateo de Vesga, ca 1622 [undated], pp. 278–284.

Vol. 6 Gobernador Don Luis de Monsalve Saavedra, Parral, October 19, 1635, pp. 291–409.

Vol. 7 General Juan de Barraza al Gobernador, Carichiqui y Peña del Cuerbo, Noviembre 14, 1648, pp. 406–412.

        Don Diego Guajardo Fajardo, Parral, September 7, 1649, pp. 551–552.

        Gobernador Don Diego Guajardo Fajardo, Parral, April 19, 1650, pp. 596–601.

Vol. 8 Fee y testimonio, Gonçalo Mesía de Munguía, escribano mayor de governación y Justicia, November 18, 1649, firmado por el governador Don Diego Guajardo Fajardo, Parral, May 30, 1650, pp. 2–9.

Diego Guajardo Fajardo, Parral, June 4, 1650, p. 13.

Ynforme que hase el Pe Fray Lorenso Canto, Santiago de Babonoyaba, May 21, 1650, pp. 13–17.

Fray Gerónimo de Birvés al gobernador, Río del Torreón, August 15, 1651, pp. 323–324.

Juan de Munguía y Villela al gobernador, Río del Torreón, August 15, 1651, pp. 324–326.

Fray Hernando de Orbaneja. San Pedro, September 3, 1651, pp. 329–330.

Vol. 9 Diego de Medina, Obispo de Durango al Doctor Don Matheo de Zagade Boqueiro, Arzobispo de México, México, June 23, 1660, pp. 185–207 (repeated on pp. 230–253).

Testimonio de Junta de Guerra, Parral, January 1, 1677 [*sic:* 1667], pp. 463–483.

Marqués de Mancera, Virrey de México a su Magestad, México, June 18, 1667, pp. 527–530.

Vol. 10 Don Joan de Gorospe y Aguirre, Obispo de la Vizcaya, año de 1669, abril, pp. 315–332.

Vol. 11 Don Juan de Cervantes Cazano, Parral, October [no day], 1654, pp. 515–541.

Vol. 14 Don Francisco Cuervo de Valdez al gobernador Joseph de Neira Quiroga, Santa María Guaxaraca, June 17, 1684, pp. 98–102.

Vol. 15 Antonio Ortiz de Otalora, Madrid, December 22, 1685, p. 239.

Real Cédula, Madrid, February 17, 1686, pp. 277–278.

Antonio de Oca Sarmiento, San José del Parral, February 18, 1667, pp. 527–534.

Vol. 16 Gobernador Juan Isidro Pardiñas, Parral, December 27, 1688, pp. 91–92.

Representación de los Vecinos de Sonora, El Capn Blas del Castillo, Alcalde Mayor de la Provincia de Sonora, and others, to the gobernador Juan Isidro Pardiñas Villar, San Juan Baptista, June 1, 1690, pp. 475–489.

Blas del Castillo y otros, San Lorenzo de Guecapa, January 9, 1691, pp. 511–520.

Juan Fernández de la Fuente al gobernador Juan Isidro Pardiñas, San Phelipe y Santiago de Janos, June 29, 1691, pp. 538–543.

Juan Fernández de la Fuente al Gobernador, San Phelipe y Santiago de Janos, August 14, 1692, pp. 586–592.

Vol. 17 Juan Fernández de la Fuente al gobernador, San Felipe y Santiago de Janos, July 26, 1692, pp. 200–205.

Juan Fernández de la Fuente al gobernador Juan Isidro Pardiñas, San Felipe y Santiago de Janos, July 31, 1692, pp. 205–210.

Juan Isidro Pardiñas al Virrey, Parral, October 6, 1692, p. 211.

Juan Fernández de la Fuente, San Felipe y Santiago de Janos, September 18, 1693, pp. 69–72.

Vol. 23 Juan de Retana al gobernador Joseph de Neyra y Quiroga, Parral, May 28, 1684, pp. 5–10.

Francisco Ramírez de Salazar al gobernador, Casas Grandes, May 12, 1684, pp. 10–13.

Fray Juan de Porras, [no place], May 14, 1684, pp. 13–14.

Fray Juan Alvarez, Casas Grandes, May 14, 1684, pp. 15–16.

Itinerario de la Visita de Pedro Tapiz, Durango, February 18, 1716, pp. 528–532.

Vol. 24 Fray Joseph Sanz, Madrid, May 18, 1717, p. 93.

Fray Joseph Sanz al S.or Secretario Don Andrés de el Corobanatia y Cúpide, Madrid, May 20, 1717, p. 101.

[Various letters and papers on the founding of Santa Ana de Chinarras, February 14, 1716, to December 15, 1717; Parral, San Francisco de Conchos, San Francisco Cuéllar, Hacienda de Tabalaopa, Santa Ana de Chinarras], pp. 120–239.

Real Cédula, Madrid, March 15, 1718, p. 271.

Real Cédula, Buen Retiro, April 25, 1719, pp. 443–444.

Vol. 27 Descripciones de las provincias internas de esta nueva España . . ., México, 1 de Febrero de 1730, pp. 195–224.

Vol. 34 Joseph Velarde Cosio al Virrey, Conde de Fuenclara, San Phelipe el Real, April 25, 1746, pp. 103–108.

Joseph de Berroterán, San Francisco de Conchos, April 26, 1746, pp. 111–113.

Vol. 35 Ynforme – Superior Gobierno 1751, Testimonio de la consulta del Governador de la Nueba Vizcaya en que ymforma el estado de los presidios de aquella gobernación, y resolución tomada sobre la extinción de los presidios de la cordillera, San Buena Bentura, April 15, 1749, Sancho Salaises and others, pp. 329–336.

Declaración de Juan de Dios Nuñes, Villa de San Phelipe el Real, April 3, 1749, pp. 336–338.

El Conde de Revilla Gigedo a su Magestad, México, July 10, 1751, pp. 587–593.

Joseph Días del Carpio al Gobernador, San Phelipe el Real, April 30, 1749, pp. 338–340.

Juan Francisco de la Puesta, San Phelipe el Real, June 15, 1749, pp. 342–351.

El Marqués de Altamira, México, December 23, 1749, pp. 364–376.

Vol. 36 Joseph de Berroterán, Real Presidio de Conchos, October 5, 1748, pp. 41–43.

El Marqués de Altamira, Mexico, December 5, 1748, pp. 43–57.

Exhorto de D.n Antonio Gutiérrez de Noriega, San Felipe el Real de Chihuahua, February 23, 1754, pp. 475–478.

Mateo Antonio de Mendoza, Segundo Cuaderno de Campaña, Años de 1754 y 1755, San Felipe el Real, February 26, 1755, pp. 561–571.

Vol. 39 Ynforme. Joseph García de Salcedo, San José del Parral, March 4, 1674, pp. 203–216.

Fray Francisco de Orosco al Gobernador, Durango, May 15, 1677, pp. 292–309.

Lope de Sierra Osorio, San Joseph del Parral, November 13, 1677, pp. 318–329.

CPP: Colección del Padre Pastells *(continued)*

Vol. 41 Expediente sobre erecciones de Iglesias y Territorios de Varios Obispados, Año de 1763. Pedro Obispo de Durango, September 7, 1761, pp. 471–504.

DHM: Documentos para la Historia de México (published; Vicente García Torres, editor)

1645 Jesus. Relacion de lo sucedido en este reino de la Vizcaya desde el ano de 1644 hasta el de 45 acerca de los alzamientos, danos, robos, hurtos muertos y lugares despoblados de que se saco un traslado para remitir al padre Francisco Calderon, provincial de la provincia de Mexico de la Compania de Jesus. . . . Nicolas de Zepeda, San Miguel de las Bocas, abril 28 de 1645, mas addendum de 11 de septiembre de 1645. Cuarta Serie, Tomo III. Mexico City: 1857.

1666 Memorial del Padre Comisario General. Fr. Antonio Valdez, Parral, 11 de octubre de 1666. Documentos para la Historia de Mexico, Cuarta Serie, Tomo III, pp. 237–240. Mexico City: 1857.

1667a Mandamiento del Senor Virey, Marques de Mancera, sobre las doctrinas de Casas–Grandes que estaban en los Yumas, Jurisdiccion de San Felipe del Parral. Plus enclosures: carta de Antonio de Oca Sarmiento, Guadiana, Septiembre 22 de 1667, y carta de Francisco de Gorraez Beaumont, Mexico, Octubre 25 de 1667. Cuarta Serie, Tomo III. Mexico City: 1857.

1667b Otra Carta. Antonio de Oca Sarmiento, Guadiana, septiembre 22 de 1667. Cuarta Serie, Tomo III. Mexico City: 1857.

1667c Otra Carta. Andres Lopez de Garcia a fray Antonio de Valdes, ministro provincia. Parral, Agosto 26 de 1667. Cuarta Serie, Tomo III. Mexico City: 1857.

1667d Carta. Andres Lopez de Gracia a D. Antonio Oca Sarmiento. Parral, Agosto 16 de 1667. Cuarto Serie Tomo III. Mexico City: 1857.

1668 Memorial del Padre Procurador General de la Orden de San Francisco. Fr. Antonio Carrillo. Plus enclosures: decretos, parecer, Auto de Junta, e Informe de Oficiales Reales de Durango con fechas entre setiembre 22 de 1668 y agosto 17 de 1669. Cuarta Serie, Tomo III. Mexico City: 1857.

1669 Patrocinio del glorioso apostol de las indias S. Francisco Javier en el reino de la Nueva Vizcaya, ano de 1669. Accompanying Auto dated 4 de Diciembre de 1668. por D. Antoniode Oca Sarmiento. Cuarta Serie, Tomo III. Mexico City: 1857.

1697 Relacion del estado de la Pimeria, que remite el Padre Visitador Horacio Polici, por el ano de 1697. Con cartas: Nuestra Senora de los Dolores y Diciembre 3 de 1697, Cristobal Martin Bernal, Eusebio Francisco Kino, Francisco de Acuna, Juan de Escalante, Francisco Javier de Barsejon; y 4 de diciembre de 1697 con las mismas firmas, que contiene el derrotero de su entrada al norte. Tercera Serie, Tomo I.2. Mexico City: 1856.

1698a Breve Relacion de la insigne victoria que los Pimas, Sobaipuris en 30 de marzo del ano de 1693 [*sic*] han conseguido contra los enemigos de la provincia de Sonora. Nuestra Senora de los Dolores, Mayo 3 de 1698 anos, con addendum de Octubre 25 de 98. Tercera Serie, Tomo I.2. Mexico City: 1856.

1698b Relacion de Nuestra Senora de los Remedios en su Nueva Capilla de su nuevo pueblo de las nuevas con versiones de la Pimeria, en 15 de setiembre de 1698. Nuestra Senora de Dolores y Setiembre 16 de 1698 anos. Eusebio Francisco Kino. Tercera Serie, Tomo I.2. Mexico City: 1856.

1704 Escrito a S.E. Mexico, Agosto 4 de 1704. Francisco Cuervo y Valdes, Gregorio de Salinas Baraona, Juan Ignacio de la Vega y Sotomayor, Martin de Sabalza, Juan de Salaises. Cuarta Serie, Tomo IV. Mexico City: 1857.

1707 Ano de 1707, Gobierno del Marques de la Penuela y Almirante D. Jose Chacon Medina Salazar, del orden de Santiago. Tercera Serie, Tomo I. Mexico City: 1856.

1715a Fr. Jose de Arranegui, S. Francisco de Cuellar ano de 1715. Cuarta Serie, Tomo IV. Mexico City: 1857.

1715b Noticia de la Mision de la Junta de los Rios. Juan Antonio de Trasvina Retis, San Francisco de Cuellar, Julio 10 de 1715. Cuarta Serie, Tomo IV. Mexico City: 1857.

1748 Informe acerca de los présidios de la Nueva Vizcaya. Jose de Berroteran, Mexico, abril 17 de 1748. Segunda Serie, Tomo I. Mexico City: 1854.

1778 Carta del padre Fray Silvestre Velez de Escalante escrita en abril de 1778 anos, al R.P. lector fray Juan Agustin Morfi. Santa Fe y abril 2 de 1778. Tercera Serie, Tomo I. Mexico City: 1856.

18tha Copia de un informe hecho a su majestad sobre las tierras del Nueva–Mexico *In:* Utiles y Curiosas Noticias del Nuevo–Mexico, Cibola y otras naciones confinantes. . . . [sin fecha, app 18th]. Tercera Serie, Tomo I. Mexico City: 1856.

18thb Informe del Padre Lizasoin, sobre las provincias de Sonora y Nueva Viscaya. Tomos Ignacio Lizasoin al Virrey Marques de Cruillas. Sin fecha [between 1761 and 1766 — see Bancroft, Vol. XI]. Tercera Serie, Tomo I.2. Mexico City: 1856.

18thc Apuntamientos que a las memorias del Padre Fray Geronimo de Zarate, hizo el Padre Juan Amando Niel de la compania de Jesus, no tan solo estando practico del terreno que se cita, si no es que llevaba en la mano las memorias para cotejarlas con el. Tercera Serie, Tomo I. Mexico City: 1856.

UTD: Documents Division, University of Texas, Austin, Texas

1592– 1592–1643. Vol. 12. Cunningham Transcripts.
1643   Comision y conducta de los servisios de Capitan General de la Nueva Galicia por los Senores Virreyes — Junio – 1607.

1648 Vol. 14. Cunningham Transcripts. AGI 66-6-17, Audiencia de Guadalajara. [1648: correspondencia de Nueva Vizcaya.]

1671–1685   1671–1685. Vol. 66. Dunn Transcripts. AGI 58-4-13, Audiencia de Mexico. Durango–Consultas que hizo el Gobernador de la Nueva Vizcaya al Virrey tocantes a la seguridad y defensa de aquella Provincia. Bino sin Carta. Informe que hizo a Su Magestad el Governador Don Antonio de Oca.

1683–1697   1683–1697. Vol. 16. Nuevo Mexico. AGI 67-4-11, Audiencia de Guadalajara. [1688: correspondencia de Nueva Vizcaya.]

1707   1707. Vol. 77 Dunn Transcripts. AGI 62-2-29, Audiencia de Mexico. [Report on Missions of Nuevo Leon.]

1710–1738a   1710–1738. Vol. 23. Dunn Transcripts. AGI 67-3-12, Audiencia de Guadalajara. 1726. Testimonio de los Auttos fhos sobre la Sublevacion, y Alzamiento de los Yndios Sumas; de las Misiones de SnTiago de la Zienega de el Coyame, y Junta de el Nortte – Presentado con memorial de fray Francisco Seco, Procurador general de Yndias del orden de San Francisco.

1710–1738b   1710–1738. Vol. 23. Dunn Transcripts. AGI 104-6-15, Audiencia de Guadalajara. Copia del Diario de la Campana executada de orden del Exmo Senor Marques de Casafuerte, por Dn Joseph Berroteran Capitan del Presidio de Conchos, para el reconocimiento de las Margenes del Rio del Norte, en el ano de 1729.

1715a   1715. Vol. 24. Dunn Transcripts. AGI 67-5-15, Audiencia de Guadalajara. Ytinerario. Razon de las distancias y leguas de los parages donde se hace mansion de noche en la visita del Obispado de Durango por el Yll.mo Senor Don Pedro Tapis desde quince de Febrero de el ano de mill setecientos y quince.

1715b   1699–1721. Vol. 20. Dunn Transcripts. AGI 67-3-3, Audiencia de Guadalajara. 1715, Derrotero que hizo Beasoain de la entrada a la Junta de los Rios que hizo Trasvina Retis.

1720–1799   1720–1799. Vol. 164. Dunn Transcripts. AGI 136-7-7-T.5. Indiferente de Nueva Espana. [Report on missions:] Fray Juan Miguel Menchero, Mexico, 20 de abril, 1744.

1742–1754   1742–1754. Vol. 30. Dunn Transcripts. AGI 67-5-15, Audiencia de Guadalajara. Durango – 30 de Diziembre de 1751. El Obispo – Da quenta de la visita que hizo en parte de su Obispado hasta el mismo ano de 51 y expresa con mucha puntualidad y distincion, los Pueblos, y parages por donde transito, y circunstancias que en cada uno concurren, anadiendo el numero de personas que confirmo en cada parte.

1749a   AGN, Historia, Tomo 52. Nueva Vizcaya, Ano de 1749. Autos fechos sobre la desercion de los tres Indios, Matheo, Gabriel y Aguilar de la Nacion Sisimbres Con Maria Antonia y Francisca de Paula Mugeres de Matheo y Gabriel que desertaron del Pueblo de Conchos, y Cargos que sobre ello se le hicieron al Capitan del Presidio de este nombre Dn Joseph de Berroteran, Por, El Senor Governador y Capitan General de este Reyno –.

1749b   Vol. 20. AGI 89-2-23, Audiencia de Mexico. Sup.or Govierno, 1749. Consultta del Governador de la nueva Vizcaya en que informa el esttado de los Presidios de aquella Governacion, y resolucion tomada sobre la extincion de los Presidios de la Cordillera. S.rio Dn Joseph Gorraez.

1768–1792   1768–1792. Vol. 462. Hackett Transcripts. AGN, Provincias Internas, Tomo 24. Ano de 1769. Num.o 1. Coahuila. Correspondencia con el Governador Don Jacobo Ugarte y Loyola.

UTEP: Janos Microfilm, University of Texas, El Paso
     Reels 1 and 2. (Courtesy of Dr. Rex Gerald.)

UTJ: Janos Collection, Latin American Collection, University of Texas, Austin
     Folder 1, Section 1
     Folder 8, Section 2
     Folder 11, Section 1
     Folder 12, Section 1
     Folder 15, Sections 2 and 3
     Folder 17, Section 2
     Folder 18, Section 3
     Folder 20, Section 4
     Folder 23, Section 3
     Folder 24, Section 2

UTL: Latin American Collection, University of Texas, Austin, Texas
1619   Varias Relaciones, Tomo 1, 1610–1675. Relass.on de losucsedido en la jornada q dn Gaspar de aluar y Salacar Cavallero del horden de sntiago governador y cappittan general de la Vizcaya Hizo a los Tarahumares desde los *26* de febrero deste ano de *619* asta los *20* de abril del dicho ano echa por el padre Al.o de Valencia de la conpania de Jesus q aconpana el Rl Campo –.

Municipal Archives
     Janos, Chihuahua
     San Francisco de Conchos, Chihuahua

Parish Archives
     Aldama, Chihuahua (for San Gerónimo)
     Aquiles Serdán, Chihuahua (for Santa Eulalia)
     Bachíniva, Chihuahua (for Santa María de la Navidad de Bachíniva)
     Buenaventura, Chihuahua (for San Buenaventura)
     Camargo, Chihuahua (for Santa Rosalía)
     Casas Grandes Viejo, Chihuahua (for Janos)
     Chihuahua Cathedral, Chihuahua (for San Francisco Cuéllar and San Felipe El Real)
     General Trías, Chihuahua (for Santa Isabel)
     Julimes, Chihuahua (for San Antonio de Julimes)
     Namiquipa, Chihuahua (for San Pedro de Namiquipa)
     Ojinaga, Chihuahua
     Parral Cathedral, Chihuahua
     Rosales, Chihuahua (for Santa Cruz de Tapacolmes)
     Valle de Allende, Chihuahua (for Valle de San Bartolomé)

PUBLICATIONS

Aguirre Beltrán, Gonzalo
1967   *Regiones de refugio.* Instituto Indigenista Inter-americano, Ediciones Especiales, 46. Mexico City.

Alegre, Francisco Javier, S. J.
1956–   *Historia de la Compañía de Jesús en Nueva Es-*
1959   *paña.* Vols. 1, 2, 3. New edition by Ernest J. Burrus, S. J., and Félix Zubiliaga, S. J. Rome: Institutum Historicum S. J.

Alessio Robles, Vito
1938   *Coahuila y Texas en la época colonial.* Mexico City: Editorial Cultura.

Almada, Francisco R.
1968   *Diccionario de historia, geografía y biografía Chihuahuenses,* 2d ed. Universidad de Chihuahua, Departamento de Investigaciones, Sección de Historia. Ciudad Juárez: Impresora de Juárez, S. A.

Almada, Francisco R., and others
1959   *Chihuahua, cuidad prócer: 1709-1959.* Chihuahua: Publicación de la Universidad de Chihuahua.

Anonymous
1954   *Nueva Vizcaya, Datos.* Biblioteca de Historiadores Mexicanos. Mexico City: Editor Vargas Rea.

Arlegui, Joseph
1851   *Chrónica de la provincia de N.S.P.S. Francisco de Zacatecas.* Mexico City: J. B. de Hogal.

Bancroft, Hubert Howe
1884   *History of the North Mexican States and Texas.* Vol. I. *1531-1800. The Works of Hubert Howe Bancroft,* Vol. XV. San Francisco: A. L. Bancroft & Co.

Bannon, John F., S. J.
1955   *The Mission Frontier in Sonora, 1620-1687.* United States Catholic Historical Society Monograph Series, No. 26. New York.

Beals, Ralph L.
1932   The Comparative Ethnology of Northern Mexico before 1750. *Ibero-Americana,* No. 2. Berkeley: University of California Press.

Bolton, Herbert Eugene
1911   The Jumano Indians in Texas. *Texas State Historical Quarterly* XV (1).

1912   The Spanish Occupation of Texas, 1519-1690. *Southwestern Historical Quarterly* 16: 1-26.

1930   *Spanish Exploration in the Southwest, 1542-1706.* New York: Charles Scribner and Sons.

Collard, Howard, and Elisabeth Scott Collard
1962   *Castellano-mayo, mayo-castellano.* Serie de Vocabularios Indígenas, Núm 6. Mexico City: Instituto Lingüístico del Verano con la Dirección General de Asuntos Indígenas.

DiPeso, Charles C.
1974   *Casas Grandes: A Fallen Trading Center of the Gran Chichimeca.* Vol. 3. Dragoon, Arizona: Amerind Foundation; Flagstaff, Arizona: Northland Press.

Dobyns, Henry F.
1966   Estimating Aboriginal American Population: An Appraisal of Techniques with a New Hemispheric Estimate. *Current Anthropology* 7 (4): 395-416, 440-444.

Dunne, Peter Masten, S. J.
1944   *Pioneer Jesuits in Northern Mexico.* Berkeley: University of California Press.

1948   *Early Jesuit Missions in the Tarahumara.* Berkeley: University of California Press.

Forbes, Jack D.
1959a   The Appearance of the Mounted Indian in Northern Mexico and the Southwest, to 1680. *Southwestern Journal of Anthropology* XV (2): 189-212.

1959b   Unknown Athapaskans: The Identification of the Jano, Jocome, Jumano, Manso, Suma, and Other Indian Tribes of the Southwest. *Ethnohistory* 6 (2): 97-159.

1960   *Apache, Navajo, and Spaniard.* Norman: University of Oklahoma Press.

Griffen, William B.
1969   Culture Change and Shifting Populations in Central Northern Mexico. *Anthropological Papers of the University of Arizona* 13. Tucson: University of Arizona Press.

1970   A North Mexican Nativistic Movement, 1684. *Ethnohistory* 17 (3-4): 95-116.

Hackett, Charles Wilson (ed.)
1926,   Historical Documents Relating to New Mexico,
1937   Nueva Vizcaya, and Approaches Thereto, to 1773. Vols. 2, 3. *Publications of the Carnegie Institution of Washington,* no. 330.

1934   *Pichardo's Treatise on the Limits of Louisiana and Texas.* Vol. 2. Austin: University of Texas Press.

Hammond, George P., and others
1932   *New Spain and the Anglo-American West: Historical Contributions Presented to Herbert Eugene Bolton.* Vol. I, *New Spain.* Lancaster, Pa.: Lancaster Press.

Hammond, George P., and Agapito Rey
1927   The Gallegos Relation of the Rodriguez Expedition to New Mexico. *Historical Society of New Mexico, Publications in History* IV (Dec. 1927). Santa Fe: El Palacio Press.

1928   *Obregon's History of Sixteenth Century Explorations in Western America.* Los Angeles: Wetzel Publishing Co.

1929   *Expedition into New Mexico made by Antonio de Espejo, 1582-1583, as revealed in the journal of Diego Perez de Luxan, a member of the Party.* Quivira Society Publications, Vol. 1. Los Angeles.

Hilton, K. Simon, with Ramon Lopez B. and Emiliano Carrasco T.
1959   *Tarahumara y espanol.* Serie de Vocabularios Indígenas, Núm. 1. Mexico City: Instituto Linguístico del Verano con la Dirección General de Asuntos Indígenas.

Hughes, Anne E.
1914   The Beginnings of Spanish Settlement in the El Paso District. *University of California Publications in History* 1.

Jiménez Moreno, Wigberto
1958   *Estudios de historia colonial.* Mexico City: Instituto Nacional de Antropología e Historia.

Kelley, J. Charles
1952a   Factors Involved in the Abandonment of Certain Peripheral Southwestern Settlements. *American Anthropologist* 54 (3): 356–387.

1952b   The Historic Indian Pueblos of La Junta de los Rios (Part 2). *New Mexico Historical Review* XXVIII (1): 21–51.

1953   The Historic Indian Pueblos of La Junta de los Rios (Part 2). *New Mexico Historical Review* XXVIII (1): 21–51.

1955   Juan Sabeata and Diffusion in Aboriginal Texas. *American Anthropologist* 57 (5): 981–995.

Kinnaird, Lawrence
1958   *The Frontier of New Spain, Nicolas de LaFora's Description.* Quivira Society Publications, Vol. 13. Berkeley.

Kroeber, Alfred L.
1934   Uto-Aztecan Languages of Mexico. *Ibero-Americana,* No. 8. Berkeley: University of California Press.

López–Velarde López, Benito
1964   *Expansión geográfica franciscana en el hoy norte central y oriental de México.* No. 12, Cultura Misional. Mexico City: Universidad Pontificia Urbaniana de Propaganda Fide.

Massey, William C.
1949   Tribes and Languages of Baja California. *Southwestern Journal of Anthropology* V (3): 272–307.

Mecham, John Lloyd
1927   *Francisco de Ibarra and Nueva Vizcaya.* Durham: Duke University Press.

Miranda, Joan de
1871   Relacion hecha por Joan de Miranda, clerigo, al Doctor Orozco, Presidente de la Audiencia de Guadalajara; sobre la tierra y poblacion que hay desde las minas de San Martin a las de Santa Barbara, que esto ultimo entonces estaba poblado — Ano de 1575. In *Collección de documentos inéditos relativos al discubrimiento, conquista y organización de las antiguas posesiones españolas de América y Oceania sacados de los Archivos del Reino,* vol. 16. Madrid: Imprenta del Hospicio.

Molina, Alonso de
1944   *Vocabulario de la lengua castellana y mexicana.* 2 vols. Madrid. (Originally published 1571, Mexico City.)

Morfi, Juan Agustin de
1935   Viaje de Indios y Diario del Nuevo México. Introduction and notes by Vito Alessio Robles. Mexico City: Antiqua Librería de José Porrúa y Hijos.

Mota y Escobar, Don Alonso de la
1940   *Descripción geográfica de los reinos de Nueva Galicia, Nueva Vizcaya y Nuevo León.* 2d ed. Mexico City: Editorial Pedro Robredo.

Mota Padilla, Lic. Matías de la
1870   *Historia de la Conquista de la Provincia de la Nueva Galicia.* Sociedad Mexicana de Geografía y Estadística. Mexico City: Imprenta del Gobierno, en Palacio, a cargo de José María Sandoval.

Oconor, Hugo de
1952   *Informe de Hugo de Oconor sobre el estado de las provincias internas del norte, 1771–76.* Texto original con prologo del Lic. Enrique González Flores; anotación por Francisco R. Almada. Mexico City: Editorial Cultura.

Park, Joseph F.
1962   Spanish Indian Policy in Northern Mexico, 1765–1810. *Arizona and the West* 4 (4): 325–344.

Porras Muñoz, Guillermo
1966   *Iglesia y estado en Nueva Vizcaya (1562–1821).* Pamplona: Universidad de Navarra.

Portillo, Esteban L.
1887   *Apuntes para la historia antigua de Coahuila y Texas.* Saltillo [Mexico].

Powell, Philip Wayne
1952   *Soldiers, Indians and Silver.* Berkeley: University of California Press.

Saravia, Atanasio G.
n.d.   *Apuntes para la historia de la Nueva Vizcaya.* No. 1, *La Conquista.* Instituto Panamericano de Geografía e Historia, Pub. no. 35.

Sauer, Carl O.
1934   The Distribution of Aboriginal Tribes and Languages in Northwest Mexico. *Ibero-Americana,* No. 5. Berkeley: University of California Press.

Schroeder, Albert H.
1961   A Study of the Apache Indians. Pt. I: The Apaches and Their Neighbors, 1540–1700. Santa Fe. Mimeographed.

Simpson, Lesley Byrd
1950   *The Encomienda in New Spain.* Berkeley: University of California Press.

Spicer, Edward H.
1962   *Cycles of Conquest.* Tucson: University of Arizona Press.

Tamarón y Romeral, Pedro
1937   *Demostración del vastísimo obispado de la Nueva Vizcaya.* Biblioteca Mexicana de Obras Inéditas, 7, 1765. Mexico City: Antigua Librería Robredo, de José Porrúa e Hijos.

Tello, Fray Antonio
1891   *Libro segundo de la crónica miscelánea, en que se trata de la conquista espiritual y temporal de la santa provincia de Xalisco en el Nuevo Reino de la Galicia y Nueva Viscaya.* Guadalajara.

Torquemada, Fray Juan de
1944   *Monarquía Indiana.* Vol. 3, 3d ed. Mexico City: Editorial Salvador Chávez Hayhoe.

Valenzuela, José (compiler)
1891   Carta General del Estado de Chihuahua, formado con los planos levantados por las compañías Deslindadoras del Estado, Compilados por José Valenzuela. Dedicada al Ministerio de Fomento, 1891. (Courtesy of Sr. Apolinar Frías Prieto, Chihuahua City.)

Wallace, Anthony F. C.
1956   Revitalization Movements. *American Anthropologist* 58 (2): 264–281.

Washburn, Wilcomb E. (ed.)
1964   *The Indian and the White Man.* New York: Doubleday and Company, Anchor Books.

West, Robert C.
1949   The Mining Community in Northern New Spain: The Parral Mining District. *Ibero-Americana,* No. 30. Berkeley: University of California Press.